SAN FRANCISCO
A CITY FOR ALL SEASONS

SAN FRANCISCO
A CITY FOR ALL SEASONS

INTRODUCTION BY **STEVE YOUNG**

ART DIRECTION BY **BRIAN GROPPE**

URBAN
TAPESTRY
SERIES

TOWERY
PUBLISHING, INC.

Contents

BY STEVE YOUNG

AS AN ADOPTED SON OF THE BAY AREA, I AM BLESSED WITH A unique appreciation of the most beautiful city in the world. Like most great cities, San Francisco seems to be treasured most by those who were born and raised here. For those of us who were not as lucky, an outsider's perspective becomes even more valuable. As a relative newcomer, my 13 years in the Bay Area have allowed me to appreciate the abundant beauty of the city, both natural and man-made: the inspiring bridges, the hilly streets with buildings and houses rising at impossible angles, the nostalgic cable cars, and the soul-replenishing view of the Pacific Ocean. Wherever you look, the Bay Area is ready to delight your senses with yet another amazing vista.

San Francisco is a magnificent city. But what truly makes the city beautiful is her wonderful inner self. The city has a diverse blend of people, a rich and colorful history, and a position of leadership in today's fast-paced technological society. This diversity spans the San Francisco peninsula. I live in Palo Alto, which is the home of Stanford University. It is a wonderful college community, with beautiful old homes and charming neighborhoods that comprise the heart of Silicon Valley. And yet, Stanford and Palo Alto form only one of many neighborhoods and institutions of higher learning combinations in the Bay Area, including the University of California in Berkeley, University of San Francisco, and Santa Clara University. Additionally, the list of cutting-edge companies that call San Francisco home is staggering: Sun Microsystems, Oracle, Sysco, and Apple, and the famous Internet companies of eBay, Lycos, and Excite, to name a few. Throughout the area, Silicon Valley companies continue to redefine world commerce in ways that were not even dreamed of a decade ago.

San Francisco has a blend of cultures and seems to offer something different in each of its many neighborhoods. The city itself has maintained its beauty by preserving local parks as well as the majestic Golden Gate Park. There are fantastic cultural venues such as the Opera House, the San Francisco Museum of Modern Art, and the spectacular, newly restored City Hall. The city is world renowned for its fantastic restaurants and gourmet culture. The area's sports franchises are second to none in terms of fans, loyalty, pride, and tradition. The new Pac Bell ballpark in China Basin is going to make visiting baseball teams truly jealous. Finally, the area's residents display their pride for maintaining an environment that has symbolized creative expression, tolerance, and faith in their fellow neighbors.

Neighborhoods in San Francisco are proud to retain their historic identities. The Haight-Ashbury district, often referred to simply as the Haight, is still thriving with a hippie culture. Chinatown bustles day and night, and offers amazing Chinese food in the quaintest of restaurants. The Marina, Union Street, and Pacific Heights are packed with charming apartments and houses filled with young professionals. The great shopping and fantastic restaurants that this crowd frequents can be found within a one- or two-block walk. Union Square is the downtown area famous for shopping, hotels, and theater. Fisherman's Wharf remains a popular tourist destination as well as the ferry launch where you can go to see Alcatraz or to the beautiful cities of Sausalito and Tiburon in Marin County. Muir Woods is only 30 minutes outside of the city, and the redwood trees there evoke a hushed amazement in all who come to stand in their shadows.

Even the weather in San Francisco is interesting. The summers are always a little chilly, and the spring and fall are spectacular. Of course, San Francisco is famous for its fog, or as the locals refer to it, "the marine layer." To watch the marine layer tumble in from the Pacific and blanket the area before your eyes is truly an incredible experience. My favorite month of the year is October. Of course football is usually in full swing, but when I get the chance, I love to take the drive over to Half Moon Bay and cruise along Pacific Coast Highway. There is something about that ocean air that does a body good.

What makes San Francisco so unique and special is that it forces you at every turn to keep perspective and to retain a healthy respect for the city and its inhabitants. Every culture, every industry, every institution is part of the diversity that makes this city great. I feel so blessed to be a part of this thriving metropolis that has touched everyone who has ever visited.

CABLE CARS CLANGING DOWN THE MIDDLE OF A BUSY STREET, passengers running to hop aboard. Hippies still finding their way to Haight-Ashbury to blow soap bubbles and panhandle for spare change. The soaring Transamerica Pyramid rising above the Financial District. The Civic Cen-

ter where the ballet and the symphony hold court, and where City Hall presides in domed majesty. Cybertech pioneers driving impossibly expensive foreign cars through South Bay cities like Cupertino, Sunnyvale, and Mountain View, their heads so filled with the coded patterns of tomorrow that they're barely aware of how beautiful their surroundings are. Fisherman's Wharf. Mimes in Golden Gate Park. Alcatraz. Chinatown. Ferries. Redwoods. The red-orange towers of the Golden Gate Bridge, soaring into the cloudy mist.

OK, enough with the images. There's a point to be made here: San Francisco is a fabled city that borders on being a complete illusion, even unto itself. No matter whether you're a lifelong resident or a first-time visitor, the Bay Area seems to exist as a kind of mirage, a vision seen on the fringes of the fog for which it's so rightly renowned.

True enough, the most common images are, by and large, tourist clichés. Postcard fodder. The kind of thing you hear all the time about San Francisco and its environs. While these images are more than a bit overused, they are nonetheless real. Life happens in between them, around them, embracing them. It's like the old saw about how only one in 10 New Yorkers has ever been to the Statue of Liberty. We seem to have a knack, no matter where we live, for overlooking the good stuff—right in front of us and all around us—in our ceaseless business of daily life. The mundane always, and sadly, seems to cancel the magical.

© KERRICK JAMES

So, for the record, San Francisco is a very real metropolitan area, much concerned with the vital commerce of the world, its citizens embroiled in the many snares and labyrinths of daily life. But more than any other city in the world, San Francisco is a patchwork of myths, an improvisation of images, a place where anything can—and does—happen. You simply can't distill the magic here so easily. Let the New Yorkers ignore the Statue of Liberty. Here, there are so many comparable wonders that it's impossible not to relish them.

Traditions here are measured both in centuries and in days. What's considered outlandish in mainstream America is downright commonplace in the Bay Area. Yet it is a city of both experimentation and conservatism. The Bay Area is a place that is both jarringly new and traditionally American. What's more, it is quintessentially Californian, representing the pioneering spirit that has made the state into the vibrant and unpredictable land that it is. To live here is to embrace a jangle of influences, and to enjoy the prospect of molding them into something entirely your own.

It needs to be asserted that the Bay Area is not without its challenges. With a consolidated metropolitan population of 6.6 million (fifth largest in the country), it would be silly to suggest that this is some kind of Shangri-la. Like any huge metropolis anywhere, at any point in history, it's got its share of problems. Traffic, smog, crime, bigotry, poverty, homelessness—the usual stew from Pandora's urban box.

Yet here is a city like no other, a mixture of the beautiful and the mundane, unheard of anywhere else in the world. Throughout its history—and more so now than ever before—this much is indisputable. ☛

ONE OF THE OBVIOUS REASONS FOR THE BAY AREA'S CONTINUING POPULARITY IS THE sheer beauty—natural and man-made—of the place. From one end of the area to another, delights abound. Occupying the northern part of a hilly peninsula, the city of San Francisco encompasses about 46 square miles, rendering it only moderate in area. The climate is also what you'd call moderate, if not a bit on the cool side, year-round, with foggy summers and delightful springs and autumns that seem to last well beyond their rightful time limits.

San Francisco is a city of neighborhoods, most of them arranged around geographical features or landmarks. Nob Hill, for instance, is traditionally thought of as the city's silver spoon neighborhood, where the so-called "nabobs" (originally a reference to a provincial governor from India) of yesteryear built lavish mansions and lived as if the money would never disappear. Today, it's still a tony enclave, although not quite as outlandishly wealthy as it was a century ago. Telegraph Hill, meanwhile, was known for the influx of immigrants who settled on its steep banks, building tiny houses on winding streets, houses that were eventually populated by artists and bohemians. Today, it's all very gentrified and upscale, but still retains a bit of the old boho mystique. Coit Tower, a 180-foot, stylized fire nozzle, was built atop Telegraph Hill in 1933 to honor the many who fought and endured the fires that plagued the city in its first century. Today, despite the boom in skyscraper construction that began in the late 1960s, Coit Tower still offers one of the most outstanding elevated views of the city and upper bay.

The islands of Alcatraz (home, of course, of the legendary federal prison), Yerba Buena, and Treasure Island (man-made as an attraction for the Golden Gate International Exposition of 1939-1940) are all in splendid view from Coit Tower.

Surrounding Nob Hill and Telegraph Hill are several other famous neighborhoods. North Beach, perhaps best known as the home of 1950s bohemia, is actually a sprawling mélange of cultural influences, encompassing an Italian neighborhood and, adjacent to it, Chinatown. North Beach is alive with foot traffic, restaurants, and shops galore. Among the most prominent is City Lights Bookstore, where poet Lawrence Ferlinghetti planted the banner of the Beat Generation when he published Allen Ginsberg's still-controversial poem *Howl* in 1956. The more conventional (and visually stunning) focus of North Beach, though, is Washington Square, populated by a ceaselessly interesting crowd of daily visitors, and watched over by the soaring towers of Saints Peter and Paul Catholic church. The effect is like visiting a piazza in northern Italy.

Chinatown, which has come to encompass a good bit of what has traditionally been known as North Beach, is filled with shops, restaurants, apartments, businesses, and homes. For more than 125 years, this area has been an almost sacrosanct center for Chinese culture; in the face of discrimination and isolation, Chinese immigrants found a haven here. Today, Chinatown is said to house the largest number of Chinese outside of China. It's not all bliss, though; population density is extremely high, and behind the facades of the shops are a good many crowded workplaces. Still, residents and the hordes of visitors alike enjoy a fascinating blend of authentic Chinese establishments alongside those that exist mainly to satisfy the endless stream of tourists.

Also adjacent to the traditional North Beach area is Fisherman's Wharf. While locals regard it largely as a tourist mecca, Fisherman's Wharf has a rich history involving several immigrant populations vying for position in what is, after all, one of the best harbors in the world. Forget the kitsch and enjoy some of the best—and certainly freshest—seafood anywhere. And, come to think of it, enjoy the kitsch as well. After all,

wax museums and boat tours can be an awful lot of fun, and here and there you find a legitimate museum or a shop worth lingering in.

Move south along the peninsula and you reach Union Square, heart of the city's shopping district, and home to grand hotels and fine dining establishments. SOMA, the area south of Market Street, is alive with galleries and museums that have taken root in old warehouses and lofts. It's also home to the Moscone Convention Center, part of the Yerba Buena Center. The San Francisco Museum of Modern Art and the Ansel Adams Center for Photography—just two of the many outstanding museums in the area—are both must-sees for art lovers of every stripe.

To the west, Civic Center features some of the finest public structures in the country. The beaux arts City Hall has recently been refurbished, its interior rotunda no less splendid than the gold dome outside. Also in the Civic Center are the relatively new San Francisco Public Library building, Bill Graham Civic Auditorium, War Memorial Opera House, San Francisco Performing Arts Library and Museum, and Louise M. Davies Symphony Hall.

The central areas of San Francisco are no less interesting. The Downtown and Financial District areas overlap to the point that few make the distinction anymore. Beginning in the late 1960s, a series of building booms began to transform the San Francisco skyline. Where once few tall buildings had stood, there began to rise magnificent skyscrapers like the regional headquarters for Bank of America—the tallest with 52 stories—and the distinctive Transamerica Pyramid, which at 853 feet has become yet another of the city's many visual landmarks.

© FRED VERHOEVEN

Central San Francisco contains neighborhoods like the Mission District, the Castro, Golden Gate Heights, Richmond, and Twin Peaks, all of which are endowed with particular characteristics. To tell people what neighborhood you live in is to tell them much about yourself: your relative wealth, your racial heritage, your political leanings, your sexual orientation, and on and on into the layers of the city's polyglot social system.

Residential areas within San Francisco are generally expensive, including Haight-Ashbury, one-time home of hippie culture. In 1967, the so-called Summer of Love was experienced in this neighborhood dominated by Victorian-style structures. By most accounts the real magic lasted for only a brief spell. Happenings and concerts in the adjacent parks attracted throngs of long-haired and flamboyantly attired young people who felt the city's vibe, and who embraced its particular rendition of the countercultural upheavals of the 1960s.

Fleeing from what they perceived as the stifling culture of President Lyndon Johnson's Great Society, the freaks and heads who descended upon the "Hashbury" reveled in afternoons spent savoring such pastimes as "acid, incense, and balloons" (to cop a line from Jefferson Airplane). Within a year, Haight-Ashbury was a household name across the country, a symbol for the defiance of the psychedelic generation. Very soon, though, hunger, homelessness, violence, and frequent overdoses took center stage, and the original hippies hightailed it to more sanguine locales in Marin County or points north. The period's acid rock is an enduring legacy of the hippie period, with distinctive recordings from the Grateful Dead, Jefferson Airplane, Santana, and scores of other bands still sounding fresh and spontaneous.

While still attracting a fair share of tie-dyed seekers, the Haight today has mellowed from its late-1960s peak. The vintage head shops are mainly gone. The area is often described as gentrified. But a number of cafés and boutiques remain, keeping the Day-Glo memories alive.

Throughout northwestern San Francisco are a number of parks, one of which—Golden Gate—rivals the world's finest. This park, in particular, is a sight worth seeing

in any season. One of the world's largest, it was carefully constructed—like Central Park in New York—to enhance the city by bringing abundant nature within its boundaries. Hence the lakes, streams, bridges, and wide expanses of greenery were built in the late 1800s atop an area known as the Great Sand Wastes. Despite intense pessimism that anything could be made to flourish in what was considered a miniature desert, Golden Gate Park now stands as a testament to nature. There are playgrounds, conservatories, gardens, museums, a planetarium, an aquarium, a polo field, athletic fields, and a golf course, all conspiring to make this a wonderful place to kick back and forget time and tide alike.

To the west lies Ocean Beach, a three-mile stretch of shoreline offering numerous fine vantage points of the Pacific; to the south, an 18-hole golf course snakes around beautiful Lake Merced in Harding Park. North of Golden Gate Park are Lincoln Park and the Presidio, the onetime army outpost whose manicured lawns provide entrée to the Golden Gate Bridge.

The Golden Gate. No Cook's Tour of San Francisco would be complete without either beginning or ending at this stunning site. Even without the bridge, this inlet is a beautiful thing to behold; viewing it from any angle reveals the power of the ocean surge as the Pacific and the Bay engage in eternal communication. But with the completion of the Golden Gate Bridge, the passage was ordained to stand as San Francisco's best-known symbol.

© FRED VERHOEVEN

The bridge itself is one of those structures that almost defy imagination: you look at it and you can't believe that what you're seeing is real. Built from 1933 to 1937, the bridge grace-fully blends with the high cliffs of the Golden Gate to tie San Francisco's peninsula with Marin County to the north. Walk-ing or driving the 4,200-foot main bridge is equally rewarding, with the art deco towers soaring overhead like dream structures, often reaching into banks of low clouds. The bridge is to San Francisco what the Eiffel Tower is to Paris, or the Statue of Lib-erty is to New York: a testament to the ability of man-made beauty not only to enhance nature, but to grant some sort of transcendence amid the bustle of everyday city life.

THE CITY ITSELF IS BY NO MEANS THE ONLY SOURCE OF BEAUTY. THE ENTIRE BAY AREA, and beyond, is a string of wonders.

Starting in the North Bay Area, there's Point Reyes National Seashore, with its lighthouse serving as a guide for ships that ventured too close to this wild and stormy seascape. The San Andreas Fault runs through here in a distinctive way, allowing visitors to see the fault line that continues to make life in these parts something of an exercise in anticipation. The park's Earthquake Trail runs along the fault and highlights points of interest, such as the spot where the entire peninsula was jolted as much as 20 feet to the north during the 1906 earthquake. Another North Bay attraction is Muir Woods National Monument, which features some of the most impressive redwoods in the state, with some topping the 250-foot mark. The hiking trails that meander through these majestic trees are favorite attractions for tourists and area residents alike.

Marin County—just across the Golden Gate from San Francisco—is home to a number of cities (many residents call them villages) that are best described as upscale and picturesque. Mill Valley and Sausalito are perhaps the best known of these enclaves, and have been wildly popular in the past 30 years or so; San Rafael is the largest, with residential, commercial, and industrial areas spreading out from the old mission, and

with the arches of the Frank Lloyd Wright-designed Marin Civic Center showcasing modern development. A visit to Marin County shows why the area is so popular: the foggy shoreline rises up into gentle mountains (not an oxymoron in this case), and wildlife is abundant and beautiful.

The East Bay Area is a vast world of cities unto itself, with a population topping 2.2 million in the Oakland metropolitan area alone. The East Bay is connected to San Francisco by the BART (Bay Area Rapid Transit), ferries, and the San Francisco-Oakland Bay Bridge; further south there's the San Mateo Bridge and the Dumbarton Bridge. The cities lining the East Bay include Richmond, Albany, Berkeley, Oakland, Alameda, San Leandro, Hayward, Newark, and Fremont.

Berkeley is known as a cutting-edge intellectual and cultural center. The home of the University of California (U.C.) at Berkeley—which dominates (some say polarizes) city life—the city is a pioneer in everything from politics to dining to nuclear science. In addition to its revolution-making activities, Berkeley is also quite an attractive city, with magnificent views of the bay from several of its hills, and with the fine University of California Botanical Garden featuring nearly 13,000 species of plants arranged in themed gardens.

Oakland, while very much a part of the Bay Area, tends to see itself as the most independent of the area's cities; whenever the talk turns to San Francisco, Oaklanders wonder why *their* city isn't the one that comes first in the conversation. Oakland sees itself as the more level-headed twin leader of the Bay Area. A rail and shipping center, Oakland has developed wide industrial bases for its economy without sacrificing the intrinsic natural resources that make the entire area special. Jack London Square, a historic district named for the author who once lived there, features shops and dining, as well as such landmarks as Heinold's First and Last Chance Saloon, an 1883 establishment frequented by London, and the waterfront area where the first ferry service to San Francisco was instituted in 1850.

© FRED VERHOEVEN

The South Bay and Silicon Valley are much too vast to cover in any sort of cursory way. San Jose alone is one of the fastest-growing cities in the country; its new international airport stands to become a busy transportation and distribution hub for the entire region. Suffice it to say that this part of the San Francisco Bay Area teems with creativity, innovation, and progress. That's about as good a summary statement as you'll get, because this area is also extremely diverse, ranging from office parks and skyscrapers to freeways and sprawling shopping complexes; from traditional subdivisions to lavish homes built in the beautiful hills. Santa Clara, Mountain View, Sunnyvale, Cupertino, Palo Alto, Redwood City, San Mateo, Menlo Park, San Bruno, Pacifica—the names are as distinctive as the communities, which tend to blend high-tech and conventional commercial centers with carefully designed residential areas, creating a unique collection of communities that are (to swipe a popular area term) symbiotic in their relationships to each other, not to mention to San Francisco to their north.

San Jose, one of the first cities in California, is today one of the largest, with a metropolitan population that's surpassed the 1.5 million mark. Until World War II the city was mainly known as an agricultural center, but during the war years it emerged as a manufacturing center for such items as aircraft parts and electrical components. Aerospace firms moved in, and after them, the computer folks, many of whom settled in the Santa Clara Valley to the north of San Jose, creating what has become known the world over simply as Silicon Valley. The result, for San Jose and the entire valley, was an unprecedented spurt in growth, which continues unabated. For example, San Jose's population more than tripled between 1960 and 1980. While there's still a good deal

SAN FRANCISCO

of agricultural activity—distribution, mainly, with some processing activity as well—San Jose is now an international center for a wide array of manufacturing and production. The San Jose Municipal Rose Garden and Alum Rock Park are reminders of the magnificent natural surroundings in which this economic activity has flourished.

Silicon Valley itself is harder to pin down. As a pioneering collection of communities located north and northeast of San Jose, its rise has been rocketlike, and its boundaries are still growing to encompass more and more of the South Bay area. Fueled in part by the brain power from Stanford University in Palo Alto, the area has—since around World War II—been transformed from hilly orchards and farming communities into the economic engine for the cyber-revolution. Sunnyvale, Cupertino, Los Altos, and Mountain View are city names likely to show up on software packages and computer shipping boxes; here are the homes (and often birthplaces) of such semiconductor and computer companies as Apple Computer, Adobe Systems, Hewlett-Packard, Lockheed, and Netscape Communications (to name a very, very few). About a decade ago, what had begun as a computer manufacturing center began morphing into an economic community with a strong emphasis on R&D and software development.

K EEP TRAVELING NORTH, UP THE PENINSULA, AND YOU'RE RIGHT BACK WHERE WE STARTED this little excursion: San Francisco, spiritual and cultural hub for the entire Bay Area. And the point to end with is this: we've barely scratched the surface. The San Francisco Bay Area is too rich, too diverse, and too big to be captured in any one set of images or anecdotes.

We didn't mention, for instance, any of the rich history of the region, from its rise during the Gold Rush of 1849 to its downfall in the earthquake of 1906. Although nearly destroyed by the quake (which, modern estimates say, measured greater than 8 on the Richter scale) and four days of fires that raged after it hit, San Francisco quickly rebuilt: Within a decade, the city was playing host to a the Panama-Pacific International Exposition, and was boasting of its resilience in the face of such calamity.

Nor did we mention the wild affinity area fans hold for professional sports franchises—the San Francisco Giants, the 49ers, the Oakland A's, the Raiders, the Golden State Warriors (also in Oakland), and the San Jose Sharks. Each has its loyal legion of fans and fanatics, and each adds immeasurably to the experience of living in the Bay Area.

And we mentioned only a couple of the area's outstanding institutions of higher education. In addition to Stanford and UC-Berkeley, there are the private University of San Francisco and the public San Francisco State University. In Oakland you have Holy Names College, Mills College, and the renowned California College of Arts and Crafts. And in San Jose there is San Jose State University and, nearby, Santa Clara University. That, once again, is just listing a few.

As for dining, shopping, museums, parks, recreation, galleries, hotels—forget about it. Best just to state the obvious, and acknowledge that the Bay Area offers more in the way of entertainment and recreation than any place you'll find.

On we could go, trying to define the area's character and trying to list just some of its many assets. But that's already been tried, many times, and, no matter how gallant the outcome, it's always a futile chore. San Francisco and the Bay Area are more than a collection of attractions, or an amalgam of beautiful vistas, or a vibrant economic center. San Francisco is a spirit, as deep as the fog that wanders the city's hills. ✍

SAN FRANCISCO

WHEN SPANISH EXPLORERS first laid eyes on San Francisco Bay in 1769, the magnificence of the beauty before them was stunning. Today, an estimated 6.8 million people call the Bay Area home.

 PERCH ATOP EITHER OF SAN Francisco's two famous bridges commands an incredible view of the Bay Area. One of the longest—1.2 miles—and strongest suspension bridges in the world, the Golden Gate Bridge (OPPOSITE) has linked the city with Marin County since 1937. Stretching 8.25 miles, the Bay Bridge (ABOVE) joins the city with neighboring Oakland.

ALF THE FUN OF SAN FRAN-
cisco is getting there. Long
a popular destination for
hitchhikers, the city today
bustles with savvy drivers—some
equipped with the latest in high-
tech satellite navigation systems.

A H, THE JOYS OF THE MORN-
ing commute. With gridlock
high on its fortunately short
list of problems, the Bay
Area suffers from traffic jams that
can prove challenging even on the
best of days.

The Streets of San Francisco was a popular television program in the 1970s, but long before that, the city's Financial District bustled with the activity of trolleys, cars, and crowds.

DIAGONAL CROSSING O. K. 7 A.M. – 7 P.M. MON-FRI ONLY

MODERN SAN FRANCISCO reverberates with the energy of a city that is constantly on the move.

GOLD!

Not since the Gold Rush has there been so much glitter in San Francisco. The Pacific Stock Exchange (bottom left) is the hub of the city's business, an area made richer in recent years by the entrepreneurial efforts of Jeremy Lent (opposite). Lent's Internet-based credit card company, NextCard, has been taking the electronic financial frontier by storm since its inception in 1997.

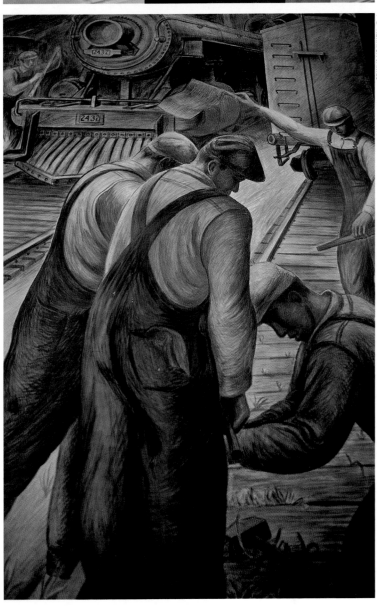

L ONG KNOWN FOR ITS CABLE
cars, San Francisco also res-
onates with the rhythms of
trains and electric buses.
Today's commuters have the
added luxury of BART—Bay
Area Rapid Transit (TOP RIGHT).

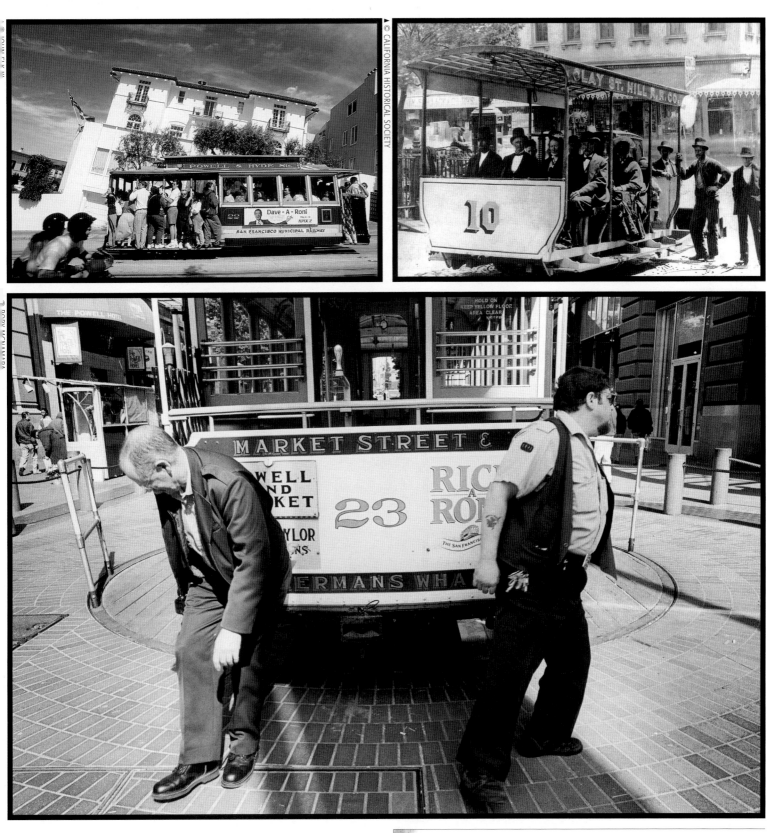

BORN IN 1873, SAN FRAN-cisco's cable car system was the first moving National Historic Landmark in the United States. At its peak, the system supported some 600 cars, and although the number has dwindled to around 40, the renovated cars are still a major attraction.

IGH ATOP TELEGRAPH
Hill rises Coit Tower
(OPPOSITE TOP). At 210 feet
tall, the circular structure—
named after local philanthropist
Lillie Hitchcock Coit—offers a
spectacular view of the city.
The hairpin curves of Lombard
Street—known as the crookedest
street in the world—compose part
of that view (LEFT AND OPPOSITE
BOTTOM). Adorned with rows of
hedges, shrubs, and hundreds
of colorful flowers, the historic
Russian Hill street presents a
challenge for both man and
machine.

WITH ALL THE HILLS AND dales that pepper the Bay Area, it's little wonder some of its occupants need to take time out for recharging. Even bike messenger Court Bell (OPPOSITE) takes a breather now and then.

WHETHER YOU DRIVE A classic car or a newer model, San Francisco's Filbert Street (OPPOSITE TOP) is most inclined to encour- age a little proactive parking. As one of the city's steepest stretches of pavement, Filbert has one section that boasts a 31.5-degree pitch.

NATURAL DISASTERS POSE an unfortunate reality for San Francisco residents — from the devastating 1906 and 1989 earthquakes to the 1991 firestorm that swept the Oakland hills. Using tiles painted by sur- vivors of the October 20 fire, ceramic artist Gail Smithwalter assembled the Firestorm Tile mural, on display outside the Rockridge BART station (BOT- TOM LEFT).

LOMA PRIETA EARTHQUAKE OCTOBER 17, 1989

SEISMOGRAPH TRANSMIT...

I T'S UP TO FOLKS LIKE GE-
ologist Pat Williams (OPPOSITE)
to keep tabs on the Bay Area's
earthshaking activity as he
inspects the rock wall of a mining
shaft beneath the University of
California, Berkeley campus.

Residents seem to keep a sense
of humor about the threat of
quakes and, if the real thing
doesn't do it for you, plenty of
artificial alternatives exist to
simulate the seismic experience.

ONE NOTICEABLE AFTERMATH of Bay Area earthquakes is the ongoing cycle of construction they provoke. The city—whether rebuilding or just building anew—continues to move forward with such modern landmarks as the $140 million Main Library (BOTTOM RIGHT), opened in 1996 .

© THOR SWIFT

HIGH TECHNOLOGY ABOUNDS in the San Francisco area— there's even a museum to honor it. In nearby San Jose, the three-level Tech Museum of Innovation (OPPOSITE TOP AND OPPOSITE, BOTTOM LEFT) shows the role of technology in everyday life. Visitors to a Seybold San Francisco Publishing Conference (TOP) get their first look at the iMac, developed under the leadership of charismatic Apple cofounder and CEO Steve Jobs (BOTTOM RIGHT). Other innovators in the burgeoning high-tech field include Excite Communities' Scott Derringer (OPPOSITE, BOTTOM RIGHT) and Intel Chairman Andy Grove (BOTTOM LEFT).

THE INCREDIBLE YERBA
Buena Gardens attracted
its first tenant in 1993 and
has been going strong ever
since. An arts and cultural complex, the $87 million project is
anchored by the Moscone

Convention Center (OPPOSITE
BOTTOM)—named after the city's
assassinated mayor, George
Moscone. An interactive arts
center for youngsters, Zeum
(OPPOSITE TOP) forms a part of
the gardens' rooftop attractions.

AS FIXTURES ON THE SAN Francisco scene, the famous Brown twins, Vivian and Miriam—or is that Miriam and Vivian?—appear at functions everywhere. Of course, a long day of shopping at the stores of Union Square (OPPOSITE) or touring through the city would have the best of folks seeing double—or more.

AFRAID TO DRIVE UP AND down San Francisco's hilly streets? Then public transportation is the way to get around. The municipal railway system—known as MUNI—is responsible for all cable cars, streetcars, trains, and buses, both conventional and electric. With routes throughout the city, MUNI can deliver you to almost any destination.

広島駅

GOLDEN GATE TIGERS

GOLDEN GATE TIGERS

25 BRYANT	J CHURCH	23 CRESCENT	CALIFORNIA-25TH	3RD ST
26 VALENCIA	CHURCH EXPRESS	27 NOE	WEBSTER-JACKSON	
26 VALENCIA EXPRESS	JUDAH EXPRESS	29 VISITACION VALLEY	26TH-CASTRO	KANSAS-17T
15 3RD-KEARNY EXPRESS	N JUDAH	33 ASHBURY	3RD-PALOU	ARLET
15 3RD KEARNY	66 QUINTARA	34 WOODSIDE		UNION
42 3RD EVANS	66 QUINTARA LIMITED	35 EUREKA	GLEN PARK BART	BROADW
40 COMMUTER	71 NORIEGA LIMITED	36 MIRALOMA	MISSION	MARINA BL
4 FREEWAY EXPRESS	71 HAIGHT-NORIEGA	37 CORBETT	FOREST HILL STA.	GENEVA-MIS
7		51 SILVER	PERSHING DRIVE	

ONCE A 30-BLOCK ENCLAVE, San Francisco's Japantown began experiencing a re-birth with the opening of the Japan Center in 1968 (OPPO-SITE, TOP AND BOTTOM RIGHT).

Known by locals as *Nihonmachi,* the area's many traditional celebrations, such as the Cherry Blossom Festival (OPPOSITE, TOP AND BOTTOM LEFT), keep the community's spirit alive.

© SHARON SELDEN

WITH ITS COLORFUL BANners and street markets, Chinatown offers an excursion into the riches of the Orient—West Coast-style. An estimated 120,000 Chinese-Americans live in the Bay Area, and this historic neighborhood, with Portsmouth Square at its hub, serves as home to many of them.

HE CHINESE NEW YEAR is a time for wild celebration on the streets of Chinatown, where parades, dragon dances, vibrant costumes, and lots of firecrackers fill the night air. Other evenings, it's the street lights and brightly lit signage along main thoroughfares such as Grant Avenue (OPPOSITE) that provide the area's aura.

TRAVELING NORTH ALONG Grant Avenue delivers you to San Francisco's North Beach neighborhood—aka Little Italy—where restaurants such as the garlic-rich Stinking Rose (TOP) and Calzone's (BOTTOM LEFT) have been dishing up Italian delicacies for years.

francisco

italy

ANY WITH ITALIAN HER-itage call North Beach—a neighbor to Chinatown—home. And, according to at least one mural artist, the rela-tionship between the city and its Italian residents occurred through a bit of divine intervention.

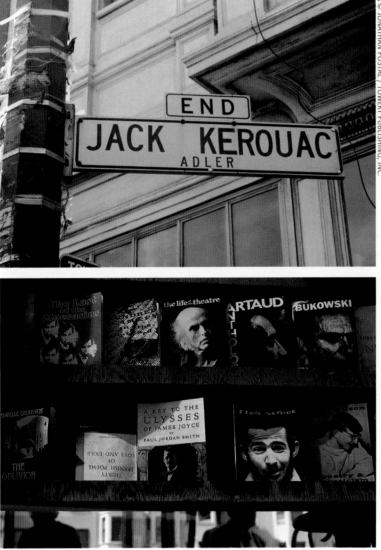

© JONATHAN POSTAL / TOWERY PUBLISHING, INC.

DURING THE 1950S AND 1960s, San Francisco's North Beach community served as ground zero for the Beat Generation, a group of young writers—championed by Lawrence Ferlinghetti (ABOVE) and his City Lights Bookstore— whose literary contributions were often overshadowed by their lifestyles. Fame, mixed with little fortune, played evil tricks on some of the group's members— Jack Kerouac among them. His health destroyed from drinking, Kerouac died in 1969 at age 47. The author of *On the Road* has the alley next to City Lights— ironically a dead end—named in his honor.

this city that grows with my dreams
dances with each new step,
creating intricate universes that expand through my senses
and hope that beats warm against the rythm
of my deepest heart .....
Todd

VESUV

WHEN THE SHADOW OF THE GRASSHOPPER
FALLS ACROSS THE TRAIL OF THE FIELD MOUSE
ON GREEN AND SLIMEY GRASS AS A RED SUN RISES
ABOVE THE WESTERN HORIZON SILHOUETTING
A GAUNT AND TAUTLY MUSCLED INDIAN WARRIOR
PERCHED WITH BOW AND ARROW COCKED AND AIMED
STRAIGHT AT YOU ITS TIME FOR ANOTHER MARTINI

S PONTANEOUS WRITING — the method preferred by the Beat elite—remains an art in North Beach even today. When they weren't squirreled away writing poems and novels, the Beats spent plenty of time in Vesuvio Cafe (TOP AND BOTTOM LEFT), a hot spot that is still good for a stiff martini.

A CITY FOR ALL SEASONS

ONE WAY

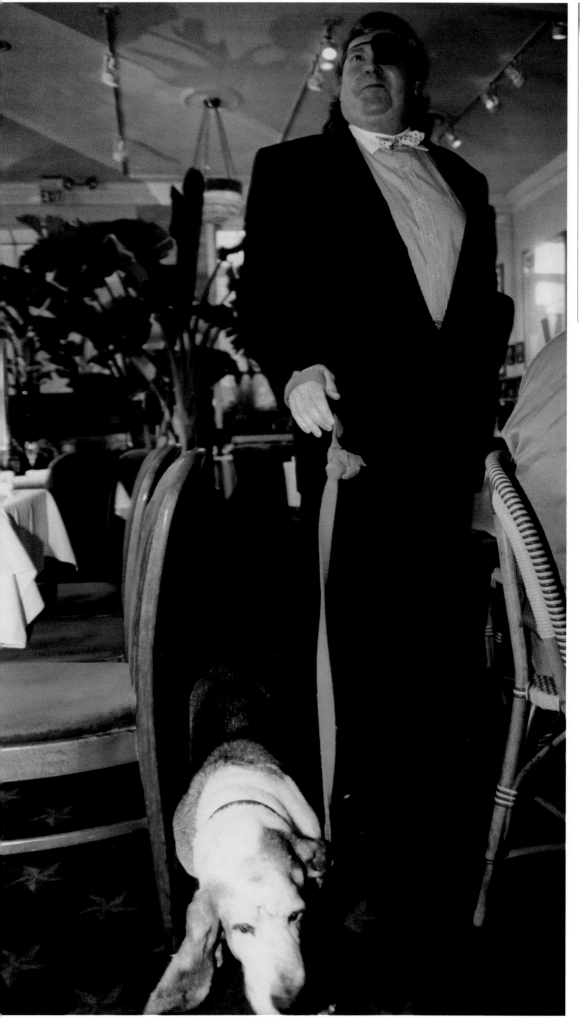

SINCE THE EARLY 1960S, celebrated and notorious Bay Area columnist Warren Hinckle (LEFT) has been upending the status quo. For 17 of those years, he was accompanied literally everywhere by his dog, Bentley. To much fanfare and coverage, the aging basset hound's last meal took place at the restaurant Stars. San Francisco also serves as home base for writers Armistead Maupin (OPPOSITE, TOP RIGHT) and Jewelle Gomez (OPPOSITE BOTTOM), while hard-boiled detective novelist Dashiell Hammett got a city street named after himself— even though he spent only a few years as a local resident.

© JEFF MYERS

© JONATHAN POSTAL / TOWERY PUBLISHING, INC.

THE APPROPRIATELY NAMED View Lounge atop the San Francisco Marriott provides an exhilarating glimpse of the city's scenic expanse (TOP). But for the best take on the bay and the Golden Gate Bridge, head to Fisherman's Wharf for a serving of cioppino at Alioto's (OPPOSITE). If it's Mediterranean cuisine you long for, food prepared by Moose's chef Brian Whitmer should fit the bill (BOTTOM RIGHT), while North Beach's Black Cat and owner/chef Reed Hearon (BOTTOM LEFT) boast a menu as varied as the city itself.

A HOY, MATIES! FOR MORE than 100 years, sailors— and all others—arriving in the Bay Area have been welcomed by the heavenly tastes of Boudin sourdough French bread and Anchor Steam Beer, two of the finer San Francisco treats.

© JAMES LEMASS

THE INVITING WATERS of San Francisco Bay and Oakland's inner harbor serve both utilitarian and pleasurable purposes. A mock sea battle (BOTTOM RIGHT) harks back to a time before the Gold Rush, when ships from Boston and other faraway cities would come to the bay to barter for pelts and other goods.

TRUE TO THE CITY'S WATERY roots, the San Francisco Maritime National Historical Park traces the history of seafaring life in the Bay Area. One part of the park, Hyde Street Pier, features *Balclutha*, a square-rigged, three-masted Cape Horn sailing ship first launched in 1886 (OPPOSITE AND BOTTOM RIGHT). But while sailing may have changed over the years, one thing remains constant: the tattooed sailor.

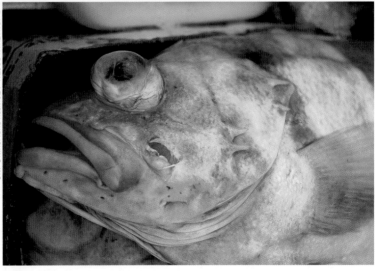

THE WATERS SURROUNDING San Francisco can prove challenging for both man and beast. Fishing once was a major industry in the Bay Area, though sites like the famous Fisherman's Wharf have given way to tourist attractions over the years.

ONE OF THE BEST-KNOWN tourist spots in San Francisco, the Fisherman's Wharf area offers shopping, fun, and good food. Among the many sights to see are Ghirardelli Square, original home to the famous chocolate factory, and Pier 39 (OPPOSITE), an old cargo pier with a great view of Alcatraz.

AN ORIGINAL CASTING of Auguste Rodin's *The Thinker* greets visitors to the California Palace of the Legion of Honor (OPPOSITE, TOP RIGHT). Located in Lincoln Park on cliffs high above the ocean, the palace's more than 20 galleries display a range of European art from the 14th through the 20th centuries. It's marine life that draws the crowds in Golden Gate Park, where Steinhart Aquarium (OPPOSITE, TOP AND BOTTOM LEFT) houses hundreds of species of fish. Not to be outdone, Pier 39—a veritable shopping mecca—displays a whale of a wall, courtesy of mural artist Wyland (ABOVE), and is home to Underwater World (OPPOSITE, BOTTOM RIGHT), where visitors travel through an aquatic wonderland along a 300-foot-long transparent tunnel.

SAN FRANCISCO IS HEAVEN ON EARTH !!!

Precita Valley Vision © 1996 All Rights Reserved
Mural by Susan Kelk Cervantes

FROM GREENPEACE TO beach cleanups, from angelic flyovers to heavenly messages: For every cause, San Francisco offers a mission or a mural.

OFTEN THOUGHT OF AS A complex city made up of many parts, San Francisco nonetheless exudes a real knack for stating the obvious.

COASTAL REDWOODS ARE among the oldest species of tree alive today—believed to have preceded humankind. Yet it's people who have fought to save the redwood forests over the years—Earth First! protestors among them. Jedediah Smith Redwoods State Park (OPPOSITE), founded in 1929, was one of the earliest such areas established to protect the giant trees.

ORTHERN CALIFORNIA'S natural beauty comes alive at Golden Gate Park, a 1,000-acre treasure founded in 1870. Stretching for two miles out to the ocean, the park features numerous attractions, including Stow Lake (OPPOSITE, TOP LEFT) and the Japanese Tea Garden (ABOVE).

WITH ITS YEAR-ROUND
temperate climate and
indisputable natural
beauty, the Bay Area is
the perfect spot for the outdoor
artist in all of us.

T HE ONLY REMAINING ARCHI-
tectural masterpiece built
for the 1915 Panama-Pacific
International Exposition,
the Palace of Fine Arts in the
Marina District helped the city
celebrate the opening of the
Panama Canal. With its reflecting pool and its domed rotunda,
the building is the site of the
Exploratorium, an entertaining,
hands-on science center for both
kids and grown-ups.

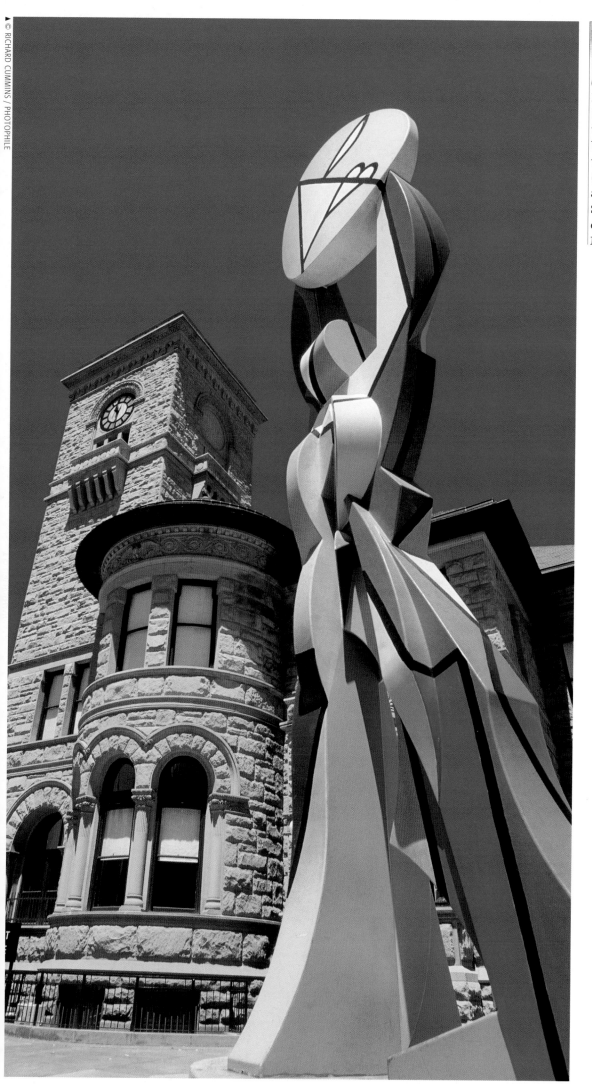

PUBLIC SCULPTURE TAKES on many forms in the Bay Area—from tributes to well-known figures including Buddha (OPPOSITE, TOP LEFT) and Sun Yat-sen (OPPOSITE, TOP RIGHT) to Christian figures such as the bronze sculptures outside the ultramodern St. Mary's Cathedral (OPPOSITE, BOTTOM LEFT). And, assuming you know the way to San Jose, you can get a colorful eyeful as well at the San Jose Museum of Art (LEFT).

RELIGIOUS ICONOGRAPHY becomes a specialized art form given the right inspiration. Each year, professional artists flock to downtown San Rafael to participate in the Italian Street Painting Festival, a fundraising event for the city's Youth in Arts program (OPPOSITE TOP). While all the works aren't religious in nature, the Spanish domes of nearby Mission San Rafael Archangel influence at least some of them. The gilded bronze doors of Grace Cathedral (LEFT) were made from casts of Ghiberti's *Gates of Paradise*, located on the doors of the baptistery of the Santa Maria del Fiore Cathedral in Florence, Italy.

OR SAN FRANCISCO'S active gay and lesbian community, the thriving Castro district is home to numerous community events. The neon marquee of the Castro Theatre (TOP), a stunning, depression-era cinema, still shines today as a beacon for the area. Prior to the showing of the theater's classic and art movies, David Hegarty (BOTTOM) takes to the pipe organ and serenades the gathering crowd.

ROM METROPOLITAN Community Church Easter services at the cross on Mount Davidson (LEFT) to the bonnets of an Easter parade, community pride abounds in the Castro. Ever active in city events, the San Francisco Gay Men's Chorus spreads some holiday cheer to those in the AIDS ward of Davies Medical Center (BOTTOM).

IMPLE EXPRESSIONS OF
faith take on many forms
in San Francisco. From
Christianity to Buddhism
and everything in between,
the city's diverse religious life
makes common what in other
cities would be a rarity.

SAN FRANCISC

MILITARY FORMATION IS nothing new to the Bay Area. The 1,480-acre Presidio (OPPOSITE) served as a military post for more than 200 years, but today is part of the National Park System and features hiking, biking, scenic views, and 620 historic buildings. Standing in the shadows of the Golden Gate Bridge, Fort Point has a spot on the National Register of Historic Places. Constructed between 1853 and 1861 as protection from sea attack during the Civil War, the site now contains a museum.

WITHIN THE BOUNDARIES of the Presidio lie portions of the Golden Gate National Recreation Area (OPPOSITE) and San Francisco National Cemetery. Around 30,000 soldiers came to rest in the 19th-century, cypress-tree-shrouded burial ground, where some headstones predate the Civil War.

THE BAY AREA COMMEM-orates historic events in thought-provoking ways. Near the California Palace of the Legion of Honor, sculptor George Segal has created a gripping tribute to persecuted victims in his piece *The Holocaust* (CENTER AND OPPOSITE). A memorial that is the focal point of Yerba Buena Gardens features 12 glass panels that preserve the words of Dr. Martin Luther King Jr. behind a cascading waterfall.

I have the audacity to believe that peoples everywhere can have three meals a day for their bodies, education and culture for their minds, and dignity, equality and freedom for their spirits. I believe that what self-centered men have torn down men other-centered can build up.

誰人たれとも、肉体のために日に三度の食事を、心のために教育と
文化を、精神のために尊厳、平等、自由を得る権利がある。
躊躇することなく信じる。利己主義の人間が破壊してきたもの、それは
利他主義の人間によって築かれると信じる。

OAKLAND
All Nations

© LISA HOFFMAN

IT SAYS A LOT ABOUT A CITY when a man who once ruled the state and aspired to the presidency is now its CEO. Oakland may live in the shadow of its neighbor across the bay, but don't tell Mayor Jerry Brown (OPPOSITE, BOTTOM LEFT) or any of the city's other roughly 370,000 residents. Writer Jack London called Oakland home in his early years, and the city pays tribute to him today with a statue in a historic square named—appropriately—Jack London Square.

I N TIMES OF PROTEST AND
celebration, or in moments
of zealous protection, San
Franciscans from the common
citizen to Mayor Willie Brown
(OPPOSITE, TOP LEFT) always seem
to find a way to come together.

© JONATHAN POSTAL / TOWERY PUBLISHING, INC.

© ERIC SLOMANSON / ZUMA

THE POWER OF THE WORD carries a great deal of weight in California, a state known for its more liberal — all things being relative — views. KQED 88.5 FM's Michael Krasny (TOP RIGHT) hosts a wealth of opinions on local matters during his weekday program, *Forum*. And you can bet the names of California's elected officials — U.S. Congresswoman Nancy Pelosi and Senators Barbara Boxer and Dianne Feinstein among them (FROM LEFT, BOTTOM RIGHT) — get mentioned during the live public affairs show.

THE HALLS OF GOVERNMENT in the Bay Area have a reputation for being quite lively. Two formidable components of the area's political stew are City and County of San Francisco Board of Supervisors President Tom Ammiano (BOTTOM) and San Mateo County Superior Court Judge Quentin L. Kopp (OPPOSITE).

WITH SO MANY DIVERSE populations contributing to the mix, activity in San Francisco's recently re-furbished City Hall is frequently aswirl.

THE ARTS FLOURISH IN the environs of the Bay Area. Since 1993, Carey Perloff (OPPOSITE TOP) has been guiding the Tony Award-winning American Conservatory Theater, a nonprofit company founded in 1965. The San Francisco Opera, a fixture since 1923, and the San Francisco Symphony, performing in Louise M. Davies Symphony Hall, help complete the cultural palette.

FROM THE CLASSICS TO THE avant-garde, San Francisco theater thrives. The antics of the San Francisco Mime Troupe (TOP LEFT) will have you splitting a gut in laughter, but it's most likely to be black humor audiences will encounter at Bindlestiff Studio, an underground theater in the South of Market area (BOTTOM).

FROM THE REAL TO THE surreal, a lot depends on your cinematic angle. The genre at Yerba Buena Center for the Arts ranges from oddball westerns to film noir under the direction of film and video cu- rator Joel Shepard (TOP). At the Werepad (OPPOSITE), an art warehouse in Protero Hill, expect the unexpected from organizers Jacques Boyreau, Scott Moffett, and Vikki Vaden. On the small screen, life in *The Real World*— MTV's city-roving documentary that throws unknown roommates together for six months of living in the camera's eye—got a little too real following its 1994 San Francisco-based season when cast member Pedro Zamora died of an AIDS-related illness. Cast members (BOTTOM LEFT) Pamela Ling (LEFT) and Judd Winick (RIGHT) developed a close friend- ship with Zamora's partner, Sean Sasser (CENTER), who is himself living with HIV.

CRIME THAT PERMEATES inner-city neighborhoods is nothing to smile about. Officer Tim Kiely of the Tenderloin Task Force (BOTTOM) hopes the happy-face sticker on the butt of his gun will help break the ice with the area's children, many of whom have parents in prison. Although he's clearly got a hot hand, vintage clothing collector Ricky Quisol (TOP) typically gets his bangs from the drum set as he plays with local bands, including the Hobnobbers and Atomic Cocktail.

UNTIL 1963, SOME OF the most notorious, high-security prisoners in the federal system served their time in Alcatraz Penitentiary. Among those who have spent time inside the island prison—a short, 15-minute boat ride from San Francisco—are former guard John Hernan (RIGHT), an ex-prisoner named Leon (OPPOSITE CENTER), and Phil Bergen (OPPOSITE BOTTOM), a former captain of the guards.

A LOOMING CONCRETE island in the distance, Alcatraz is known equally well as the Rock. Its mysterious beauty belies a foreboding past.

WHILE PARTICIPANTS IN the annual New Year's Day swim to Alcatraz wear clothing designed to avoid hypothermia, runners in the San Francisco Examiner's Bay to Breakers footrace barely give it a thought. The 7.46-mile run has become as well known for its costumed contestants as it has for its buff ones—leading to a subevent dubbed, appropriately, Bare to Breakers.

F ISH GOTTA SWIM AND
Californians gotta surf.
From the nude beaches of
Devil's Slide in San Mateo
to the waves off Santa Cruz,
the lure of the Pacific Ocean
beckons.

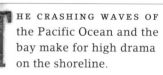
THE CRASHING WAVES OF the Pacific Ocean and the bay make for high drama on the shoreline.

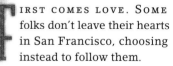

FIRST COMES LOVE. SOME folks don't leave their hearts in San Francisco, choosing instead to follow them.

T HEN COMES MARRIAGE. What more scenic spot can there be for a wedding portrait than the Golden Gate?

Then comes baby in a baby carriage. In hospitals throughout the Bay Area, newborns enter the world ready to take on its many challenges.

IN ADDITION TO ITS EVER growing human population, the Bay Area supports a wealth of animal life, the most exotic of which call the San Francisco Zoo home.

© PEGGY PATTERSON / GEOIMAGERY

L ET'S FACE IT: No MATTER what kids do, they have a way of pulling it off with angelic charm. Throughout San Francisco, folks—and fountains—are putting on a happy face (PAGES 155-157).

156

158

A TRUE RELIC OF OLD SAN Francisco, the Cliff House (OPPOSITE) has been around in one incarnation or another since 1863. Built in 1909, today's version—the third— features restaurants that overlook Seal Rock—although barking sea lions rather than seals sun themselves there. Below the cliffs, a second longtime attraction, the Musée Mécanique (TOP), displays a variety of antique mechanical items from fortune-telling machines to Merlin (BOTTOM RIGHT). Not ones to hide behind clever foreign names for their drawing power, the traveling carnies at an Oakland Coliseum swap meet put it all out there for customer consideration (BOTTOM LEFT).

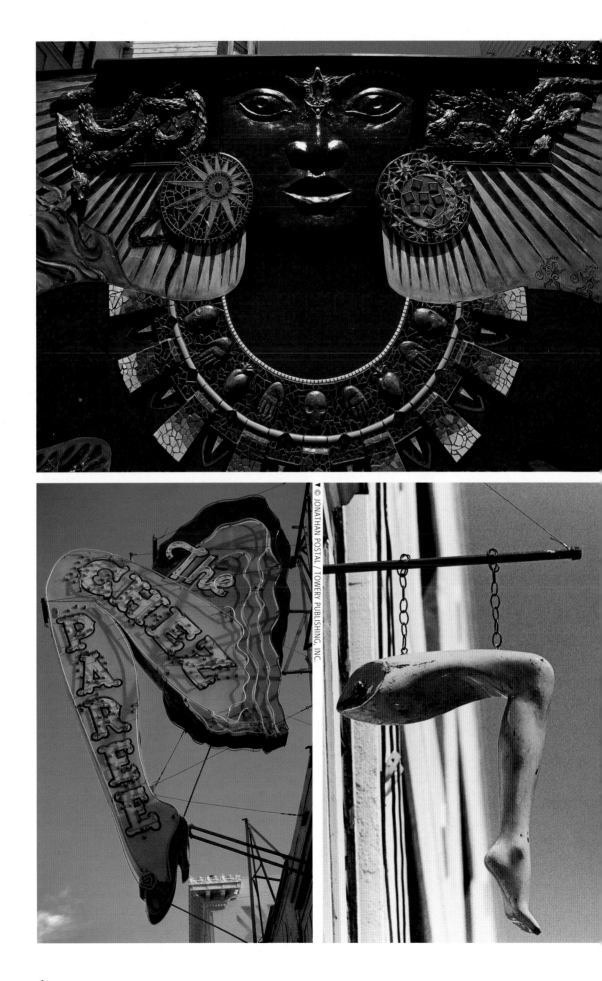

See SUSIE
DANCE THE
CAN-CAN

WHY?

TATTOOED TWINS

WHY

ALIVE

—Maya Hayuk—

T HOSE WACKY SAN FRAN-
ciscans always seem to have
a leg up when it comes to the
more unusual things in life.

Planetarium

T HE WONDERS OF SAN Francisco cause some folks to flip head over heals, proving that what goes up must come down. To learn even more about gravitational pull and the earth's mysteries, visit the California Academy of Sciences' Earth and Space Hall in Golden Gate Park (OPPOSITE BOTTOM) and the Exploratorium (BOTTOM), housed in the Palace of Fine Arts.

THOUGHTFUL CONTEMPLA-
tion, whether scholarly or
otherwise, can take place
anywhere, even in a jump-
ing town like San Francisco. Of
course, a combination laundromat
and café sounds like a great re-
treat for washing away the blues.

From herbs to acupuncture, the wisdom of centuries of Eastern medicine lies behind storefront windows in the Bay Area. Attempting to take its place alongside the ginseng and echinacea is the counterculture drug of the 1960s—marijuana. A leader for its legalization for medicinal purposes, Dennis Peron (OPPOSITE, BOTTOM RIGHT) helped guide Proposition 215—the initiative to make pot available with a doctor's prescription—to victory in 1996.

HAIGHT

BAY AREA MUSIC AWARDS HALL OF FAME

JERRY GARCIA

THE 1960S SPAWNED A wealth of talent that thrives even today. Late in the decade, underground cartoonists Spain Rodriguez (BOTTOM LEFT) and Robert Crumb (BOTTOM CENTER) joined forces with five colleagues to create *Zap*, a groundbreaking comic book that vividly depicted the sex, drugs, and rock and roll of the time. Applying his artistry in a different vein, Don Ed Hardy (BOTTOM RIGHT) is widely regarded as the premier tattoo artist in the United States. And from the visual to the aural, concert promoter Chet Helms (OPPOSITE) organized the Summer of Love 30th Anniversary Celebration in 1997 and remains active in the local music scene.

Now you see him, now you don't. Wavy Gravy (ABOVE) has been clowning around since the 1960s, but now he does it for a cause—several causes actually, since he represents numerous charitable groups. Known as the perpetual Nobody for President candidate—because If Nobody Wins, Nobody Loses—his true name is Hugh Romney and he once played a significant role in the counterculture movement, a by-product of which was People's Park in Berkeley.

THE MUSICIAN'S LIFESTYLE comes across as glamorous to many, but it's not without its problems as well. From MC Hammer (TOP) to the Further Festival, featuring members of the Grateful Dead (CENTER), to the *taiko* drummers at the Cherry Blossom Festival (BOTTOM), cranking up the volume has become part of the show. Hearing Education and Awareness for Rockers (H.E.A.R.) cofounded by Kathy Peck (OPPOSITE) in 1988, provides information to musicians and music fans on hearing loss, tinnitus, and hearing protection—advice now heeded by long-time rockers such as Eric "Professor Sludge" Lencher (OPPOSITE).

A VIBRANT MURAL IN THE Mission District sets a festive mood and serves as a reminder that life's simple pleasures often evoke the greatest happiness.

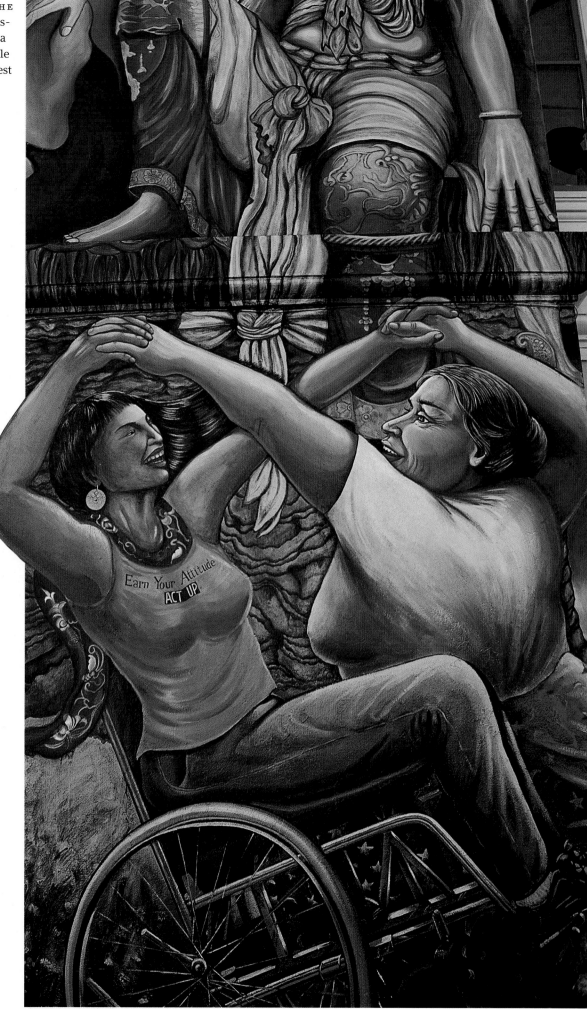

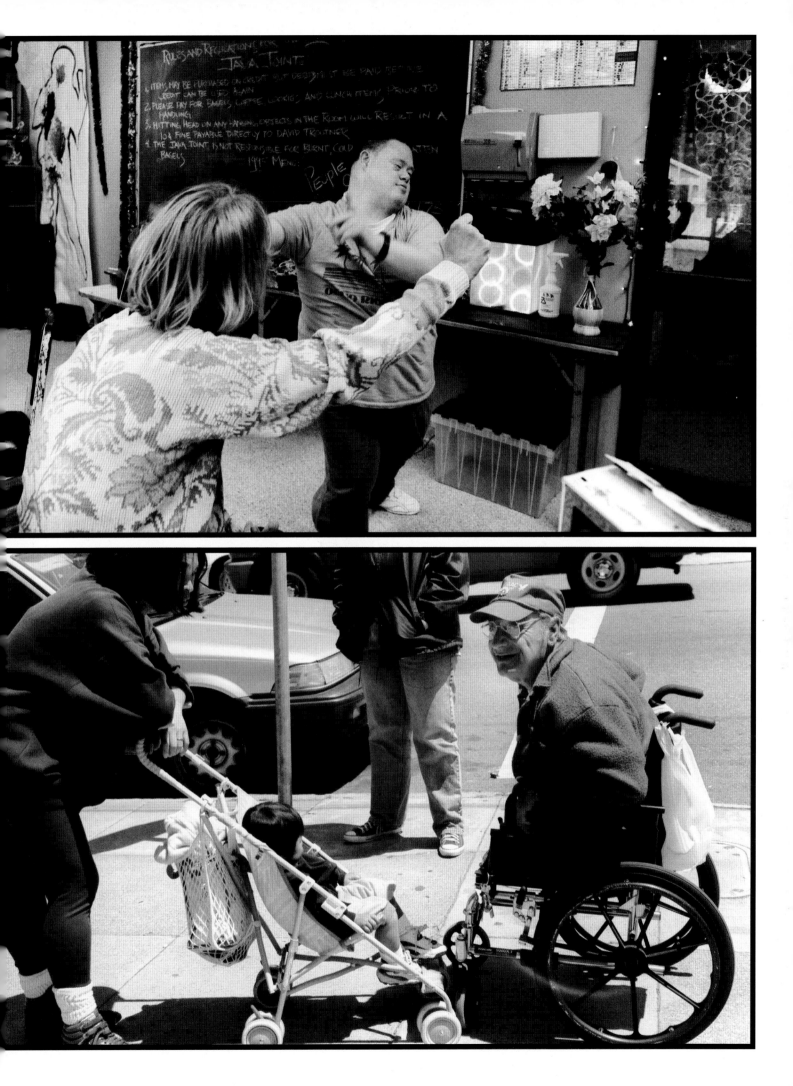

SAN FRANCISCO

ALL KINDS OF EVENTS are cause for breaking into dance around San Francisco. Each year, the symphony hosts the Black and White Ball, a fund-raiser that attracts some 1,000 dancers (ABOVE). Even the pros get around. Swing band Steve Lucky and the Rhumba Bums, featuring Lucky and Miss Carmen Getit (PAGE 180), provide a steady beat for the feet, while swing dance teachers Diane Thomas and Rob van Haaren (PAGE 181) share their lindy hop skills with students throughout the Bay Area.

THE DELICATE CREATION OF fine instruments—whether musical or otherwise—requires skill and much patience. Stanford University physicist by day and violin maker by night, Bill Atwood (LEFT) knows the best of two worlds. UC Berkeley's Tom Lawhead (OPPOSITE TOP) represents the last of a dying breed as a glassblower who crafts specialized instruments for scientific researchers. And for luthier Dan Ransom (OPPOSITE BOTTOM), who's created pieces for the rich and famous, a good guitar is all in the details.

ET THERE BE MUSIC FOR ALL
ages and audiences. Robert
Hansen (OPPOSITE TOP) bids
farewell to listeners of the
Golden Gate Park Band, which
has performed on Sundays and
holidays in Spreckels Temple of
Music for more than 100 years.
From 1972 until his retirement
performance in 1999, Hansen
was at the helm. Michael Tilson
Thomas (OPPOSITE BOTTOM) has
been conductor of the San Francisco Symphony since 1995, and
it's practice that makes perfect
for a San Francisco State University student (LEFT).

ON CERTAIN FESTIVE OCCA-sions in San Francisco, it's considered acceptable to mask your true identity. But no matter what flag you wave, the city demonstrates a unique openness to all lifestyles. Just ask Terence Smith (TOP RIGHT), who—dressed in drag as Joan Jett-Blakk—hosts a live variety and talk show, periodically presented at Josie's Cabaret and Juice Joint, a local comedy club.

PARKING FOR IRISH ONLY
ALL OTHERS WILL BE TOWED

Sᴀɴ Fʀᴀɴᴄɪsᴄᴏ's ɢᴀʏ ᴀɴᴅ lesbian population is estimated at around 210,000, with thousands more in the surrounding Bay Area. The city's annual Gay Pride Parade begins with Dykes on Bikes (ʙᴏᴛᴛᴏᴍ ʟᴇꜰᴛ) in the lead, followed by a procession of elected officials, public servants, proud parents, and leather-clad beauties of both sexes.

B AY AREA CAR CLUBS KEEP the cruisin' spirit alive with their classic automobiles of yesteryear—all souped up and ready to take to the streets.

A WAY FROM THE RUNWAYS and fashion mavens of modern style, the average joe has his or her share of taste—from a true heads-up hairdo to more conservative attire. Young fashion designer Noto (OPPOSITE BOTTOM) has begun making a name for herself in San Francisco circles. Longevity, meanwhile, plays a role in the fashion careers of the Hat Guys (TOP), whose shop in Oakland favors the classic flair of felt and fedoras. Albert Ribaya's Martini Mercantile Co. (BOTTOM) also makes its mark in the growing field of vintage attire.

THE FAST-FOOD CHAIN known as the Doggie Diner closed its doors in the late 1980s, but that didn't stop the rock group Devo from puttin' on the dog in their own right below one of the defunct restaurant's last remaining mascots. Nor does the departure mean that four-legged residents of the Bay Area can't belly up to the bar and slurp down a cold brew every now and then. But if bagels top beer on your list of delights, plenty of bakeries and specialty shops—including one that's the Katz' meow—dot the local landscape.

S AN FRANCISCANS SHARE a deep devotion to their pets. From blessing ceremonies to burial grounds, four-legged friends often ascend to places of great significance in the lives of their masters.

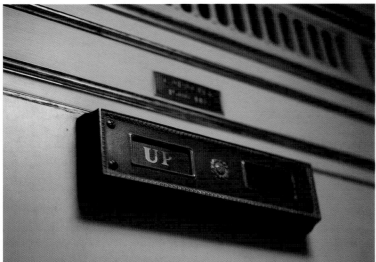

A VERITABLE TON OF LODG- ing locations await visitors to the Bay Area, not the least of which is the decadently decorated Hotel Triton (TOP RIGHT AND BOTTOM LEFT). As president of Joie de Vivre Hospitality, a collection of hotels, restaurants, and lounges, Chip Conley (BOT- TOM RIGHT) operates what *Condé Nast Traveler* calls "the hippest hotels in town."

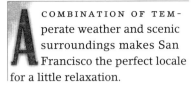A COMBINATION OF TEMperate weather and scenic surroundings makes San Francisco the perfect locale for a little relaxation.

S HARING A DIFFICULT problem with cities across the United States, San Francisco continues to struggle with the plight of its homeless citizens.

S EEKING SHELTER IN THE Bay Area can become quite an exercise in patience and persistence. Suffering from a significant shortage in affordable housing, many area residents long for a place to call home.

M i casa es su casa AT Casa Sanchez (OPPOSITE AND BOTTOM LEFT), a Mexican restaurant where a logo tattoo translates into free lunch for life. Culinary delights and their accompanying artwork abound in the Bay Area.

ALL THAT GLITTERS ISN'T gold, after all. Much of the sparkling that occurs in the Bay Area results from the region's wines and mineral waters, guaranteed to satisfy any palate.

N ATURAL ENERGY, WHETHER harnessed or running free, always finds the perfect backdrop among the hills of Northern California.

THE WARM COLORS OF THE fall harvest—especially depicted in a rich fresco from Coit Tower (OPPOSITE)—go hand in hand with Halloween. Located in the Haight, Labyrinth Phassions & Costumes—along with owner Jennifer Jensen (TOP LEFT)—must have a devil of a time keeping up with the demands brought about by another season of ghosts and goblins.

No Bay Area autumn would be complete without the ground attacks and airborne antics of the San Francisco 49ers. Over the years, three names have become synonymous with the team. Although he was quarterbacking for the Kansas City Chiefs when he retired in 1995, Joe Montana (RIGHT) spent the bulk of his career on the 49ers' roster. Upon Montana's departure, Steve Young (OPPOSITE, BOTTOM RIGHT) stepped in, taking up where Montana left off by lobbing pass after pass to wide receiver Jerry Rice (OPPOSITE, BOTTOM LEFT).

SAN FRANCISCO

WHATEVER THE TEAM, sports in the Bay Area score high in the game of raw emotion. The face of former Golden State Warriors Coach P.J. Carlesimo (OPPOSITE, TOP LEFT) says it all about his short tenure in the area. When Philip Mathews (OPPOSITE, TOP RIGHT) became head coach of the University of San Francisco Dons in 1995, he described his style as intense—an approach he continues to maintain. Sporting his own version of a game face, one Oakland Raiders fan readies himself for some football.

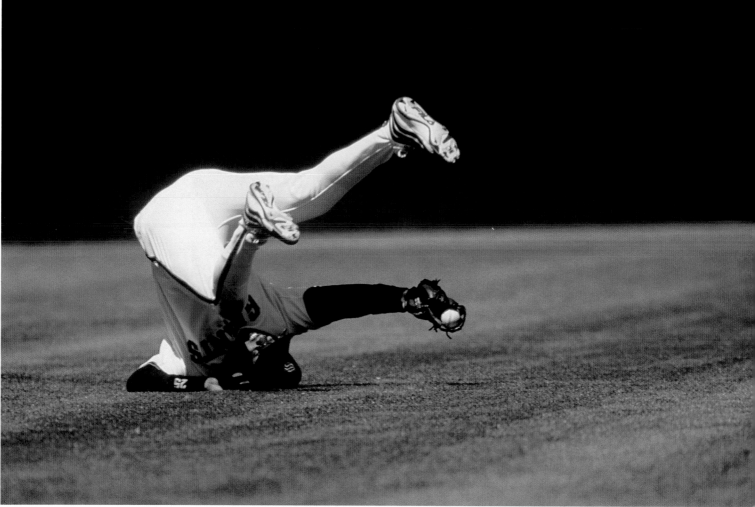

© DAN KRAUSS

SINCE HIS REELECTION IN 1999, San Francisco Mayor Willie Brown (OPPOSITE, TOP LEFT) has reportedly put his professional baseball career on hold. Fortunately for the area's fans, the San Francisco Giants and the Oakland A's stand ready to fill the void.

H EY, BUB, WHAT'S THE LINE on me?" Thoroughbred racing enjoys a loyal following in the Bay Area, and has sparked the careers of jockeys such as Russell Baze (BOTTOM LEFT). One of the top 10 winningest riders in history, the still-active Baze posted 400 or more victories in seven consecutive seasons from 1992 through 1998, and was elected to the national Thoroughbred racing Hall of Fame in 1999.

CATCHING A BREEZE San Francisco style might find you with quite a lofty view of the shoreline. Beautiful from any vantage point, the bay presents a captivating setting no matter what your recreational pleasure.

ITH ALL ITS WONDROUS
beauty, the Bay Area
at sunset has no equal.
Its skies, its shorelines,
and its skyline all radiate with a
natural glow.

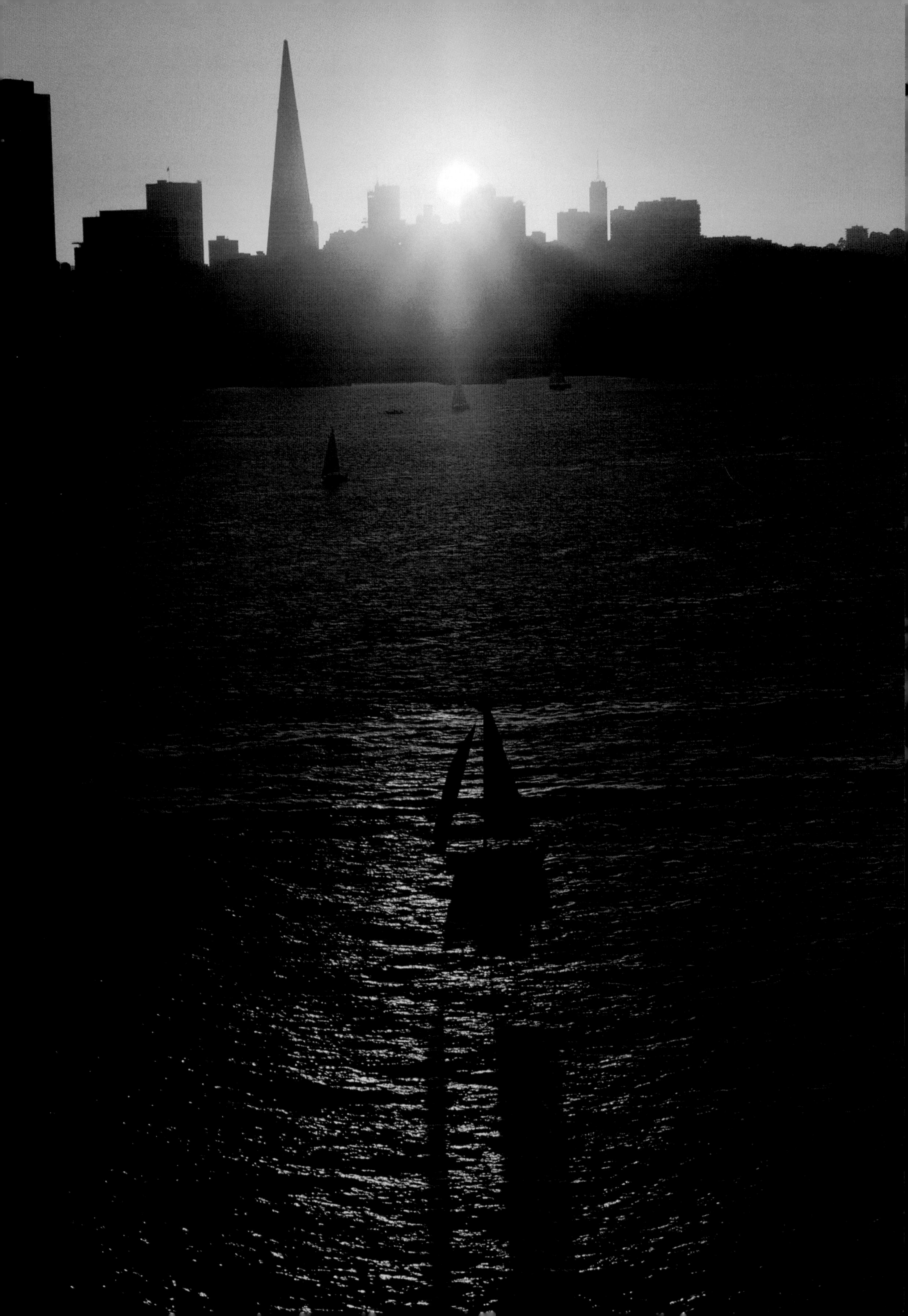

Considered one of the loveliest views in the world, the rolling landscape as seen from Mount Tamalpais depicts the Bay Area at its best. The sweeping vista that surrounds the Golden Gate Bridge (PAGES 228 AND 229) offers equally stunning scenery.

For many in the Bay Area, the livin' is easy, whether your lifestyle calls for a marina environment or the Victorian architecture of Alamo Square (PAGES 232 AND 233).

S AN FRANCISCANS MAY
not see a white Christmas
outside their doors and
windows, but a lighted
Christmas is another story as
the city celebrates the year-end
holidays.

S THE SUN BREAKS OVER the magnificent Golden Gate Bridge, nearby, Bay Area residents start to stir in the still hours of dawn.

HEN DAY IS DONE, THE quiet moments spent absorbing San Francisco's wonders truly make this place a city for all seasons.

A LOOK AT THE CORPORATIONS, BUSINESSES, PROFESSIONAL GROUPS, AND COMMUNITY SERVICE ORGANIZATIONS THAT HAVE MADE THIS BOOK POSSIBLE. THEIR STORIES—OFFERING AN INFORMAL CHRONICLE OF THE LOCAL BUSINESS COMMUNITY—ARE ARRANGED ACCORDING TO THE DATE THEY WERE ESTABLISHED IN THE SAN FRANCISCO BAY AREA.

GOLDEN GATE UNIVERSITY _____ 1835

WELLS FARGO & COMPANY _____ 1852

GUMP'S SAN FRANCISCO _____ 1861

FIREMAN'S FUND INSURANCE COMPANY _____ 1863

UNION BANK OF CALIFORNIA (UBOC) _____ 1864

PILLSBURY MADISON & SUTRO, LLP _____ 1874

CHEVRON CORPORATION _____ 1879

McCUTCHEN, DOYLE, BROWN & ENERSEN, LLP _____ 1883

SWINERTON INCORPORATED _____ 1888

BANK OF AMERICA _____ 1904

WESTIN ST. FRANCIS _____ 1904

PACIFIC GAS AND ELECTRIC COMPANY _____ 1905

DEL MONTE FOODS COMPANY _____ 1916

CHALLENGE DAIRY PRODUCTS, INC. _____ 1925

ZDNET _____ 1927

THE FIFTH-LARGEST PRIVATE COLLEGE IN CALIFORNIA, GOLDEN GATE University (GGU) offers opportunities for academic and professional enrichment for students throughout the region and around the world. A downtown institution with some 7,000 in annual enroll-ment at nine teaching sites and an on-line CyberCampus, the university provides higher education for professional careers through programs that integrate theory with practical experience.

DEEP HISTORICAL ROOTS

San Francisco was little more than a booming encampment of mostly boys and men seeking their fortune in California's hills, when the roots of Golden Gate University were planted with the founding of the YMCA San Francisco chapter in 1853. The facility offered a program of mental and spiritual enrichment through literary societies, lecture series, and composition classes. Eventually, those offerings evolved into Golden Gate University.

The institution has grown with the times. The YMCA educational programs were organized into a California nonprofit organization, and Golden Gate College was formed in 1923. In 1950, the school was accredited by the Commission on Higher Schools of the North-west Association of Secondary and Higher Schools and, in 1959, by the Western Association of Schools and Colleges (WASC).

The bylaws of the board of trustees, established in 1960, au-thorized Golden Gate to establish branches throughout California. Anticipating the future need for higher education, the school even-tually expanded to more than 40

campuses in California and Asia, and at military bases nationwide. Although the university no longer maintains programs at military bases, it continues to operate sev-eral off-site teaching programs in California and one in Seattle. In 1972, the institution was renamed Golden Gate University, and is now headquartered in the South of Market area at the Mission Street campus.

REAL-WORLD PROFESSIONS

The school's emphasis on professional instruction means a faculty of both full-time academics and working practitioners. For example, prac-ticing lawyers and distinguished judges teach in the law school;

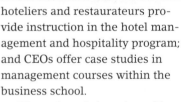

hoteliers and restaurateurs pro-vide instruction in the hotel man-agement and hospitality program; and CEOs offer case studies in management courses within the business school.

The university's real-world curriculum includes more than 130 academic programs offered in five schools: Business; Law; Professional Programs and Under-graduate Studies; Taxation; and Technology and Industry. For students with day jobs—the bulk of its student body—Golden Gate University offers invaluable con-venience through nighttime classes for professionals seeking either advancement or opportunities for a new career.

SCHOOLS AND PROGRAMS

Within the School of Tech-nology and Industry, the information technology and hotel management and hospitality programs are growing rapidly. And the School of Professional Programs and Undergraduate Studies prepares students for professional careers in a variety of fields in both the public and the nonprofit sectors. The university is perhaps best known for its oldest programs— the schools of law, business, and taxation.

Established in 1901, Golden Gate University School of Law was the third such law school with a four-year study course in Northern California, after Stanford University and Hastings College of the Law. Throughout the century, it has grown into a highly competitive school with an international reputation.

The school offers advanced, up-to-date courses on statutory, judicial, and constitutional law, and emphasizes a practical education that readies students for professions in the legal arena. While the School of Law does teach legal theory, it focuses primarily on the skills needed to be a successful practitioner. To that end, the school sponsors internships with area legal offices and courtroom simulations.

In 1908, a nighttime School of Accountancy was established, the first of its kind in the western United States. The Graduate School of Accounting was added in 1932. Today, the accounting program holds the distinction of having the best pass rate in the country for the rigorous Certified Public Accountant (CPA) examination. With the growth of the university's business programs, the accounting program became a part of the current GGU School of Business.

Due to its great success in providing accounting education, the university began offering a graduate degree in taxation in 1967. Today, the Golden Gate University School of Taxation is one of the nation's leading tax schools.

Classes are taught by area practitioners, such as CPAs and other professionals, who not only practice in their field, but also maintain a very current knowledge of tax procedures and practices. In addition, the school constantly updates its curriculum and writes its own textbooks, so students will have the skills to enter the job market immediately upon graduation.

CyberCampus

In keeping with its long-held vision of making professional education accessible to students everywhere, the university launched the ultimate in educational convenience when it opened its virtual campus on the Internet in the fall of 1997.

Currently offering seven degrees, as well as other classes in programs provided at the university's physical campuses, CyberCampus is accessed by students on five continents, most of whom administrators and instructors will never see. Courses work as asynchronous dialogues between students, their instructors, and their classmates via Web-based conferencing software. Students read on-line lectures, work on interactive problem sets, do Web research, and participate in class discussions on-line. At the end of the term, CyberCampus students take their exams under the watchful eyes of university-approved proctors.

According to university administrators, students in a live class may never ask a question or contribute in any way. Cyber-Campus actually forces dialogue because every student is required to interact with the instructor and other students.

Fully accredited by WASC, CyberCampus was named one of the 100 Most Wired Colleges by Yahoo! In 1998, the *Philadelphia Inquirer*, the *Chicago Tribune*, and the Web site www.learningwellinc.com all ranked Golden Gate University among the top 10 in the world for its CyberCampus program.

As it has since its early days, Golden Gate University continues to fulfill its mission by providing convenient access to outstanding educational opportunities leading to professional advancement.

CLOCKWISE FROM TOP LEFT: WHEN THE YMCA BUILDING WAS DESTROYED IN THE 1906 EARTHQUAKE, THE 700 STUDENTS ENROLLED IN THE ORGANIZATION'S EVENING COLLEGE ATTENDED CLASSES IN TENTS UNTIL NEW ACCOMMODATIONS WERE FOUND.

AT GRADUATION, GOLDEN GATE STUDENTS CELEBRATE THE FULFILLMENT OF MANY HOURS OF HARD WORK.

A FACULTY OF BOTH PRACTICING PROFESSIONALS AND FULL-TIME ACADEMICS GIVES GOLDEN GATE STUDENTS A WELL-ROUNDED, PRACTICAL EDUCATION.

WELLS FARGO & COMPANY

ROM CALIFORNIA, THE CRY OF "GOLD!" ECHOED ACROSS THE UNITED States and around the world. New York expressmen Henry Wells and William George Fargo eagerly joined the throngs looking west. On March 18, 1850, they consolidated their eastern operations as the American Express Company, and two years later, Wells Fargo &

Company would do business on the Pacific coast, linked with the romance and history of the Old West.

With the need for express and banking services in the 1850s, the new company busied itself buying gold dust, selling drafts, and doing general banking, shipping, and transportation business throughout the West. Customers entrusted so much gold and silver to Wells Fargo that it continued to compile precious metals production statistics until 1900. By the 1860s, it carried three-fourths of the letters mailed within the Golden State.

TRAILBLAZING THE SERVICE ECONOMY

Wells Fargo's leadership in express and banking services included the inauguration, with three other companies, of the Overland Mail Company, whose stagecoaches rushed letters and passengers across the Southwest. The firm also ran the Pony Express for its final six months when the original company went bankrupt. Concurrently, Wells Fargo expanded into Nevada with the opening of two

banking offices and 24-hour Pony Express service.

In 1866, Wells Fargo created the world's largest stagecoach network. Stages ran from the Central Pacific railhead at Cisco, California, to the Union Pacific terminus at North Platte, Nebraska, and reached booming, as well as remote, outposts across the West.

The Central Pacific Railroad gained control of the company in 1869, and its services expanded eastward. In 1888, Wells Fargo reached New York City, becoming the first express company to offer ocean-to-ocean service. Wells Fargo soon moved from coastal steamers to the interior of Mexico over a new rail net-

work that ultimately linked 300 offices.

Honesty and fair dealing allowed Wells Fargo to flourish. Through boom times and bust, customers banked on its reputation for reliability, speed, and security.

ACQUIRING SUCCESS THROUGH MERGERS

Wells Fargo doubled in size with its first of many mergers in 1905. Isaias W. Hellman, who in 1893 founded the first trust company and the pioneer Italian bank, was president of Wells Fargo Nevada National Bank. At that time, Wells Fargo & Company's Express became a separate entity, serving the United States through 10,000 offices. During World War I, it became part of a government-sponsored consolidation into American Railway Express. On April 18, 1906, another shake-up occurred, and Wells Fargo loaned express wagons to those escaping the San Francisco conflagration. The bank wired correspondents after the earthquake: "Building destroyed. Vaults intact. Credit unaffected."

Hellman worked by a simple philosophy: "Our ambition is not to be the biggest bank in San Francisco, but to be the soundest and the best." It paid regular dividends through the Great Depression of the 1930s.

IN 1866, WELLS FARGO CREATED THE WORLD'S LARGEST STAGECOACH NETWORK, RUNNING FROM THE CENTRAL PACIFIC RAILHEAD AT CISCO, CALIFORNIA, TO THE UNION PACIFIC TERMINUS AT NORTH PLATTE, NEBRASKA.

THOUGHOUT ITS LONG HISTORY, HONESTY AND FAIR DEALING HAVE ALLOWED WELLS FARGO TO FLOURISH. THROUGH BOOM TIMES AND BUST, CUSTOMERS BANKED ON ITS REPUTATION FOR RELIABILITY, SPEED, AND SECURITY.

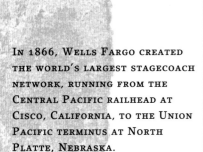

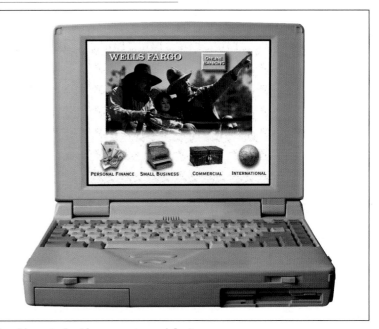

Merging with American Trust Company in 1960, Wells Fargo entered retail banking grandly, while a 1967 foray into Southern California made it a statewide bank. The 1980s saw banking deregulation, automated teller machines, and 24-hour telephone service. A 1986 marriage with Crocker Bank provided Wells Fargo with a gorgeous banking office at One Montgomery Street, complementing the nearby Wells Fargo History Museum.

Convenience grew with supermarket banks and on-line banking in the early 1990s. In 1996, the company acquired First Interstate Bank, which began in 1928 as Transamerica Corporation, a holding company for A.P. Gianinni's non-California banks. With banks in 10 states under its charter, Wells Fargo allows its customers access to their accounts anywhere, anytime. November 1998 brought new opportunities—a true merger of equals—joining Wells Fargo with its younger cousin, Norwest Corporation.

The New Frontier

Wells Fargo stands poised for the 21st century, working to become the premier financial services provider in America with more than $200 billion in assets, 100,000 employees, and 2,900 banking offices, melding a proud tradition with industry-lending capabilities. Together with Norwest Mortgage and Norwest Financial, Wells Fargo offers the industry's largest network of stores—6,000 throughout the United States and Canada, and an additional 1,000 supermarket banking stores.

A leader in retail banking cross-sell, mortgage origination, small-business lending, on-line financial services, supermarket banking, student loans, commercial real estate lending, agricultural lending, and insurance agency sales by a banking organization, Wells Fargo also specializes in Internet banking.

A pioneer in the technology frontier, Wells Fargo is the largest Internet bank in the country with more than 1 million customers and growing at 100,000 customers a month, offering on-line customers more services than any competitor. In 1998, Wells Fargo became the first American bank to offer instant decisions on-line for home equity loans; offer customers credit card bills on-line; handle more than 500, 000 Internet banking transactions for small-business customers; and launch Internet stock trading to allow investors the convenience of doing both their banking and their trading on-line. Wells Fargo also opened two cyberbanking stores in Seattle and Las Vegas, letting customers use the Internet free of charge.

These are the same kind of opportunities Wells and Fargo pursued a century and a half ago. They helped create the country's service economy, reducing time and distance relative to money. They wanted their customers' banking business, safekeeping business, delivery-of-goods business, and mail business delivering products, services, and information across the American frontier.

Today's Wells Fargo continues to deliver for its 15 million customers—anytime, anywhere.

A PIONEER IN THE TECHNOLOGY FRONTIER, WELLS FARGO IS THE LARGEST INTERNET BANK IN THE COUNTRY WITH MORE THAN 1 MILLION CUSTOMERS AND GROWING AT 100,000 CUSTOMERS A MONTH, OFFERING ON-LINE CUSTOMERS MORE SERVICES THAN ANY COMPETITOR (RIGHT).

ON MARCH 18, 1850, NEW YORK EXPRESSMEN HENRY WELLS AND WILLIAM GEORGE FARGO CONSOLIDATED THEIR EASTERN OPERATIONS AS THE AMERICAN EXPRESS COMPANY, AND TWO YEARS LATER, WELLS FARGO & COMPANY WOULD DO BUSINESS ON THE PACIFIC COAST, LINKED WITH THE ROMANCE AND HISTORY OF THE OLD WEST (LEFT).

GUMP'S
SAN FRANCISCO

IT IS NEARLY IMPOSSIBLE TO IMAGINE SAN FRANCISCO WITHOUT GUMP'S. The storied city and the legendary house of style grew up together, drawing life and inspiration from each other. Today, that legend continues with a new panache, attracting San Franciscans and world travelers alike to this home, jewelry, and gift store at 135 Post Street

to pay homage to fine quality and exquisite taste, and perchance to buy a piece of the good life.

An American mercantile institution with an international reputation and a San Francisco pedigree, Gump's today incorporates every facet of the store's past: from the days of gold rush San Francisco, through the decades when Gump's grew with San Francisco and introduced the graces of good living from all over the world to the burgeoning gentry, to the store's last half-century as the preeminent purveyor of unique, quality merchandise. Today, its focus is on advanced, contemporary, and antique design of American and Asian art objects, crafts, jewelry, gifts, and home accessories, all in an engaging gallery environment.

The common element among the offerings at Gump's—the antiques, furniture, gifts, tableware, accessories, china, crystal, silver, stationery, and jewelry—is the timelessness of quality workmanship and materials. In addition, The Gump's Galleries showcase handmade works by emerging artists and the crafts of talented artisans, and continues to introduce discriminating shoppers to fresh and established master crafts.

A SAN FRANCISCO STORY

How Gump's came to be the arbiter of good taste is the quintessential San Francisco story. Solomon Gump came to San Francisco from Europe by way of New York, and worked in the gold frame mirror shop his brother-in-law opened in 1861. At this time, the city was hardly more refined than its mining camps and muddy streets. Installed behind the bars in Barbary Coast saloons, Gump's giant, gilt-framed mirrors were a bit of civility in the riproaring tent and shack town. During barroom brawls, these mirrors were easy targets for flying bottles, bullets, and bodies. So

Gump's mirror and frame shop flourished.

A year after his arrival, Solomon bought out his brother-in-law's share of the store, and sent for his wife and children and his brother Gustav. He renamed the store S. & G. Gump: Mirrors, Mouldings, and Paintings.

At the turn of the century, taverns were gathering places of sociability for the newly rich and would-be rich alike. The artwork on the walls—installed by S. & G. Gump Company, Fine Arts provided an education in art appreciation to those who frequented the saloons, and launched many art collecting careers in San Francisco.

During their repeated forays to Europe in the quest for decorations, the Gumps bought back the sentimental Victorian landscapes and still lifes that were popular

overseas. Solomon had an eye for voluptuous nudes on canvas, which were perfect replacements for broken mirrors. Eventually, this led to a new venture for the brothers: the first art gallery in California.

Fortunes were made in a hurry and spent the same way. A phrase used to express the mood of the era was "a mansion a minute," and Gump's seemed to be decorating them just about as fast. They filled the frames hanging in the grand salons of the newly minted millionaires of the mother lode, and the railroad magnates who built extravagant mansions on Nob Hill and Van Ness Avenue. These nabobs called on the Gump brothers to provide gilded cornices, gold leaf ceilings, and other intricate and unique fixtures.

TURNING EASTWARD

Solomon's fourth son, Alfred Livingston "A.L." Gump, inherited the store just before the 1906 earthquake and fire destroyed it. There was no money to rebuild until Dodie Valencia, a "lady of the evening," offered A.L. $17,000 for a painting he had at home. Gump's was back in business, and Dodie's girls always had credit at the store.

Under his knowing eye—or more accurately, his knowing touch, since A.L. was nearly blind—Gump's inventory turned east toward the Pacific Rim, establishing renown for its oriental department and its unparalleled objets d'art and jewels. Today, Gump's remains true to its East/West character: The company offers a variety of antique and traditional Asian treasures, along with the best of contemporary Asian design.

Richard Gump, one of A.L.'s three lively offspring, became president of Gump's after the death of his father in 1947. A handsome man, Richard was multitalented: He worked as a designer for MGM Studios, and later designed many of Gump's products, including jewelry, flatware, and linens. He was also a painter and composer, and wrote two best-sellers, *Jade: Stone of Heaven* and *Good Taste Costs No More*, both published by Doubleday. His staff adored him

for his humor and taste, exemplified in his exhortation to San Francisco: "You can't afford an ugly thing at any price!"

Richard also created a new logo for the store in 1932, employing a streamlined, modern typeface. He had the logo reproduced in chrome letters affixed to the store's delivery trucks. This signature was so simple, attractive, and evocative that it remains virtually unchanged today.

In time, the store passed out of the family's hands: In 1993, Hanover Direct, Inc., an international marketing conglomerate, bought the store, including the existing Gump's By Mail. Gump's continues as San Francisco's premier purveyor of taste and style, offering daily evidence to support the Gump family's ageless axiom: "Not only is it better to buy the best, but it is often the best buy."

TODAY, GUMP'S REMAINS TRUE TO ITS EAST/WEST CHARACTER: THE COMPANY OFFERS A VARIETY OF ANTIQUE AND TRADITIONAL ASIAN TREASURES, ALONG WITH THE BEST OF CONTEMPORARY ASIAN DESIGN.

GUMP'S FOCUS IS ON ADVANCED, CONTEMPORARY JEWELRY BY IN-HOUSE DESIGNER LYNN NAKAMURA.

Fireman's Fund Insurance Company

ONE OF THE TOP 20 PROPERTY CASUALTY INSURERS IN THE COUNTRY, Fireman's Fund Insurance Company bears a name steeped in true San Francisco tradition. ◆ The name originated in 1863 during the days when the company donated 10 percent of its profits to a fund that benefited the widows and orphans of San Francisco volunteer firefighters. When the great 1906 San Francisco earthquake and fire destroyed the company's headquarters and all its records, it survived by providing all claimants with settlements of half cash and half stock. Within five years, that stock was worth considerably more than the cash owed on the original claim.

Today, Fireman's Fund is nationally respected as a dynamic, customer-oriented company serving a wide range of personal and business insurance needs. Fireman's Fund also enjoys top marks from independent financial rating organizations—such as A.M. Best Company, Standard & Poor's, and Moody's—for its financial position, capacity, stability, and ability to pay claims. Contributing to that stability are annual gross premiums written exceeding $4 billion and total assets of nearly $13.5 billion.

A Variety of Coverages

A significant number of Fireman's Fund's clients buy home owners and auto policies. The company has specialized capabilities for those who require very high limits for expensive homes and who also need to protect expensive collectibles. Fireman's Fund has also developed special insurance coverages for professionals and entrepreneurs, offering policies that can extend to offices in the home as well as to professional liability. And, the company is known for its unique Private Event Cancellation Insurance, which can cover loss from canceling or postponing private parties and receptions like weddings, retirements, or bar mitzvahs.

As for business coverage, Fireman's Fund is one of the top underwriters of package insurance policies, a concept the company pioneered in the early 1960s. It allows companies to incorporate their choices from a broad range of diverse coverage into a single policy. Fireman's Fund packages have protected some of the most recognized institutions in America, such as Sunkist Growers, YMCAs, See's Candies, and the San Diego Wild Animal Park.

Fireman's Fund also dominates the highly specialized world of motion picture insurance. Beginning in the era of the silent screen, the company covered props and sets, and over the years developed so many film coverages that its entertainment packages have be-

SOME 2,500 EMPLOYEES WORK AT THE FIREMAN'S FUND INSURANCE COMPANY CORPORATE CAMPUS, LOCATED IN THE ROLLING HILLS OF NOVATO, CALIFORNIA, JUST 25 MILES NORTH OF SAN FRANCISCO.

come the most desired policy in Hollywood. Take any week's top five major box-office films and chances are that Fireman's Fund will have insured at least one of those blockbusters.

Another special niche is ocean marine coverage, which the company has been underwriting ever since it insured schooners that brought goods around the tip of South America in the late 1800s, which turned the rough-and-tumble, post-gold-rush town of San Francisco into a refined, international port city and a commercial center. In fact, Fireman's Fund was founded by a retired sea captain. It has consistently been a leader in the industry, and recently added to its luster in this area by purchasing one of the top ocean marine cargo insurers in the country.

Another of the founding fathers was a hay-and-grain merchant, so it's no surprise that insurance for farm operations was an early expertise. Fireman's Fund pioneered crop-hail insurance in the 1870s, but has never rested on its laurels: The firm recently unveiled a global satellite positioning system to help growers map their fields. That mapping service, which is provided without charge to those who buy Fireman's Fund policies, is especially important to the many vintners in the world-famous Napa and Sonoma valleys. Fireman's Fund AgriBusiness coverage is also a national leader in coverages for farmers and growers who need to insure business property and standing crops in the field.

Fireman's Fund covers small business as well. In recent years, the company has developed American Business Coverage (ABC), one of the most successful package policies for small to medium-sized firms. In fact, Fireman's Fund has the flexibility of growing with small companies until they qualify for larger business portfolio packages, and can even help if the customer develops the need and capability to offer its services internationally. That's possible because Fireman's Fund is now a subsidiary of Allianz AG of Munich, one of the top five insurers in the world and a company

with $400 billion in assets under management. Having Allianz as a parent has become a powerful advantage partially because Fireman's Fund can exchange ideas and techniques with 57 sister companies around the world.

SHARED VALUES

Now based just 25 miles north of San Francisco, the Fireman's Fund headquarters campus is set in the quiet, rolling hills of Marin County, where the 8,700-person company directs national operations across all 50 states. The site is also home to the company's large information technology unit, which is integral to its overall customer-focused orientation. In 1998, Fireman's Fund launched the first wave of development against an aggressive, five-year, $150 million plan that is closely aligned with the company's profit and growth objectives, which are predicated on supporting agents and customers with streamlined processing, reduced long-term

operating costs, and innovative systems capabilities.

Giving something back to the community that has supported it over the years is an important part of the Fireman's Fund ethic. That's why the Fireman's Fund Foundation, the company's charitable arm, has contributed more than $30 million over the years to fund projects that support education, human needs, and community activities. Similarly, Fireman's Fund encourages employees to volunteer personal time and effort to benefit agencies working toward a better community.

Such examples of personal involvement reflect a basic set of guiding principles that are now established at Fireman's Fund. Called Shared Values, these nine principles define what Fireman's Fund is and what is important whenever a difficult business decision needs to be made. Shared Values includes action, clear thinking, competitive spirit, courage, hard work, honesty and integrity, professional mind-set, sensitivity, and teamwork.

EMPLOYEES CAN OCCASIONALLY ENJOY OUTDOOR MEETINGS AT THEIR CORPORATE HEADQUARTERS.

Union Bank of California (UBOC)

A MODEL OF WORKPLACE DIVERSITY, UNION BANK OF CALIFORNIA (UBOC) prides itself on the diversity of the communities it serves. In fact, in 1999, *Fortune* magazine declared UBOC—California's third-largest commercial bank—the number one company in the nation for women and minorities. ◆ Today's Union Bank of California, headquartered in San Francisco, is the direct descendant of several storied financial institutions rooted in California, Oregon, Washington, and Japan. The bank's name itself, taken from the 1996 merger between Union Bank and The Bank of California, signaled the opening of a new chapter in the institution's history.

ACQUISITIONS BRING STRENGTH

One merger partner, The Bank of California, was established in 1864, and through its chief founder, William C. Ralston, helped launch many of the state's early industries in the wake of the gold rush boom: woolen mills, silk factories, wineries and other agricultural ventures, canneries, shipyards, transportation (financing the western portion of the Transcontinental Railroad, steamship lines, and San Francisco's early cable cars, among others), and real estate development. Through a 1905 merger with the London & San Francisco Bank, Ltd., The Bank of California acquired offices in Oregon and Washington State that endure today.

Meanwhile, Japan-based Mitsubishi Bank, Ltd., founded in 1880 by former samurai Yataro Iwasaki, made its way into America. In 1960, it opened a Los Angeles agency office as a convenience to clients with U.S. subsidiaries. The full-service Mitsubishi Bank of California was born in 1971, as a wholly owned subsidiary. In 1984, the parent bank acquired The Bank of California.

On the other side of the UBOC family, Union Bank is also the culmination of a series of mergers. Its Bay Area roots go back to 1886, when Yokohama Specie Bank, established in Japan in 1880 and a predecessor to the Bank of Tokyo, opened a San Francisco office. The Bank of Tokyo was a majority stockholder of Union Bank in 1996, when it merged with Mitsubishi Bank, Ltd., to form Bank of Tokyo-Mitsubishi, Ltd. At that same time, the banks' California-based subsidiaries merged, creating Union Bank of California.

Union Bank of California has emerged from the series of acquisitions with strengths in many areas. These include middle market business banking; international correspondent services, especially throughout the Pacific Rim and Central and South America; private banking and personal trust; specialized lending to specific industries such as oil and gas, entertainment, and telecommunications; and community banking.

In keeping with UBOC's Asian heritage, the institution continues to provide banking services to almost every Asian company that does business in California. The bank prides itself on being able to handle complex financial needs, from trust services to global trade finance, while also being small enough to offer personalized service.

ROOTED IN THE COMMUNITY

With a network of some 250 offices in California, Washington, and Oregon, UBOC connects with local communities from the Mexican border north through

UNION BANK OF CALIFORNIA'S (UBOC) HEADQUARTERS IS LOCATED IN DOWNTOWN SAN FRANCISCO. THE GRECIAN-COLUMNED BUILDING (RIGHT) HAS BEEN THE BANK'S FLAGSHIP BRANCH SINCE ITS COMPLETION IN 1908. UBOC HAS OCCUPIED THIS CORNER AT SANSOME AND CALIFORNIA STREETS SINCE 1867.

the Los Angeles metropolitan area, the Inland Empire, the Central Valley, the San Francisco Bay Area, and up to Oregon and Washington. The bank's presence is felt along the entire Pacific Coast from Canada to Mexico.

"We offer every conceivable product through our community banking network," says Stephen Johnson, senior vice president and director of public relations and government affairs. To better serve community customers, UBOC was the first major bank to offer banking seven days a week through its partnership with grocery stores. And UBOC was one of the first banks in the country to offer Bank@Home computer-based banking capabilities to its clients. The bank's success in providing superior service is borne out by consistently high scores for customer service in numerous independent surveys.

Beyond providing a full menu of banking services, UBOC aggressively seeks opportunities to make loans to minority- and women-owned business enterprises. The

bank's community responsibility is linked to its firm belief that its own success lies in the success of local government, schools, community groups, and individual families. Advising the bank on the financial needs of low-income and underserved communities is a community advisory board, formed in July 1996 and comprised of top West Coast community leaders.

"We have a commitment to the communities where we operate," says Johnson. "In addition to the volunteer hours that individual staff may contribute, our foundation focuses on affordable housing, education, health, the environment, and welfare services. We give away millions of dollars a year in grants as a pledge to reinvest 4.5 percent of our assets annually."

UBOC's local efforts have undeniably had a positive effect on the bank's bottom line. *Fortune* magazine—in its July 1999 cover story on the 50 best companies for Asians, African-Americans, and Hispanics—points to the outstanding performance of the bank's

stock, which "has appreciated at a 34 percent compound annual rate for the past five years."

MOVE TO THE BIG BOARD

On June 16, 1999, UBOC's parent holding company, UnionBanCal Corporation, began trading on the New York Stock Exchange, moving from the Nasdaq exchange. "We've enjoyed a long and rewarding relationship with Nasdaq," notes Johnson. "But after our successful capital management initiatives earlier in the year, we felt the time was right to move to the NYSE. We believe the switch will give us additional exposure to further enhance shareholder value."

In the immediate future, Union Bank of California will continue to grow; however, that growth will be slow and measured, so as not to compromise its sterling reputation for customer service. "We're large enough to provide all the services our customers need," says Johnson, "yet not so big that we're impersonal." It's a balance UBOC's customers appreciate.

UBOC EMPLOYEES VOLUNTEER IN MANY COMMUNITY ACTIVITIES, SUCH AS HELPING AT LOCAL SCHOOLS, BUILDING HABITAT FOR HUMANITY HOMES, AND PARTICIPATING IN A NUMBER OF FUND-RAISING EVENTS TO COMBAT DISEASE. IN ADDITION, MANY EMPLOYEES PARTICIPATED IN THE SEPTEMBER 1999 CALIFORNIA COASTAL CLEAN-UP AT SAN FRANCISCO'S OCEAN BEACH (LEFT).

THIS BANK OF CALIFORNIA VAULT WITHSTOOD THE 1906 SAN FRANCISCO EARTHQUAKE AND PROTECTED ITS CONTENTS FROM THE FIRE THAT FOLLOWED (RIGHT).

B Y THE TIME THE GREAT EARTHQUAKE AND FIRE OF 1906 HAI destroyed its offices, records, and files, the Pillsbury Madison & Sutro, LLP law firm had been a venerable legal presence in Sar Francisco and the Pacific Rim for more than three decades. ◆ Founded when Evans S. Pillsbury opened his one-man law practice

in 1874 to represent the innovators and entrepreneurs of the time, the office expanded with the addition in the 1890s of Frank D. Madison, Alfred Sutro, and Pillsbury's son Horace as associates. Elevated to partners in 1905, they were joined by the newly admitted Oscar Sutro in the law firm they called Pillsbury Madison & Sutro, the name that has endured for nearly a century.

Today one of the nation's pre-eminent full-service law firms, and among the oldest in the state, Pillsbury Madison & Sutro has grown to more than 530 attorneys in offices throughout California, the East Coast, and Japan. In the *1999 Vault.com Guide to America's Top 50 Law Firms*, Pillsbury Madison & Sutro was named one of the 20 best firms to work for.

PROGRESSIVE IDEAS

Pillsbury was the first law firm of its size in the nation to elect women to the top leadership posts—naming Mary Cranston as chairman of the board and Marina Park as managing partner. The 1998 appointment of the firm's new management team signaled to the world what the firm's attorneys and staff had known for some time—that Pillsbury Madison & Sutro is truly at the forefront of gender issues and diversity efforts. This progressive position has helped the firm move aggressively into the new economy—high-tech and emerging business—while enhancing its overall strength in traditional corporate law.

"Today, we offer one of the nation's broadest intellectual property, technology, and emerging growth practices," says Cranston. "Also, we have one of the largest banking and financial institution practices for worldwide capital markets in the country. And we're renowned for successfully handling strategic, complex litigation."

The firm's broad range of services and specialties has served as a magnet for talented associates attracted to opportunities to gain expertise in these new growth areas.

LAW FIRM OF RECORD

If you look at the 125-year history of this law firm and figure that only 2 percent of American companies make it to age 75, we're 50 years beyond that. That suggests considerable staying power," says Joseph Macrum, director of marketing and communications.

Along the way, Pillsbury Madison & Sutro has distinguished itself as a law firm of record in California and Pacific Rim history. Among the firm's accomplishments is the incorporation of Standard Oil of California, the precursor to today's Chevron Corporation and still on the firm's roster of titan clients. In 1886, Clarence R. Greenhouse, an early name partner of the firm, was appointed U.S. consul general for Japan and later became a confidential adviser to the king of Korea. And in 1901, Oscar Sutro opened a branch office in the Philippines, where he was active in drafting the Philippine Code.

As for the firm's future, Pillsbury Madison & Sutro is preparing for substantial growth in the new millennium. The firm is looking to double the number of its attorneys over the next two to three years and to expand its geographic reach, with additional offices in the United States, Asia, and Europe.

"Pillsbury's long history, combined with its broad range of legal capabilities and its strong focus on the new economy, gives it a solid foundation for growth," says Cranston. "We look forward to our next 125 years."

PILLSBURY MADISON & SUTRO, LLP HAS DISTINGUISHED ITSELF AS A LAW FIRM OF RECORD IN CALIFORNIA AND PACIFIC RIM HISTORY.

A LTHOUGH CHEVRON CORPORATION STARTED BUSINESS IN LOS ANGELES in 1879 as the Pacific Coast Oil Company, the San Francisco Bay Area has always been its home base. With some 8,000 employees in San Francisco and the Contra Costa County cities of San Ramon, Concord, Walnut Creek, and Richmond, Chevron is one of the San Francisco area's—and California's—largest companies.

Acquired in 1900 by John D. Rockefeller's Standard Oil Trust and broken up in antitrust legislation 11 years later, it became Standard Oil Company of California. In 1984, the company nearly doubled in size by acquiring Gulf Oil Corporation in what was then the largest corporate merger in U.S. history. That same year, Standard changed its name to Chevron, adopting the well-known brand name of many of its products.

A publicly held company involved in all aspects of the petroleum business worldwide, Chevron focuses on exploration, production, refining, marketing, transportation, and research. Chevron also has a significant chemical business, is a leading U.S. jet fuel supplier and gasoline marketer, and owns one of the largest oil tanker fleets in the country.

Chevron explores for and produces crude oil and natural gas in 23 countries, including Nigeria, and is active in more than 20 countries and has 34,000 employees around the world. In the United States, major oil-producing areas include the Gulf of Mexico, California, the Rocky Mountains, and Texas. Abroad, Chevron production areas include Angola, Nigeria, Canada, the North Sea, Australia, Indonesia, Kazakhstan, Venezuela, China, and Papua New Guinea. In addition, Alaska and Azerbaijan are major exploration areas.

"We take pride not only in our products and services," says David J. O'Reilly, chairman and CEO, "but also in the way we conduct worldwide operations."

SUSTAINING COMMUNITIES

A company whose success depends upon the goodwill and cooperation of communities around the world, Chevron throughout its history has acted upon its guiding belief that the company is obligated to share resources, experience, and time to benefit the communities in which it lives and works.

Chevron's Partnership in Action encourages individuals and groups to work together to build and sustain their communities. Efforts range from the formation of Little League baseball in Kazakhstan to the preservation of a rain forest in Papua New Guinea.

"We must always, without fail, earn trust and respect," says O'Reilly. "To be a welcome member of any community is an essential part of our corporate vision. As a company, it is our hope that we are viewed not only as a good neighbor, but as a vital and important community asset."

With such high standards and thorough attention to basic principles, Chevron, not surprisingly, has met with early success in reaching its goal to be first among its competitors in total stockholder return for the period 1999 through 2003. In 1997, Chevron turned in the best financial performance in its 118-year history, and through 1998, Chevron had declared a dividend increase for 10 straight years.

Heading into the new millennium, Chevron is well under way toward its goal to be, as O'Reilly says, "better than the best."

CHEVRON EXPLORES FOR AND PRODUCES CRUDE OIL AND NATURAL GAS IN 23 COUNTRIES, INCLUDING OFFSHORE NIGERIA (LEFT).

SEVEN CHEVRON REFINERIES, INCLUDING THIS ONE IN PASCAGOULA, MISSISSIPPI, TRANSFORM CRUDE OIL INTO GASOLINE, JET FUEL, LUBRICANTS, AND OTHER CONSUMER AND INDUSTRIAL PRODUCTS (BOTTOM).

McCutchen, Doyle, Brown & Enersen, LLP

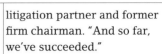

IN 1883, WHEN CHARLES PAGE AND CHARLES P. EELLS JOINED FORCES TO establish a law practice in downtown San Francisco, they had no idea that their firm would one day grow into one of Northern California's largest law firms. ◆ Although McCutchen, Doyle, Brown & Enersen, LLP no longer bears its founders' names, the firm has continuously

existed as an active partnership of practicing lawyers since its beginning as Page & Eells. Founded during the waning days of the Barbary Coast, the firm took on primarily admiralty cases involving ship ownership, cargo losses, collisions at sea, and other casualties of maritime commerce. At the turn of the century, the firm had one of the nation's first law office branches when it established an outpost in Nome, Alaska, to provide legal services to participants in the Yukon gold rush. One client, Charles D. Lane, became involved in a bitter dispute over several rich mining claims on Anvil Creek near Nome. The firm successfully defended his claim, and the litigation subsequently became the subject of a 1906 novel, *The Spoilers*, by Rex Beach.

Although the firm underwent several name changes before adopting the current one in 1967, McCutchen's dedication to its mission has endured. "We are committed to providing effective, fairly priced, ethical legal representation," says David Balabanian,

litigation partner and former firm chairman. "And so far, we've succeeded."

HANDMAIDENS TO PROGRESS

With 300 lawyers and offices in San Francisco, Palo Alto, Walnut Creek, Los Angeles, and Taipei, McCutchen offers full legal services and representation on a broad spectrum of global and local legal matters, ranging from antitrust to white-collar crime.

"One of the interesting things in law practice is that it reflects the needs of society instantaneously," says Balabanian. In order for a law firm to succeed, he adds, "We have to not only keep up, but also be ahead of developments and anticipate issues that could have legal consequence. We are handmaidens to progress."

Today's progress focuses on high technology, especially given McCutchen's stronghold in Northern California. As a result,

THE *Banking and Law* MURAL DECORATING THE WALL OF SAN FRANCISCO LANDMARK COIT TOWER WAS PAINTED IN 1934 AS A PUBLIC WORKS ART PROJECT. AMONG THE LAWYERS LISTED IN THE PAINTING ARE CLARENCE DARROW, OLIVER WENDELL HOLMES, ABRAHAM LINCOLN, AND E.J. MCCUTCHEN OF MCCUTCHEN, DOYLE, BROWN & ENERSEN, L.L.P.

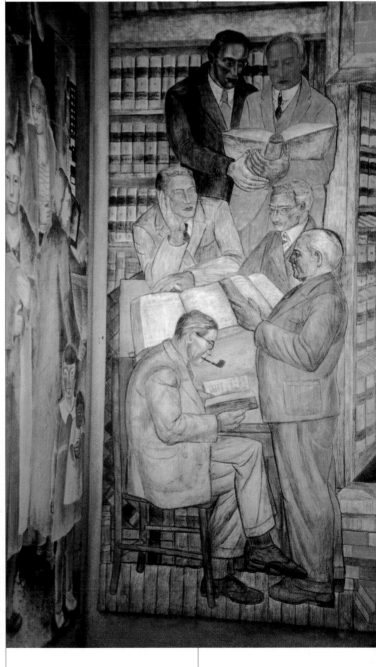

the firm has committed staff and resources to expanding its office in Palo Alto, the nucleus of Silicon Valley and an incubator for countless high-tech companies.

Carol Dillon, a real estate partner and member of the firm's executive committee, opened the branch in 1994 with only three people. By 1999, the staff had grown to more than 50 lawyers. "We represent cutting-edge semiconductor, hardware and software, Internet, and biotech companies," says Dillon. "For every concept you can think of, and some that are hard to imagine, there is a start-up here in the Valley."

COMMITTED TO DIVERSITY AND COMMUNITY SERVICE

A successful law firm by any measure, McCutchen holds itself to high standards in a myriad of areas. In measuring success, Balabanian says, "I'm inclined to emphasize the percentage of our lawyers who are women, minorities, and gays and lesbians. The fact that we have a diverse group of lawyers who reflect the composition of the community makes us better able to understand and respond to that community."

Honored by the City and County of San Francisco with the 1998 Business That Makes a Difference award, McCutchen was recognized for making a positive difference in the employment and economic advancement of women. Of the nation's top 100 largest law firms, McCutchen has the second-largest percentage of female equity partners. A roster of associates' and partners' backgrounds reads like a who's who of the nation's top law schools, proving that the firm has not sacrificed academic excellence in its commitment to diversity. The firm's outstanding personnel help McCutchen achieve its mission to be progressive as well as responsive.

Once the best minds have been hired, they are allowed to take part in McCutchen's decision making. "We are a very democratic law firm at a time when large law firms are increasingly moving toward more highly managed or hierarchical structures," says Balabanian. In a 1998 survey of midlevel associates, *The American Lawyer* ranked McCutchen's Palo Alto office at the top in the state and number two in the nation for work environment, including a perfect score for the office's work-

ing relationship between associates and partners.

A hallmark of McCutchen attorneys is a deep sense of civic commitment, as evidenced by the firm's attitude toward pro bono work. The goal throughout the firm is to deliver a minimum of 50 pro bono hours annually, which attorneys easily exceed every year. Children's rights, gays in the military, the environment, domestic violence, refugee rights, and freedom of the press are a small sampling of the issues addressed in pro bono cases. For this work, McCutchen has been honored with innumerable awards, including being one of only a handful of firms to receive an A rating for its pro bono program from *The American Lawyer*, and formal recognition from many of the nonprofit organizations it has championed.

Ultimately, explains Balabanian, the reward of these pro bono hours is a staff that is grounded in the real world. "There's a great risk in a big corporate law firm of insulating itself from the community at large," he says. "We have a professional obligation to make sure that the legal system is accessible and responsive to everyone."

F OR MORE THAN A CENTURY, SWINERTON INCORPORATED HAS BUILT UPON its reputation for constructing many of San Francisco's signature buildings. From the Phelan flatiron building in 1908, to the War Memorial Opera House and the Veteran's Building, both completed in 1932, to Ghirardelli Square in the 1960s, to the San Francisco Museum

of Modern Art (SFMOMA) in 1995, Swinerton has made its mark on nearly every decade of the city's architectural history since the turn of the century.

Despite its longevity in the construction business and its maturity in the market, Swinerton still performs like a young, growing company. In its 110th year of operation in 1998, the company ranked 17th among the top 50 general builders in America, according to the trade weekly *Engineering News-Record*. In addition, Swinerton was the fastest-growing firm on that list.

"We always hire the best talent available," says Swinerton's Chairman of the Board David Grubb, citing one of the reasons for the company's staying power. Over the course of more than a century of construction, Swinerton has introduced or been among the first to put into practice an im-

pressive number of innovations that revolutionized the building industry. Swinerton's formula for longevity is built on quality materials, processes, and people; a priority on safety; and a reputation for integrity. In fact, many of the industry standards in these areas were set by Swinerton.

COMPANY FOUNDATIONS

I n 1888, a 28-year-old Swede named Charles Lindgren formed a partnership in Los Angeles with two other Southern California newcomers and named it Boyd, Sharples & Lindgren, Brick Masons and Contractors.

In 1900, Lindgren entered into a partnership with a Berkeley engineer named Lewis Hicks, and they began operations in San Francisco as Lindgren Hicks. Toward the end of the decade, Lindgren parted with Hicks and joined with his brother

Fred in incorporating the Lindgren Company. After the devastating 1906 earthquake, Lindgren hired the best talent available in the city, choosing Alfred Bingham Swinerton, then a junior at Stanford University, as an estimator. A mining engineering student at the time of the earthquake, Swinerton got a good look at the earthquake rubble and decided to become a builder.

In 1913, Swinerton became vice president, and the company expanded operations and earnings by continuing to prove its integrity and its use of innovative technology on the most challenging projects of the day. By 1923, the company's board of directors, recognizing Swinerton's role in the growth of the company, changed its name to Lindgren & Swinerton.

A young engineer named Richard Walberg joined the firm in the late 1920s as a project manager. In time, he proved his leadership

ability during the Great Depression and forged into post-World War II economic growth with military and industrial projects of increasing complexity and diversity. A new general partnership, Swinerton & Walberg, was formed in 1942 to manage these complex projects.

In the early 1960s, the various Swinerton companies and partnerships began consolidating into one organization, Swinerton & Walberg Co. Upon the death of Swinerton in 1963, Walberg succeeded him as chairman of the board, and Swinerton's son, William, became president of the company. Today, Swinerton & Walberg—the Swinerton organization's main construction subsidiary—is still one of the premier builders in the West.

The company headed into the new millennium with offices in the major metropolitan areas in the western states. Growth led to the creation in 1996 of a holding company structure, Swinerton Incorporated, the parent company of the diverse stable of subsidiaries. Its leadership was composed of Grubb as CEO and chairman of the board; Jim Gillette as president of Swinerton Incorporated, the parent company; and Gordon Marks as president and chief operating officer of Swinerton & Walberg. This seasoned management team began focusing on market diversification to better serve customers into the 21st century.

HISTORY OF INNOVATIONS

Swinerton's history has been punctuated by innovations that have advanced the building industry. For example, in the 1880s, Lindgren helped introduce to the West Coast a stronger brick made of sand and lime, with no straw, which had typically been used in making bricks at that time.

As a pioneer in steel-reinforced concrete construction in California, Hicks oversaw the construction of the reinforced concrete Greek Theatre. Completed in 1903, the structure still stands on the campus of the University of California-Berkeley as one of the first uses of this technology in the state. This process proved to be instrumental in the rebuilding of San Francisco after the catastrophic earthquake and fire of 1906.

The 10-story, $1.5 million Southern Pacific Building at the end of Market Street was the largest office building west of Chicago when it was built in 1915. In 1928, while building the Sir Francis Drake Hotel near Union Square, the company became among the very first contractors in the West to mix concrete at a central plant and have it delivered to the job site in trucks. Even during economic recessions, the company continued to innovate. During the 1980s, Swinerton & Walberg built the nation's first spiral escalator in the San Francisco Shopping Centre.

Today, in the Internet age, the company continues to lead the industry. "We're now managing jobs using the Internet, with many paperwork processes performed electronically," says Grubb. "The owners, architects, consultants, and subcontractors can all access the same critical documents, making it very interactive and streamlined so that we get ahead much faster and more efficiently."

When all is said and done, the final measure of success, according to Grubb, is to ensure that employees are taken care of and customers are satisfied. "That's what it's all about: happy employees and loyal customers," he says. With more than a century of success behind it, Swinerton Incorporated sees a bright new era in the 21st century, for itself and for San Francisco.

CLOCKWISE FROM TOP LEFT: GHIRARDELLI SQUARE (1964), ONE OF THE NATION'S MOST SUCCESSFUL AND RECOGNIZED RETAIL CENTERS, REPRESENTS SWINERTON & WALBERG'S WORK AT ITS FINEST.

ONE OF THE SWINERTON ORGANIZATION'S EARLY PROMINENT PROJECTS WAS STABILIZING THE FAIRMONT HOTEL AFTER THE DEVASTATING 1906 EARTHQUAKE.

THE OLD SAN FRANCISCO PUBLIC LIBRARY (1917) STILL SHINES AS ONE OF SAN FRANCISCO'S JEWELS AND ONE OF SWINERTON'S PRIDE AND JOYS.

WESTIN ST. FRANCIS

THE HISTORIC ST. FRANCIS HOTEL WAS CONSIDERED THE MOST MODERN and luxurious hotel west of the Mississippi in the early 1900s when it opened its doors after two years of construction. Incorporating only the finest and highest-quality materials, the hotel's $2.5 million price tag ensured that the structure would be built to last;

its location at the doorstep of Union Square, San Francisco's virtual living room, sealed its status right from the start. As integral to the city's legacy as the cable cars that have stopped just outside the front doors since its beginning, the hotel has defined San Francisco hospitality since 1904.

Today, as the flagship of the Westin brand of Starwood Hotels & Resorts Worldwide, Inc., the landmark is known as Westin St. Francis. "We recognize the history and heritage that our hotel represents, given that it was built just after the turn of the century," says Michael Cassidy, area managing director, "and through the new millennium, we will continue to uphold that history and heritage

in a style and manner that is first class."

A Storied History

Through the years, the hotel has played a central role in many events—famous and infamous—in the social, political, business, and humanitarian life of San Francisco. A year after its opening, the Westin St. Francis hosted a banquet to celebrate the end of bubonic plague in San Francisco. In the immediate aftermath of the 1906 earthquake, the hotel fed hundreds of newly homeless residents and displaced guests from the quake-damaged Palace Hotel in makeshift dining facilities in Union Square.

Celebrated guests have included singers, musicians, writers, screen and theater stars, Olympic and professional athletes, war heroes, and potentates such as Emperor Akihito of Japan and his father, Emperor Hirohito; Queen Elizabeth II; King Juan Carlos of Spain; the Shah of Iran; and all of the U.S. presidents since William Taft. Heads of state are traditionally honored during their stays with the unfurling of their national flag at the Union Square entrance. In an unprecedented event, on March 2, 1983, the hotel proudly flew the stars and stripes alongside the Union Jack when President Ronald Reagan played host to Queen Elizabeth II. The occasion also marked the first time a formal state dinner was held outside of the White House.

Accommodating the highest standards of protocol and first-class service are the norm for the legendary hotel. Even out-of-the-ordinary requests receive extraordinary service. Actress Ethel Barrymore's pet chimpanzee was looked after by the staff; President Richard Nixon's midnight Oreo craving was fulfilled without hesitation; and when silent-screen

star Anna Held demanded her daily bath in 30 gallons of milk, she got it.

Serving Guests One at a Time

The associates who provide the high caliber of service in this hotel have a high sense of pride, enthusiasm, and energy for their work," says Cassidy. "Some of our team members have been with our hotel for upwards of over 50 years of service."

As bell captain at the Westin St. Francis since 1947, George Cross has literally carried the baggage of every president and major celebrity who has stayed in the hotel. Most remarkably, he has enjoyed his job for more than five decades, and has viewed the changes of time through the people who have entered the hotel's doors. One of Cross's highlights includes being on hand to greet General Douglas MacArthur upon the hero's return from Asia. And Cross recalls the family of Earl Warren, who eventually became chief justice of the U.S. Supreme Court, as "terrific and down-to-earth."

In fact, most of the celebrities Cross encountered in his early years at the hotel were warm and approachable. Now, in addition to being more aloof, "they're a bit too casual," he says. "People dressed better then. Even when they were traveling all night in sleeper cars, they'd come in in the morning all dressed up." The beginning of the end of that sartorial era came at the dawn of flower power. "The white gloves went away in the mid-'60s," he observes nostalgically.

But one unusual tradition remained. For 31 years, until he retired in 1993, the legendary Arnold Batliner laundered the hotel's coins in the basement. Not wanting to soil the white gloves of the genteel female guests, the hotel installed a machine that Batliner invented to wash every

THE MAGNETA GRANDFATHER CLOCK HAS WITHSTOOD THE TESTS OF TIME AND CONTINUES TO PRESIDE OVER THE POWELL STREET LOBBY IN THE WESTIN ST. FRANCIS HOTEL.

coin exchanged within the hotel. Batliner, who died in 1995, earned international renown as much for the longevity of his employment as for the unusual nature of his job. Today, ladies rarely don white gloves any more, credit cards have greatly reduced the use of change, and the washing machine has been inducted into the permanent archives of the hotel, yet Batliner is still remembered as a key figure in the hotel's history. In his honor, long-time St. Francis employee Rob Holsen is carrying on the tradition, washing coins once a week.

Constantly refining the terms of first-class service, the Westin St. Francis continues to find innovative ways to serve guests. It was the city's first hotel to offer wireless phones in each room, introduced in the mid-1990s. Despite being the city's second-largest hotel, "We have built a reputation of serving our customers one at a time," Cassidy emphasizes.

Accommodating Growth

pon opening, the hotel was comprised of two wings in the form of the letter H. The hotel structurally withstood the ravages of the 1906 earthquake, but the great fire that followed gutted its interior. A temporary building was constructed and opened on Union Square around the Dewey Monument within a mere 40 days after the catastrophe, and in November 1907, a scant 19 months later, the St. Francis reopened with 450 rooms. A third wing to the main building was added in 1908, and a fourth wing in 1913, making the St. Francis, then with 600 rooms, the largest hotel on the Pacific Coast.

The jet airliner and the prosperity of the 1960s caused an explosion in tourism and business travel to San Francisco. In August 1967, the St. Francis had an occupancy rate of 99.6 percent and was turning away business because of a lack of rooms. It was time to expand, and a 32-story tower was constructed and married to the main building. The tower was crowned with an elegant dining room named Victor's, for Victor Hirtzler, the legendary master chef of the hotel from 1904 to 1926. Considered the father of California cuisine, he helped put San Francisco on the culinary world map.

In time for the turn of the millennium, the hotel was burnished with a $65 million renaissance, adding luster to an already shining star. The restoration included renovations to guest rooms, the facade, the grand ballroom, and the lobby, and included the addition of a $2 million fitness center and spa. It also encompassed the completion of the Imperial Floor, located on the 32nd floor atop the Tower Building, comprising two lavish special-event venues: Victor's and the adjoining private room, Alexandra's. Each features spectacular panoramic views of the city, with their design inspired by the decor of lavish, 19th-century Russian palaces. Upon opening, Victor's and Alexandra's were instantly hailed as the West Coast's most sumptuous special-event venues.

Today, the hotel has a total of 1,192 guest rooms, 10 specialty suites, and 71 smaller suites; 28 ballrooms and meeting rooms; and a shopping arcade. San Francisco's venerable bar The Compass Rose and Dewey's

AS INTEGRAL TO THE CITY'S LEGACY AS THE CABLE CARS THAT STOP JUST OUTSIDE THE FRONT DOORS, THE WESTIN ST. FRANCIS HAS DEFINED SAN FRANCISCO HOSPITALITY SINCE 1904.

sports bar are both just off the Powell Street lobby.

The six specialty suites in the Tower, each commanding a different view of the city, are decorated in different styles from Mediterranean to Asian. Her Majesty Queen Elizabeth II and His Royal Highness Prince Philip enjoyed the elegance of the Presidential Suite during their historic 1983 visit, and the suite now is named the Windsor Suite in the queen's honor. Four additional specialty suites are in the main building: the London Suite, MacArthur Suite, Chairman's Suite, and State Suite. During the royal visit of Queen Elizabeth II and Prince Philip, President and Mrs. Ronald Reagan stayed in the elegant London Suite, named for Dan London, renowned manager of the St. Francis from 1938 to 1970.

MEET ME UNDER THE CLOCK

San Francisco society has been meeting under the clock since November 30, 1907, when the first master clock introduced to the West—the great Magneta grandfather clock—was installed in the hotel's spacious, 6,000-square-foot Powell Street lobby.

The master clock originally controlled all other clocks in the hotel, with wires connecting the "slave" clocks to the Magneta's main mechanism. This novel concept proved problematic when Russian delegates to the United Nations' World Security Conference were housed on the hotel's 10th floor in 1945. Unfamiliar with the master clock concept, they promptly snipped the suspicious-looking wires in an effort to assure their security—thereby stopping all the clocks in the hotel.

Although no longer the hotel's master clock, the Magneta has withstood the tests of time and continues to preside over the Powell Street lobby, which was renovated in 1991. Throughout the restoration program, the famous lobby retained its grand and historical appeal with the addition of an inlaid marble floor similar to the 1904 original. A handwoven, tufted area rug replicating an antique French royal carpet graces the center of the room. The ornate woodwork found throughout the lobby has been completely retouched with a fresh laminate of gold leafing. Above, pink and blue pastels highlight the elaborate rosettes adorning the ceiling.

San Francisco's Legendary Bar

Perhaps nowhere else in San Francisco is the time capsule preserved more carefully than the magnificent Compass Rose. Refurbished in 1982, the room off of the Powell Street lobby originally served as the fine dining room of the hotel, its interior inspired by the Cluny Museum in Paris.

With its beautiful, fluted columns framing the high, ornate ceilings and rich, wood-paneled walls, the room today looks much like it did when the hotel was built in 1904, coming full circle from a number of radically different incarnations, including a stint as a luxurious library, complete with 4,000 books, and as the ultramodern Patent Leather Bar and Orchid Room. Its current name refers to the multipointed design that appears on the background of all compasses, known as the compass rose. The name alludes to the exotic elegance of custom-made artwork, sculpture, and museum-quality objects brought to the room from all points on the compass at a cost of more than $1 million.

Starwood Corporate Family of Hotels

Through a 1998 marriage of Westin and Starwood Hotels & Resorts Worldwide, Inc., the Westin St. Francis hotel became the big sister property to the city's venerable Palace Hotel and the Sheraton Fisherman's Wharf, as well as four other Bay Area hotels. When it opened in the summer of 1999, W San Francisco, in the Yerba Buena District, became the eighth area property in the Starwood family of hotels.

Starwood—through its St. Regis, Luxury Collection, Westin, Sheraton, Four Points, and W subsidiaries—is one of the leading hotel and leisure companies in the world, with more than 700 hotels in 76 countries and 130,000 employees at its owned and managed properties.

PERHAPS NOWHERE ELSE IN SAN FRANCISCO IS THE TIME CAPSULE PRESERVED MORE CAREFULLY THAN THE MAGNIFICENT COMPASS ROSE. WITH ITS BEAUTIFUL, FLUTED COLUMNS FRAMING THE HIGH, ORNATE CEILINGS AND RICH, WOOD-PANELED WALLS, THE LEGENDARY BAR TODAY LOOKS MUCH LIKE IT DID WHEN THE HOTEL WAS BUILT IN 1904.

PACIFIC GAS AND ELECTRIC COMPANY

IN 1854, A TINY POWER PLANT ON THE CORNER OF FIRST AND HOWARD LIT the streets of San Francisco with gaslights for the first time. This innovative company was the direct ancestor of today's Pacific Gas and Electric Company, founded in 1905. In almost a century, Pacific Gas and Electric Company has evolved through the acquisition and merger of

more than 200 power and natural gas companies. Today, it serves one in 20 Americans and thousands of businesses in Northern and Central California.

The utility's 70,000-square-mile service area stretches from Eureka in the north to Bakersfield in the south, and from the Pacific Ocean in the west to the Sierra Nevada in the east. It encompasses one of the most robust economies in the world, one that includes 970 wineries, 38 gold mines, and 2,682 bakeries, as well as the technology powerhouses of Silicon Valley.

Pacific Gas and Electric Company is a subsidiary of PG&E

Corporation. PG&E Corporation also provides energy services and products throughout North America through its National Energy Group, which includes four wholesale and retail businesses: PG&E Energy Services, PG&E Energy Trading, PG&E Gas Transmission, and PG&E Generating.

FOCUSING ON CUSTOMER SERVICE

In addition to providing reliable utility service, Pacific Gas and Electric Company offers a wide range of services, from gas pilot lighting to flexible payment methods to safety pro-

grams. The company's call centers have the capacity to handle more than 500,000 calls per hour in up to 140 languages.

The Smarter Energy Line provides customers with a convenient point of contact for answers to their energy efficiency questions. Through a do-it-yourself home energy survey or a simple phone conversation with a certified energy adviser, customers can find out where their energy dollars are spent and how best to use energy wisely. Other energy efficiency programs for homes and businesses include incentives, equipment guides, and technology centers.

EMPLOYEES OF PACIFIC GAS AND ELECTRIC COMPANY GO TO GREAT HEIGHTS (TOP LEFT AND RIGHT) TO ENERGIZE 13 MILLION CALIFORNIANS. FROM HELPING FARMERS SAVE POWER IN THE FIELD (BOTTOM RIGHT) TO HARNESSING MOUNTAIN RIVERS FOR ELECTRICITY (BOTTOM LEFT), THE COMPANY DELIVERS ENERGY AND A WIDE RANGE OF SERVICES.

WITH ASSETS SUCH AS 70,000 MILES OF GAS PIPE (TOP LEFT) AND 1,000 CUSTOMER SERVICE EMPLOYEES TAKING CALLS IN MANY LANGUAGES (TOP RIGHT), PACIFIC GAS AND ELECTRIC COMPANY SERVICES A 70,000-SQUARE-MILE AREA THAT STRETCHES FROM EUREKA TO BAKERSFIELD AND FROM THE PACIFIC OCEAN TO THE SIERRA NEVADA.

The company also provides customers with information on gas and electric safety, storm and earthquake readiness, and safety programs for youth. Businesses can find out about surplus real estate and equipment for sale, electric and natural gas vehicles, and California's economic outlook.

EMBRACING CUSTOMER CHOICE

After nearly 100 years of both supplying and delivering energy, Pacific Gas and Electric Company has embraced sweeping changes in California's energy industry. In 1996, the California legislature opened the state's electricity generation market to retail competition. This historic action made California the first in the nation to restructure its electricity industry statewide, and gave all of the utility's electric customers—as well as those of seven other providers—the option of choosing their supplier.

Whether a customer buys power or gas from another energy supplier or remains a full-service utility customer, Pacific Gas and Electric Company delivers that energy over its wires and pipes, safely and reliably.

Customer choice is also leading utilities to focus more on what consumers want and to find new ways to be cost-efficient and innovative. Since 1993, the company's rates for residential electric customers have decreased by 12.5 percent, with more decreases expected by 2002. "Our goals for the future are to be the best at

what we do—safe, reliable energy delivery; responsive customer service; and efficient performance," says Gordon R. Smith, president and chief executive officer.

INVOLVED IN THE COMMUNITY

The company works with local governments and nonprofit groups to help those most in need and to improve the quality of life for everyone. The utility's many community projects range from relocating raptors' nests away from power poles and planting trees, to economic development programs that encourage businesses to move to or stay in Northern and Central California.

Each year, five employees receive the Mielke Award for outstanding community service, in which $5,000 is donated by the company to the employee's chosen nonprofit organization. In the past, this program has benefited such diverse groups as the Boys & Girls Club of Santa Maria and the Central California Forum on Refugee Affairs. Also, millions of dollars each year are donated by shareholders, customers, and employees to The Salvation Army's Relief for Energy Assistance through Community Help (REACH) fund. In recent years, the company has given about $8 million annually to nonprofits of all kinds, with an emphasis on education, job training, and business development.

Pacific Gas and Electric Company invests start-up funds in more than 20 business incubators—

support centers where new firms are nurtured. Affordable housing gets a boost from the corporation's investment in building and retrofitting hundreds of low-income units. And the utility promotes education with contributions and matching gifts to schools and universities.

"One thing that's constant is the active partnership we have with our neighbors to meet the needs of communities we serve in Northern and Central California," says Smith. "We're as much connected to this area by shared concerns and values as we are by our electric wires and gas pipelines. We're rooted here, committed to delivering the best service in the most environmentally responsible way possible, and dedicated to continuing our decades of community involvement."

PACIFIC GAS AND ELECTRIC COMPANY HAS A LONG HISTORY IN CALIFORNIA. FOUNDED IN 1905, THE COMPANY EVOLVED FROM A TINY POWER PLANT ON THE CORNER OF FIRST AND HOWARD STREETS WHICH LIT THE STREETS OF SAN FRANCISCO WITH GASLIGHTS FOR THE FIRST TIME IN 1854.

Del Monte Foods Company

TS ROOTS MAY BE IN THE FOOD CANNING BUSINESS, BUT THE DEL MONTE® FOODS Company of today and tomorrow is growing by inspiring great meals at home and on the go. ◆ Back in 1916, when four major canning companies joined to market premium canned goods under the Del Monte label, Americans took their meals as a family around a dining room table.

Today's frenetic lifestyles have dramatically altered our eating occasions—whether engaged in together or alone. Mealtimes, more often than not, may involve kitchen counter eating while doing homework or dashboard dining on the way to soccer practice.

Still, most consumers prefer sitting down to an enjoyable meal, one that is more than just another routine event in their busy schedules. Del Monte is addressing the realities of the consumer's pace, time constraints, and desires. "We've adjusted, like any successful company, to what the marketplace wants," says Irv Holmes, senior vice president of marketing. "Consumers are very limited with their time, yet have a very strong desire for healthful foods and delicious meals at home and on the go."

In response to these market forces, Del Monte has unified two key strategies: first, helping consumers with creative ways to use the company's revered quality products in simple, healthful, and tasty meal preparations; and second, developing new products that meet the needs of consumers.

The first strategy has led to creating easy-to-fix, Can Do® meal recipes needing just "20 minutes or less" to complete. These creative recipes also inspire numerous consumer innovations—delicious variations on a theme, or as the slogan says, "Add imagination and serve!" These recipes lead many consumers to endorse Del Monte's popular Hey, I Can Do That! program.

The second strategy has spawned the introduction of a variety of foods within the company's category-leading lines of canned fruit, vegetable, and tomato products. Fruit Pleasures®, FruitRageous®, and Orchard Select® top Del Monte's fruit category creations. The recently acquired Contadina® brand brings the "freshest ideas in Italian cooking"

to the tomato category. Del Monte's specialty vegetables are growing in popularity, along with the expanded use of pull-top lids. Newly introduced plastic packaging for single-serve Fruit Cup® is perfect for desk-side dining or on-the-go nourishment.

Industry Breakthroughs

Del Monte is no stranger to innovation. Throughout its history, the company has led the industry with several breakthrough concepts. In 1917, for instance, an ad in the *Saturday Evening Post* suggested that con-

sumers ask for the Del Monte brand, introducing the packaged food industry's first brand-loyal marketing campaign.

Del Monte remains uniquely in the forefront with its unified agricultural research, seed production, and grower advisory programs that yield the best possible raw product quality. In 1970, Del Monte was widely praised for being the first national company to voluntarily include meaningful nutrition information on product labels. Subsequently, it became the first national brand to introduce a companion line of no-salt-added

vegetables, and it perfected the method of producing a companion line of unsweetened, juice-pack fruits.

A Heritage of Quality

In 1916, four major canning operations merged to form the California Packing Corporation, or Calpak, but the company's true beginnings can be traced to the California gold rush and the exploding population's need for preserved foods.

The Del Monte brand first appeared in 1886 on coffee specially blended for the prestigious Hotel Del Monte in Monterey. In 1891, the Oakland Preserving Company used the name to identify its premium quality canned fruits. In 1899, 18 Pacific Coast canning companies merged to form the California Fruit Canners Association, which continued to use the Del Monte brand as its premium label. The association's largest peach cannery, located at the time in San Francisco, is now the popular waterfront retail center known simply as the Cannery. The California Fruit Canners Association was one of the four entities that formed Calpak, whose headquarters were established in San Francisco, where Del Monte proudly remains today.

Del Monte Foods is the largest producer and distributor of premium-quality, branded processed fruit, vegetable, and tomato products in the United States, and is the number one brand in all three of its product categories. This strong consumer franchise is backed by 14 production facilities and six distribution centers strategically located throughout the United States.

Del Monte's beginnings and lifelong heritage are inexorably linked to superior quality, an attribute that has prevailed in all its undertakings, and is clearly evident today as the company inspires great meals at home and on the go.

IN THE FUTURE, WHEN SCHOOLCHILDREN READ ABOUT THE HISTORY OF TH] information age, they will find ZDNet featured as a pioneer in on-line publishing, and one that reported on the era as it unfolded. ◆ "There's no question we were early adopters," says Dan Rosensweig, CEO of ZDNet Endowed with content from its parent, ZDNet evolved from the Interne

division of technology publishing giant Ziff-Davis. In 1996, it was officially established under the name ZDNet, although its precursor ZiffNet had maintained an on-line presence through CompuServe for 12 years.

HELPING PEOPLE USE TECHNOLOGY

If you come to ZDNet, you'll be able to find products, services, tips, and information, all about technology and the Internet," says Rosensweig. "We help individuals, companies, and small businesses understand the power of technology and find the right technology solution for their needs, whether they're first-time buyers or corporate-enterprisewide buyers. ZDNet is designed to help them make the right decision, buy the right product from the right vendor, then use that product to its maximum capability."

ZDNet's Web site, www.zdnet.com, also offers definitive news reporting and analysis of technology in general. For example, coverage of the Microsoft antitrust case in 1999 was updated as often as 12 times each day. Not only did ZDNet provide up-to-date information, but also in-depth analysis of the case's impact on the computer industry. And high-tech crises like the onslaught of the Melissa virus in the spring of 1999 brought out the journalistic excellence of the firm's 200-strong editorial staff in breaking and covering the developing news.

"As technology has become more pervasive, it has developed more impact on people's lives in more ways than it ever had in the past," says Rosensweig. "Technology intersects people's lives in so many ways."

Accordingly, ZDNet has added a variety of features to its Web site. For example, GameSpot has become the Internet's largest independent gaming site due to the popularity of computer games, especially among teenagers and children, whose first introduction to technology often begins with games. Another example, ZD Inter@ctive Investor, has earned Barron's ranking as a top 10 investing site to help users make sense of the volatile stocks in the high-tech industry, which in the past two decades has fueled economic growth around the world.

"The Web is obviously a new medium," Rosensweig says. "We're taking advantage of this and providing tens of thousands of open doors for users to come in. We want to give users information the way they want to get it, any time they want to get it."

Harnessing the personalization capabilities of the Internet, ZDNet is able to customize the information delivered to users according to a path they designate. As a result, ZDNet has developed strong bonds with users, as evidenced by research that shows users spend 70 percent more time on ZDNet than on other sites in the technology category, and come back 40 percent more often in the course of a month.

"Think of ZDNet as an early form of a smart site that can un-

"IF YOU COME TO ZDNET, YOU'LL BE ABLE TO FIND PRODUCTS, SERVICES, TIPS, AND INFORMATION, ALL ABOUT TECHNOLOGY AND THE INTERNET," SAYS PRESIDENT AND CEO DAN ROSENSWEIG. "WE HELP INDIVIDUALS, COMPANIES, AND SMALL BUSINESSES UNDERSTAND THE POWER OF TECHNOLOGY AND FIND THE RIGHT TECHNOLOGY SOLUTION FOR THEIR NEEDS, WHETHER THEY'RE FIRST-TIME BUYERS OR CORPORATE-ENTERPRISEWIDE BUYERS."

derstand the user and do some anticipating in response to what the user wants," says Rosensweig. "When you're making a mission-critical decision—whether you're parents deciding on the right computer for your child, or an enterprise information systems manager buying $10 million in computers for your company—our unbiased, trusted information about technology products, services, and companies has a huge potential impact. The depth, breadth, and quality of information on our site allow users to start here on their first day of using technology, and continue to move up the technology knowledge ladder."

Effective Advertising Vehicle

ith its loyal user base, ZDNet is one of the few on-line content publishers that actually operate in the black. In June 1999, analysts

with Goldman Sachs' Investment Research division rated the firm's stock a market out-performer, noting that "ZDNet will continue to be well positioned in capturing a large portion of the on-line advertising dollars that are being spent on technology content sites."

Citing ZDNet's multibranded sites across different demographic groups, ability to leverage print content and assets from Ziff-Davis, growing international presence, and loyal audience of more than 2 million registered users and 8 million visitors in April 1999, analysts deemed ZDNet a strong company, driven primarily by advertising revenues and poised for healthy growth into the new millennium.

A Future-Oriented Company

As ZDNet continues to evolve, it is striving to reach a broader audience beyond the current dominance of

well-educated, high-net-worth men. For instance, the firm has established strategic alliances and programs such as its partnership with iVillage, a leading site for women. And as prices for technology decrease, younger users can be expected to seek out ZDNet's product information reviews and listings.

Globally, the Ziff-Davis brand is already well known. Four wholly owned international sites and alliances with 16 licensees worldwide are helping to build ZDNet into a leading international brand for technology information, products, and services.

"We're not following the curve," says Rosensweig. "We're out in front of it. We've been on the Internet since the beginning. We saw it early. We embraced it. We participated in it. We contributed to it. And we are thriving in it."

ONE OF THE FEW ON-LINE CONTENT PUBLISHERS THAT ACTUALLY OPERATE IN THE BLACK, ZDNet MADE ITS INITIAL PUBLIC OFFERING (ZDZ) ON THE NEW YORK STOCK EXCHANGE ON MARCH 31, 1999. IN JUNE 1999, ANALYSTS WITH GOLDMAN SACHS' INVESTMENT RESEARCH DIVISION RATED THE FIRM'S STOCK A MARKET OUT-PERFORMER, NOTING THAT "ZDNet WILL CONTINUE TO BE WELL POSITIONED IN CAPTURING A LARGE PORTION OF THE ON-LINE ADVERTISING DOLLARS THAT ARE BEING SPENT ON TECHNOLOGY CONTENT SITES."

CHALLENGE DAIRY PRODUCTS, INC.

S INCE ITS FOUNDING, CHALLENGE DAIRY PRODUCTS, INC. HAS BEEN A LEADER in marketing. It started advertising in 1911, and advertises and promotes its butter throughout the West with an award-winning campaign in television and outdoor advertising. Today's theme line aptly sums up both Challenge and its products: Making a Stand for Quality.

On January 2, 1911, the Challenge Cream & Butter Company opened for business with a staff of four people. In a rented storeroom in Los Angeles, they sold the products of cooperative creamery associations in Riverdale and Tulare. The new company owned a wagon, but had to rent a horse to pull it. That first day, Joe Spence, the delivery salesman, set out in a wagon with 132 pounds of Challenge butter— and returned that evening with 120 pounds.

After going through two salesmen during the first couple of months of business, Clyde Mitchel, the general manager, began going out with two pounds of Challenge butter in a black satchel packed with ice. He would tempt grocers with butter on a cracker, and if that failed, he would leave a pound with them to try on their own tables. In this way, the business was built up— slowly at first, then faster and faster, because of the high quality of Challenge's product.

In the 1920s, all Challenge retail butter for Northern California was cut in the San Francisco plant from the bulk butter churned at Danish Creamery in Fresno. Challenge then purchased a dairy in San Francisco that processed fluid milk, and grew to have 25 home delivery and retail grocery store routes by the 1950s. At that time, Challenge had a fluid milk and butter-cutting plant in San Francisco that employed 63 people. Also, a new ice-cream and fluid milk plant was built in Berkeley with 153 employees. All around the Bay Area, Challenge had branch offices, whereas today, distribution of all products is from an efficient center in San Leandro.

Very early, the management of Challenge recognized the elements of successful butter marketing: consistent quality, consistently promoted. By refusing to sell any butter that didn't meet the highest standards, Challenge built a reputation for quality. The company has undergone several reorganizations since 1911, but the trade name of Challenge has endured to become the symbol of its tradition

of unparalleled quality and customer service.

RETAIL DIVISION

T he present-day Challenge Dairy Products, Inc. offers a complete selection of Challenge butter products for retail stores. Challenge butter is the best-selling brand throughout the West and is the market leader in California. The company also markets Danish Creamery butter, the number three market leader in California. Other states where Challenge products can be found include Alaska, Arizona, Hawaii, Idaho, Montana, Nevada, New Mexico, Oregon, Texas, Utah, Washington, and Wyoming.

Challenge and Danish Creamery brands of premium butter are 93 score, Grade AA butter, produced in a modern, USDA-approved plant by Danish Cream-ery located in the San Joaquin Valley. Challenge butter has received the Gold Medal award for quality of both salted and unsalted butter by Food Service Chefs of America every year since 1994.

FOOD SERVICE DIVISION

C hallenge Dairy also markets Challenge butter to the food-service trade, including approximately 3,400 restaurants, hotels, bakeries, commissaries, and cafeterias. Along with other dairy and non-dairy-food items, Challenge butter is distributed in California through eight branch distribution centers using company-owned refrigerated trucks, and in Oregon, Washington, Nevada, Arizona, and Hawaii through food-service distributors. Challenge Dairy is the only statewide, full-time dairy serving all major metropolitan areas in California.

Challenge's eight Food Service branches sell approximately 1,000 items, including premium cheese and other dairy items, salad dressings, salads, desserts, eggs, oils, and pickles. Since April 1,

"THE SUCCESS OF THE CHALLENGE ORGANIZATION IS BASED UPON OUR CONTINUING TRADITIONS OF QUALITY AND SERVICE," SAYS JOHN D. WHETTEN, CEO AND PRESIDENT OF CHALLENGE DAIRY PRODUCTS, INC.

998, the company has been the exclusive Ben & Jerry's Ice Cream distributor for food service in both Northern and Southern California.

Food Ingredients Division

A separate Food Ingredients Division sells Challenge-brand butter to food processors. In addition, whey, agglomerated powdered milk, sweetened condensed milk, lactose, and blends produced for Challenge Dairy by other companies are sold under the Challenge label. Sales by the Food Ingredients Division are made throughout the United States and to other countries.

Since quality ingredients produce quality goods, it is not surprising that the South San Francisco-based chocolates maker, See's Candies, has used butter from Challenge in its premium candies since 1923.

Challenge Firsts

Throughout its history of commitment to quality, Challenge has pioneered numerous methods of production, packaging, and marketing. Among the company's firsts was the use in Los Angeles of lighted commercial outdoor billboards for advertising in 1911. The company also developed the first metal

churn, which was more durable and sanitary than the old wooden ones. Challenge revolutionized the packing and shipping of butter, and developed the first lab sampling of all butter to ensure quality. Shipping bulk butter in corrugated cases instead of wooden containers was a Challenge idea, too.

"The success of the Challenge organization is based upon our continuing traditions of quality and service," says John D. Whetten,

CEO and president of Challenge Dairy Products, Inc. "We are grateful for the many steadfast dairymen and employees who have been dedicated and determined to have the finest-quality product for Challenge to sell."

Challenge has become a part of the West. Based on its long history of service and quality, the company will continue to serve the West for many years to come.

BELIEVING QUALITY INGREDIENTS PRODUCE QUALITY GOODS, SOUTH SAN FRANCISCO-BASED CHOCOLATES MAKER, SEE'S CANDIES, HAS USED BUTTER FROM CHALLENGE IN ITS PREMIUM CANDIES SINCE 1923 (TOP).

BASED ON ITS LONG HISTORY OF SERVICE AND QUALITY, AND UNDER THE LEADERSHIP OF WHETTEN, CEO, AND SENIOR VICE PRESIDENT JIM WEBB (LEFT), CHALLENGE WILL CONTINUE TO SERVE THE WEST FOR MANY YEARS TO COME (BOTTOM).

TRANSAMERICA CORPORATION

SEVENTY-ONE YEARS AFTER ITS FOUNDING BY LEGENDARY SAN FRANCISCO banker A.P. Giannini, Transamerica Corporation entered a new phase in its remarkable history in 1999, when it was acquired by the Dutch insurance giant Aegon NV ◆ Following the trend in the late 1990s toward worldwide consolidation of financial services companies,

Transamerica Corporation and Aegon combined forces to achieve the global reach and scale required to stay competitive. Under this alliance, the new organization became one of the world's largest insurance companies, providing financial security to people and groups through products such as life insurance, annuities, pension products, mutual funds, and reinsurance. The Transamerica name was retained and Transamerica's trademark Pyramid building became the new company's U.S. headquarters.

Transamerica's other businesses continue to rank among the top players in their related fields. For example, in transportation equipment leasing—such as intermodal containers—Transamerica ranks among the world's leaders. The company ranks among the nation's top competitors in commercial finance—financing the products of manufacturers, distributors, retailers, and consumers in a wide range of industries, and

making asset-based loans to businesses. Transamerica's real estate information companies, which monitor payments of property taxes for lenders and provide them with tax payment processing and guaranteed flood hazard determination services, lead the nation.

SHARED HERITAGE OF SERVICE

That Transamerica would eventually become a life insurance concern seemed an unlikely course for the holding company that Giannini established in 1928 to serve his diverse operations, including Bank of America. For 30 years, the structure enabled him to offer a variety of financial services to the general public in keeping with his dream of serving the ordinary working class.

In 1956, Congress passed the Bank Holding Company Act, which prohibited an institution from owning both banking and nonbanking companies. To comply, Transamerica was forced to

choose a direction. It was widely thought that Transamerica would take the banking route, but instead the company divested its banking activities and nurtured the growth of its modest life insurance group.

Eventually, the company grew into a major corporation that included such diverse subsidiaries as a motion picture company, an airline, and a hotel chain. By the early 1980s, Transamerica had grown to nearly 30,000 employees. A period of restructuring followed, as the company refocused on its original core finance and insurance businesses. In the 1990s, the company continued to simplify its structure and to focus on creating shareholder value by maintaining leadership in each of its major businesses.

POWER OF THE PYRAMID

Throughout its history, Transamerica has consistently put an emphasis on performance. Like the pyramid that has become the company's

symbol and logo, Transamerica stands solid, strong, and safe, even under the force of the winds of change. Like the Pyramid building, Transamerica is integral to the fabric of San Francisco.

Built in 1972, the 48-story Transamerica Pyramid is one of San Francisco's most distinctive landmarks and its tallest building, reaching a height of 853 feet. Architect William L. Pereira chose the slender, pyramidal configuration because it allows more light to reach the street and offers advanced safety features, especially related to earthquakes. Moreover, the building design made room for the adjacent, half-acre Redwood Park, which harbors the world's only urban redwood grove of some four dozen trees.

A Success Story

Transamerica measures itself by four primary principles: creating value for shareholders, serving customers, respecting employees, and being a positive force in the communities in which it does business. By all measures, Transamerica is indeed a San Francisco success story.

Built in 1972, the 48-story Transamerica Pyramid, headquarters of Transamerica Corporation, is one of San Francisco's most distinctive landmarks and its tallest building, reaching a height of 853 feet. Architect William L. Pereira chose the slender, pyramidal configuration because it allows more light to reach the street and offers advanced safety features, especially related to earthquakes.

HE ACADEMY OF ART COLLEGE PRIDES ITSELF ON ITS DEDICATION TO THE career preparation of artists and designers. "We maintain a disciplined approach to the study of art and design," says Elisa Stephens, president. "Our focus is on the classroom and the student. Each semester, we bring to the Academy the best faculty from all over the country. Our instructors are professionals who impart to students years of experience and the skill and training needed to be successful in their chosen profession."

It is this vision that led Richard S. "Pappy" Stephens, an advertising art director of *Sunset* magazine, to open the Academy of Advertising Art in 1929. His new school consisted of 46 students meeting in one room on San Francisco's Kearny Street.

With his wife, Clara, as administrator, Stephens sought to give aspiring artists and designers the skills needed to become successful. His practice of hiring professional artists to bring real-world problems, solutions, and practical experience to his students set the philosophy of the Academy: Hire today's best practicing professionals to teach the art and design professionals of tomorrow.

When Richard A. Stephens succeeded his father as president in 1951, he added a foundations department to ensure that all students comprehended the basic principles of traditional art and design. In 1966, the Academy officially became a college, with approval from the California Department of Education to issue a bachelor of fine arts degree. In another decade, the master of fine arts was offered. With top industry leaders as instructors and access to the most advanced facilities and equipment, the Academy's enrollment growth topped more than 2,500 students in 1992. That was the same year that the presidency was turned over to the third generation in the family, Elisa Stephens, granddaughter of the school's founder. Today, the Academy of Art College is the largest private art and design school in the nation, spanning 16 buildings, boasting a student body numbering more than 5,500, and representing nearly every country in the world.

Associate in arts degrees and certificates, as well as bachelor of fine arts and master of fine arts degrees, are awarded in 10 art and design majors: advertising design, computer arts, fashion, fine art, graphic design, illustration, industrial design studios, interior architecture and design, motion pictures and video, and photography. In addition, personal enrichment courses are offered days, evenings, and weekends.

True to the school's focus on preparing students for jobs in the fiercely competitive arts and design fields, an aggressive career services department assists students with presentation and interviewing skills in order to maximize their opportunities with recruiters. Notable examples of companies who recruit the college's students include Disney, DreamWorks, Pixar, Sony, Columbia Tristar, and George Lucas' Industrial Light & Magic, all of which regularly schedule calls for portfolio review at the Academy.

"We are proactive every day," says Stephens. "Our curriculum is reviewed regularly to ensure that our students receive relevant information that will allow them to develop the best portfolio and achieve a career in the arts. And we employ exclusively a profes-

ACCORDING TO ELISA STEPHENS, PRESIDENT OF THE ACADEMY OF ART COLLEGE IN SAN FRANCISCO, "STUDENTS RECEIVE RELEVANT INFORMATION THAT WILL ALLOW THEM TO DEVELOP THE BEST PORTFOLIO AND ACHIEVE A CAREER IN THE ARTS." THE WORK OF DOMINGO JOHNSON IN THE ADVERTISING DEPARTMENT (LEFT) AND KAREN SCHMUCKER IN GRAPHIC DESIGN IS EVIDENCE OF THE COLLEGE'S COMMITMENT TO TRAINING ART AND DESIGN PROFESSIONALS.

Bob learns the value of sharing.

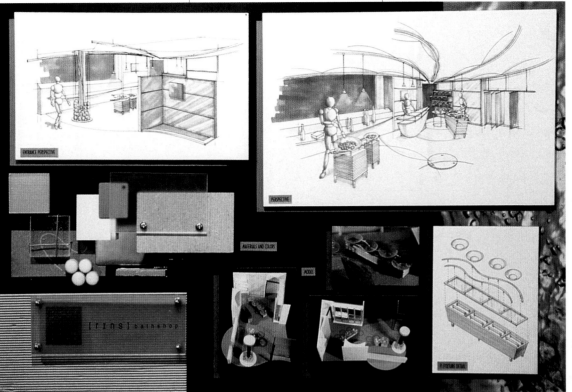

sional faculty because they can convey information relevant to today's marketable skills."

INTO THE FUTURE

It is not an accident that the Academy is headquartered south of Market Street in the heart of Multimedia Gulch, where cutting-edge technology is simultaneously the tool and the creation of the future art and design professional.

Perhaps the school's most successful challenge has been the growth of its computer arts program. Originally conceived as a service department for layout functions in the advertising and graphic design majors, the sizable computer arts department became a major with the revolutionary advent of desktop publishing, and has become the Academy's fastest-growing department.

Stephens' ability to recognize prevailing technology and to employ it in the school has allowed the Academy to continually ride the crest of the wave in cutting-edge technology, even as standards shift and evolve with lightning speed.

"We educate our students using state-of-art technology and offer them the most advanced facilities available," says Stephens. "The Academy constantly reviews the equipment needs of our departments in order to remain an institution on the cutting edge of technology. The arts are moving so fast in today's digital environment that you have to be immersed in this dynamic urban environment to stay current."

It also doesn't hurt that San Francisco is a beautiful city in which to be an artist. In Stephens' view, San Francisco is the perfect setting for the Academy's future plans: expansion of the motion picture/video program. Recognizing the city's leading role in the multimedia industry and its voracious need for talent to fuel that growth, Stephens can foresee the industry's dovetailing perfectly with the school's special effects, directing, cinematography, editing, and computer animation functions.

"We have all the components for making an entire special effects movie, as well as video games and a full range of TV programs," says Stephens.

The expansion into this new area is one more example of how the Academy of Art College is successfully evolving to meet the changing needs of its students. With roots tracing back for more than seven decades, it is a tradition that is sure to be continued for many generations of students to come.

SAN FRANCISCO

City College of San Francisco — 1935

Landor Associates — 1941

Washington Township Health Care District — 1948

MBT Architecture — 1954

KTVU Fox 2 — 1958

Hilton San Francisco — 1964

McKessonHBOC — 1967

Gap Inc. — 1969

Hill & Knowlton, Inc. — 1969

Walker — 1969

ADAC Laboratories — 1970

Semiconductor Equipment and Materials International (SEMI) — 1970

Custom Chrome, Inc. — 1971

Webcor Builders — 1971

Bayer Corporation — 1974

ZiLOG Inc. — 1974

CITY COLLEGE OF SAN FRANCISCO

CITY COLLEGE OF SAN FRANCISCO IS ONE OF THE NATION'S LARGEST MULTI-campus colleges. Serving nearly one out of every seven of the city's 723,000 residents every year, the annual student body is more than 92,000. With classes offered at 150 locations in neighborhoods throughout the city, the institution is truly a community college. ◆ Originally established in 1935, City College separated from the San Francisco Unified School District in 1972 to become part of the San Francisco Community College District. Over the years, City College's enrollment has grown substantially, and the makeup of the student body has changed dramatically. Today, the classroom is more than 60 percent women and 67 percent ethnic minorities, compared to the Class of 1935, when 42 percent of the students were women and 19 percent ethnic minorities.

Accustomed to forging new academic paths, City College was the first college to train women as aircraft mechanics, and one of the first schools to offer a hospitality program. A current college catalog, which is comprised of more than 100 programs, includes classes from the nation's only Gay, Lesbian, and Bisexual Studies department.

TRAINING WORKERS OF TOMORROW

The success of City College in serving the community can be attributed to the school's ability to listen and respond to changing educational needs in the marketplace. Students, alumni, academic partners, educators, and community and business leaders meet at regularly scheduled focus groups and listening sessions to discuss the current trends in the workforce.

"What we're hearing," says Dr. Philip R. Day Jr., chancellor, "is that the economy of the future is going to depend upon the quality of the workforce." As a result, an entire division of City College is dedicated to workforce education: If a local company needs skilled workers to produce its products or service its customers, City College can develop customized programs to train its personnel. For example, the college provides special skills training for mechanics to service the fleet of aircraft for major airlines like United at San Francisco International Airport.

"To start the program, we'll bring in the equipment, and find the faculty and staff to teach it, but the company pays the college directly for this invaluable service," explains Day. "The bottom line is that they make it work for us, and we make it work for them."

Those already in the workforce benefit from City College as well. Public safety workers take language courses like Spanish and conversational Vietnamese in order to communicate with clients who seek their help, often in an emergency situation. In addition, the college serves the immigrant community through its noncredit English as a second language (ESL), citizenship, and vocational courses.

City College also works with traditionally overlooked segments of the community. For example, Pacific Gas & Electric (PG&E) partners with City College in a welfare-to-work initiative that places 100 percent of the program's welfare-recipient students in the workforce upon graduation. And an entire division of the college is dedicated to serving the educational needs of older adults.

SUCCESS IN THE FUTURE

City College annually awards more than 1,000 associate degrees and more than 700 vocational and technical certificates. Close to 300 City College students transfer to the University of California system, while 1,200 students transfer to the

MONICA DAVEY

"WE TAKE PRIDE IN THE ACCOMPLISHMENTS OF OUR STUDENTS," SAYS DR. PHILIP R. DAY JR., CITY COLLEGE OF SAN FRANCISCO CHANCELLOR. "THE SCHOOL'S SUCCESS IS NOT ABOUT BRICKS AND MORTAR, THE NUMBER OF CAMPUSES, OR HOW MUCH WE OWN. IT'S ABOUT THE PEOPLE WE SERVE AND WATCHING THEM GROW AND DEVELOP."

California State University system.
In addition, City College is the
single largest source of students
for San Francisco State University.
The college assists more than 700
students in receiving high school
equivalency certificates, and
helps students pass health sciences licensure exams at well
above national rates. City College
accomplishes all this with the
commitment and determination of
a top-notch faculty of more than
750 full-time and 1,000 part-time
instructors, and a great support
staff.

The success of City College,
however, is not just measured by
the numbers. "We take pride in the
accomplishments of our students,"
says Day. "The school's success is
not about bricks and mortar, the
number of campuses, or how

much we own. It's about the
people we serve and watching
them grow and develop."

City College has become more
than a stepping-stone to a bacca-
laureate degree. Although the
institution is concerned with preparing people for furthering their
education, it also prepares people
for the workplace through more
than 100 short- and long-term
training programs geared specifically to the current market.

With a nursing program regarded as one of the best in the
nation, the health services field is
one of City College's most sought-
after programs. "We know that
the health field is going to continue
to boom," says Day, "and recently
we've become the national center
for biotechnology." In 1998, the
National Science Foundation

awarded City College a $5 million
Advanced Technological Education
grant to build a new biotechnology
center, called Bio-Link, and to
create a national network of community colleges similarly engaged.

In maintaining the optimum
balance between assessing the
needs of local businesses and
serving the local community, City
College constantly looks to the
horizon to see where the opportunities lie. "There's a lot of business
out there, and we can handle it.
City College is a partner in the
pursuit of the highest quality of
life in the San Francisco Bay Area,"
emphasizes Day. By providing
local business and industry with
an educated and high-quality
workforce, City College will continue to play a vital role in the
future of San Francisco.

LANDOR ASSOCIATES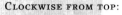

A SAN FRANCISCO-BASED BRAND AND DESIGN CONSULTING FIRM, LANDOR Associates follows closely the guiding principle of its founder, the late Walter Landor: Products are made in the factory, brands are built in the mind. ◆ The firm's worldwide staff, now 700 employees strong, is strategically positioned to shape the corporate identities of domestic and multinational companies. Many of the firm's clients have become household names and internationally recognized symbols. FedEx, Lucent, SGI, Andersen Consulting, Delta Airlines, Canadian Airlines, Microsoft, Nagano Olympic Winter Games, Atlanta Centennial Olympic Games, Xerox, Hewlett-Packard, Agilent, Levi's, and Netscape represent just a sample of the diverse Landor portfolio.

Landor has offices in nearly every design capital in the Americas, Asia, and Europe. In addition to its San Francisco headquarters, full-service consulting studios are located in New York, Seattle, Cincinnati, Mexico City, London, Paris, Hamburg, Sydney, Tokyo, and Hong Kong. Marketing offices are based in Bangkok, Madrid, Miami, Milan, São Paulo, Seoul, Stockholm, and Taipei.

KLAMATH HOUSE

A talented industrial designer, Landor followed in his architect father's footsteps in pre-World War II Germany. While he was overseeing construction of the British pavilion at the 1939 World's Fair in New York, war broke out in Europe, and Landor decided not to return home. Instead, he bought a car and drove cross-country, stopping in San Francisco where he was captivated by the city's beauty.

In 1941, Landor and his wife, Josephine, began working out of their Russian Hill apartment, designing packaging for local companies. Before long, the company had grown and Landor's reputation had spread. By the end of Landor Associates' first decade, the M.H. de Young Memorial Museum had mounted an exhibition on package design, honoring his work.

In 1964, Landor purchased the decommissioned ferryboat *Klamath* at the Port of Redwood City. Restoring it to its original splendor, Landor docked it at Pier 5, and moved his design studio and offices aboard. A quarter of a century later, he sold the company to the worldwide marketing communications conglomerate Young & Rubicam Inc. By that time, Landor Associates had outgrown the ferryboat, and the offices were moved to the firm's present location on Front Street.

Although the *Klamath* has since been sold, Landor Associates maintains the image of the ferry as its icon of innovation, or as author Tom Wolfe once called it, the "flagship of package design." Today, all Landor offices around the world are in buildings named Klamath House.

DEVELOPING INNOVATIVE CONCEPTS

For Italian book and magazine publisher Mondadori, Landor created the name, identity, and store design for Biblioteq bookstores, based on what was then

CLOCKWISE FROM TOP: "TODAY, WE FOCUS ON POWER APPLICATIONS MOST CRITICAL IN CREATING BRAND PERCEPTIONS," SAYS CLAY TIMON, CHAIRMAN, PRESIDENT, AND CEO OF LANDOR ASSOCIATES, A SAN FRANCISCO FIRM THAT SHAPES THE CORPORATE IDENTITIES OF DOMESTIC AND MULTINATIONAL COMPANIES.

THE NEW BRANDING SYSTEM FOR CANADIAN AIRLINES EXTENDS TO NUMEROUS CONSUMER TOUCH POINTS, INCLUDING AIRCRAFT LIVERIES, CABIN INTERIORS, IN-FLIGHT PRODUCTS, GROUND VEHICLES, AND CORPORATE COLLATERAL.

PIONEERING RETAIL ENTERTAINMENT IN THE EARLY 1980S, LANDOR CRAFTED A RELAXED AND SOCIAL ATMOSPHERE FOR BIBLIOTEQ TO BROADEN CUSTOMER BASE AMONG LESS AVID READERS.

a new retail concept: entertainment book retailing. This precursor to today's spacious bookstore with café and cross-merchandising was the first bookstore-as-entertainment environment. Today, branded environments and retail design are separate divisions within the firm.

Still blazing trails, Landor extends to the latest frontier: Web site development. "More and more people today come in contact with our clients through their Web site," says Clay Timon, chairman, president, and CEO. "Take an airline, for example. What we call the power application of the brand will be the aircraft first and the Web site second. With a petroleum company, only 10 percent of its income may come from retail—the other 90 percent from exploration—yet its power applications are retail and the Web site, so that's where we focus our energy."

The process of shaping corporate identity begins with the discovery phase, understanding a client's branding and identity needs. Creating a strategic platform follows. "We distill it down to a brand driver—

our trademark word—that sums up the core of a brand. It could be one or two words, a sentence or paragraph, or a montage of pictures and colors," says Timon.

The next step is where the ink meets the paper. In Landor's early days, it might have involved delving into the work of fashioning business cards or stationery. "Today, we focus on power applications most critical in creating brand perceptions," says Timon. "When we work with Frito-Lay, for instance, the power application is not in the package itself, it's the whole shelf presence of the products. So when we design for Frito-Lay, we don't show them a bag and ask how it looks. We show the entire shelf."

Firmly Rooted in San Francisco

Every advertising and marketing communications conglomerate offers brand identity consulting services. While the competition has added clients piecemeal by gobbling up boutique firms around the world, Landor Associates developed naturally from the firm's infancy.

Throughout six decades of creating, building, and revitalizing brands, advertising firms have tried to mimic Landor's approach to graphic, interactive, and interior design—marrying brand, image, and identity management. However, the oldest brand consulting firm is also one of the world's largest, and its longevity has spawned innovations that are now standard in marketing communications. Landor Associates provides industry leadership and continues to break new ground in the branding field it pioneered.

Furthermore, while competitors have stationed headquarters in New York or London, Landor remains firmly rooted in San Francisco. "That fact alone makes us unique," says Timon. "For 25 years, we were housed on a ferryboat docked at Pier 5. Being a design firm on a boat in San Francisco differentiated us from all of our competitors."

In keeping with its heritage and Timon's vision, Landor Associates continues to be recognized as the benchmark of the brand-building industry.

In celebration of the long-awaited prequel to the *Star Wars* series, *Episode I: The Phantom Menace*, Landor created these vivid promotional packages for its longtime client Frito-Lay. With this incredibly successful promotion, Landor wove together two classic brand icons: Each bag of Lay's potato chips features a character from the movie, including Jar Jar Binks, the first completely computer-generated movie character.

WASHINGTON TOWNSHIP HEALTH CARE DISTRICT

ALONG THE SOUTHEASTERN SHORES OF SAN FRANCISCO BAY LIES A CLUSTER of communities surrounded by sweeping vistas and well-planned technical and industrial parks. A high-technology center that is also home to a diverse residential community, the area has managed to keep pace with its economic growth and change while retaining much of its small-town charm.

Washington Township Health Care District is an integral part of this community. A not-for-profit health care provider, Washington is owned by the very community that established it, serving the residents of Fremont, Newark, Union City, and south Hayward.

The community's grassroots effort to create a district hospital in the late 1940s was difficult, but the obstacles they faced only served to stiffen their resolve. Despite funding troubles, criticism-filled newspapers, and problematic state laws regarding the formation of hospital districts, the community's determination was unbending. Its perseverance led to the successful 1948 ballot measure to establish the Washington Township Health Care District. Ten years later, Washington Hospital admitted its first patient, and since then has grown into an integrated health care system that today serves as southern Alameda County's top health care provider.

INVESTING IN THE COMMUNITY

Governed by a five-member, publicly elected board of directors, Washington offers a full range of acute care services and features some of the most advanced, leading-edge technology available today. Washington stands out as an exemplary model against a backdrop of turmoil in health care, including hospital bankruptcies and mergers. In 1999, Moody's Investors Service rated it as one of the few successful hospitals in the state, citing a strong financial position, longevity in the leadership of its board of directors and management team, and responsiveness to the community.

"Washington Hospital is woven into the very fabric of this community," says Nancy Farber, chief executive officer. "The strength of our close ties to the people of this region allows our health care system to be responsive to the local needs. That's why we're so much more than just a hospital."

The district's 308-bed, acute care hospital serves as the hub for a far-reaching system of facilities, services, and community outreach programs. Community services include the free Washington Community Health Resource Library, offering the public access to up-to-date health information and resources; the Health Insurance Information Service, which provides free counseling to callers regarding an increasingly confusing health insurance industry; dozens of free health classes on topics ranging from home health care to proper nutrition; and no-cost health outreach programs that provide important health services, screenings, and immunizations for local families.

"It's important for people to understand that all of our excess revenue goes back into services that will benefit this community," says Farber. In addition to its reinvestment in the health of the community, Washington Hospital also invests in technology so that equipment and facilities remain up to date.

STATE-OF-THE-ART CARE

Washington's 350 physicians have access to the latest in medical technology and services in order to provide high-quality care for their patients. These services include advanced diagnostic equip-

A COMMUNITY-OWNED HEALTH CARE DISTRICT, WASHINGTON'S STAFF AND PHYSICIANS ARE COMMITTED TO PROVIDING THE MEDICAL SERVICES NECESSARY TO MEET LOCAL HEALTH CARE NEEDS.

ment at Washington Hospital, including both open and traditional MRI units, computerized catheterization laboratories, mammography equipment, a spiral CT scanner, and radiographic fluoroscopy equipment.

In addition, the hospital's cardiology program offers a comprehensive continuum of care, from diagnosis to surgery to rehabilitation. In 1999, the hospital's cardiology services were recognized as one of the top 100 programs in the nation by an industry leader in the collection of health care data.

Total joint replacement and spinal care at Washington Hospital have earned a reputation of clinical excellence. Washington was selected in 1999 to serve as one of 10 beta sites across the country to test new stealth technology, which uses image-guided systems to perform surgeries.

Washington's oncology program features a wide range of services, from advanced treatments to support and counseling for patients and their families. In 2000, the newly rebuilt Washington/Stanford Radiation Oncology Center will open, featuring the latest in linear accelerator technology.

Childbirth and Family Services at Washington Hospital features a modern birthing center with private suites and the Washington/ Packard Children's Special Care Nursery, a Level II nursery for newborns with special medical needs.

Washington's comprehensive range of facilities and services also includes 24-hour emergency care; critical care services; state-of-the-art operating rooms and diagnostic equipment; urgent care clinics located throughout the community;

the Washington Outpatient Surgery Center; the Washington Outpatient Rehabilitation Center; and a student health clinic serving 8,000 students at a local community college.

While Washington's leadership merits recognition, it would not be the foremost facility it is today without its exceptional nursing staff. Washington's compassionate, highly skilled nurses provide the backbone of the hospital's quality patient care. Patients can easily identify Washington's registered nurses because each wears a white uniform with a lapel pin that boldly displays "R.N." Additionally, each floor of the hospital features a display case of nursing memorabilia, which acknowledges the nurses' important roles within the hospital industry, and—more important—in direct patient care.

Washington's strength has been its ability to adapt and keep pace with change by introducing new programs and services that meet the needs of the community. In a changing health care environment, Washington stands firm on its commitment to provide high-quality health care services. Says Farber, "Our physicians, employees, and volunteers remain steadfast in their resolve to provide the health services needed in this community at the highest levels of care. In a time when change is all around us, it is good that certain things remain constant."

IN THE MONTHS PRIOR TO THE HOSPITAL'S OPENING, NURSES BEGAN PREPARING THE FACILITY TO PROVIDE COMPASSIONATE, STATE-OF-THE-ART PATIENT CARE SERVICES. THE NURSING STAFF'S TRADITION OF EXCELLENCE CONTINUES TO THIS DAY.

KTVU Fox 2

A STRONG, INDEPENDENT STATION AT ITS INCEPTION IN 1958, KTVU FOX 2 DID NOT HAVE THE PROGRAMMING RESOURCES OF ITS NETWORK AFFILIATE COMPETITORS, BUT IT PUT ITSELF ON THE MAP WITH POPULAR ENTERTAINMENT PROGRAMMING. KTVU IS NOW ONE OF THE MOST SUCCESSFUL TELEVISION STATIONS IN THE UNITED STATES.

A STRONG, INDEPENDENT STATION FROM ITS INCEPTION IN 1958, KTVU Fox 2, owned by Cox Enterprises Inc., is now one of the most successful television stations in the United States. ◆ In its infancy, KTVU did not have the programming resources of its network affiliate competitors, but it put itself on the map with popular entertainment programming such as *Roller Derby*, *Creature Features*, *Dialing for Dollars*, and original children's programs like *Romper Room*, *Charley & Humphrey*, and *Captain Satellite*. In those days, KTVU remained the number four station in the nation's fifth-largest market.

That began to change in 1987 when the station joined Fox. Critics scoffed at the fledgling network, seemingly an outsider looking to access the audience that all but channeled into the established networks, namely ABC, CBS, and NBC.

More than a decade later, the Big Three has become the Big Four. Fox, in recent years, ranks second or third nationally, showing particular strength among younger viewers. And through the years, the jewel in the Fox crown has been KTVU.

In November 1998, KTVU dominated the ratings sweeps, winning its first sign-on-to-sign-off number one ranking in its history, and dominating in the late-news arena with the *10 O'Clock News*.

"We're the most successful Fox affiliate in the country," Jeff Block, vice president and station manager, states without hubris. "We're proud to say that we are the number one TV station in the Bay Area. We are certainly one—if not the only—Fox station in the country that consistently beats the other networks. And we've done that since the early 1990s."

Top-Rated Newscast

The cornerstone of KTVU's success has been its top-rated news operation, led by news anchors Dennis Richmond and Leslie Griffith. Year after year in Bay Area critics' polls and readers' surveys, KTVU's *10 O'Clock News* consistently wins the best newscast designation; not surprisingly, the *10 O'Clock News* consistently wins in the ratings sweeps, and the mystery each time is by how much.

The recognition reaches beyond the local coverage area. The Rocky Mountain Media Watch, a Denver-based media watchdog, honored KTVU News in a recent survey of newscast content of 102 stations in 52 markets. Cited "for presenting quality programs that provide empowering information to viewers," KTVU News was one of only two stations in the country to be so highly rated. "KTVU-TV, San Francisco . . . whose newscasts stand out for quality, intelligence, and creativity . . . is notable for the depth of stories and compelling subject matter," the survey commends.

With the *KTVU Morning News* from 5:30 to 7 a.m.; *Mornings on 2*, a local news and information program from 7 to 9 a.m.; the *Noon News*; and the *10 O'Clock News*, KTVU is dedicated to providing Bay Area television viewers with the best news all day long, seven days a week.

In addition, the Bay Area's number one station for sports, KTVU is home on the airwaves for the Bay Area's most popular sports teams. Televising Giants baseball since 1958, the year the team traded its New York jerseys for San Francisco gear, KTVU also broadcasts the five-time Super Bowl Champion San Francisco 49ers football games. Ken Norton Jr., the team's hard-hitting linebacker, joins KTVU Sports Director Mark Ibanez for the weekly pregame football show *49ers Playbook*. Then, after every 49ers game, former 49ers great and Hall of Fame nominee Ronnie Lott mixes it up with Ibanez on *The Point After*.

THE KTVU PATH TO SUCCESS HAS BEEN TO LEAD IN INFORMING AND ENTERTAINING ITS LOCAL AUDIENCE. ACCORDING TO JEFF BLOCK, VICE PRESIDENT AND STATION MANAGER, KTVU'S FUTURE IN THE BROADCAST BUSINESS WILL REMAIN LOCAL: "WITH THOUSANDS OF OPPORTUNITIES TO COMPETE NOW, WITH THE INTERNET AND CABLE, THE ONE THING WE CAN DO TO DIFFERENTIATE OUR-SELVES IS TO EXCEL IN LOCAL PROGRAMMING."

STAYING NUMBER ONE

A s great as an organization like ours can be, we're always working to improve," says Block. "It's comparatively easy to go from fourth to third place, from third to second, and from second to first. It's far more challenging to stay number one. The only way to do that is to always work on improving, keep changing, and keep leading."

Taking the lead in technology, in November 1998, KTVU was the first station in the Bay Area to throw the switch on its digital broadcasting transmitter in early compliance with FCC requirements. To showcase the higher-resolution capabilities of the breakthrough technology, the station led the market when it televised in high-definition television (HDTV) the San Francisco Chinese New Year Parade celebrating the Year of the Hare in February 1999 (lunar year 4697). Because of the scarcity of HDTV-produced shows, KTVU's digital telecast of the parade has also run frequently on other digital stations across the country throughout the year—never mind that the Lunar New Year season was long over.

THE CORNERSTONE OF KTVU'S SUCCESS HAS BEEN ITS TOP-RATED NEWS OPERATION, LED BY NEWS ANCHORS LESLIE GRIFFITH AND DENNIS RICHMOND.

LOCAL NEWS AND INFORMATION

T he KTVU path to success has been to lead in informing and entertaining its local audience. According to Block, its future in the broadcast business will remain local.

"With thousands of opportunities to compete now, with the Internet and cable, the one thing we can do to differentiate ourselves is to excel in local programming," says Block. "Information, sports, news—nobody can do it better. It is our strength in local information that has created that level of expectation, of credibility, in the news story."

Regardless of the season, in times of disaster and celebration, KTVU has continued to provide integrity in news and information, as well as liveliness in entertainment. As the ratings margin between KTVU and its competitors continues to widen, Block's goal in the next millennium, he jokes, is to beat the other stations combined.

Hilton San Francisco

OCCUPYING A FULL CITY BLOCK IN SAN FRANCISCO'S THEATER DISTRICT, AND BOASTING 1,900 GUEST ROOMS AND 110,000 SQUARE FEET OF FUNCTION SPACE, THE HILTON SAN FRANCISCO IS A VERTICAL CITY WITHIN A CITY.

OCCUPYING A FULL CITY BLOCK IN SAN FRANCISCO'S THEATER DISTRICT, and boasting 1,900 guest rooms and 110,000 square feet of function space, the Hilton San Francisco is a vertical city within a city. ◆ The size and generated revenue of the Hilton San Francisco—the largest hotel on the West Coast—rival that of actual California

cities. The "population" of the Hilton on any given day tops 6,000, exceeding the population of the city across the bay, Emeryville (population 5,740). The Hilton's 54-member security force outnumbers the 17-member police force of nearby Half Moon Bay, a city of more than 11,000 people. One million dollars a month pour into San Francisco's coffers from taxes the Hilton alone generates.

If the Hilton San Francisco is a city, then General Manager Holger Gantz is the mayor. The exclusive four-diamond rating awarded for 23 years in a row, bestowed by the American Automobile Association (AAA), mirrors the consistent ranking of San Francisco as the number one favorite destination among world travelers, as shown by readers of *Condé Nast Traveler* and *Travel & Leisure*, and the 16 million yearly visitors to the city by the bay.

A Star Is Born

When the hotel opened its doors in 1964, big-finned Cadillacs and triple-taillight Impalas lined up at the Motor Entrance on Ellis Street. The hotel's 19,000-square-foot Continental Ballroom was one of the largest in the world. Featuring 1,200 guest rooms, the Hilton became an obvious destination for conventions. More than 150 organizations, including the American Medical Association and the Republican National Convention, booked their meetings before the doors even opened.

The hotel that now occupies an entire city block and three massive buildings evolved at a fast pace. In 1971, the Hilton completed the addition of the 46-story Tower One. Designed by architect John C. Warneke, the luxury tower offered guests an impressive panorama of the city. At more than a thousand rooms and more than 200 suites in the combined buildings, the Hilton was larger than any other hotel west of Chicago.

In 1989, a third tower was added and the hotel underwent total renovation in a $210 million project, which increased guest rooms and expanded the meeting and banquet facilities to 110,000 square feet. Since then, $6 million to $8 million has been invested annually in the ongoing program of renewing the Hilton's first-rate guest rooms, meeting rooms, and public spaces. The new, 23-story O'Farrell building features an 11,000-square-foot lobby with 15 registration bays, inlaid marble, and million-dollar chandeliers. Above the reception area, several

THE NEW, 23-STORY O'FARRELL BUILDING FEATURES AN 11,000-SQUARE-FOOT LOBBY WITH 15 REGISTRATION BAYS, INLAID MARBLE, AND MILLION-DOLLAR CHANDELIERS.

levels of meeting rooms and exhibit space are crowned with the 30,000-square-foot Grand Ballroom.

The City that Knows How

Staff responsiveness counteracts the feeling that the Hilton San Francisco is a link in a chain of more than 500 Hilton hotels worldwide. Reflecting its hometown's diverse populace, the 1,200-member Hilton San Francisco workforce includes native speakers of 50 languages.

"All the things you wouldn't expect to be done in a big hotel get done here," says Gantz. The hotel has one of the lowest turnovers of staff in the city, in part because of an enlightened attitude that equips all staff with the tools to handle guest needs.

Imprinted on every house phone is the Guest Service Hotline number, and all employees are prepared to help solve whatever problem a guest might present on the spot. In a typical year, the 24-hour hot line handles 17,000 calls. Hilton code instills that caring for guests and solving any dilemma they might face is the duty of all employees, who rise to the challenge of becoming more resourceful about concerns well outside their job descriptions.

Says Gantz, "We took a good concept, the Guest Service Hotline, and made it better by adding the element of employee empowerment. Guests have told us they are extremely pleased to have help all around them at a moment's notice."

Top-Notch Security

On a typical day, 1,200 conventioneers check out the same day as 1,100 conventioneers from the next group check in. The luxury hotel straddles the border between one of the city's poorest neighborhoods (the Tenderloin) and one of the most prosperous (Union Square). Yet safety is not an issue for guests because it is the main issue for the Hilton's Security and Safety Department, a 54-member, highly skilled team.

Training is a key factor in the success of the department. Ongoing courses cover more than 150 subjects, including emergency response training and CPR. The Ambassador Program trains officers to provide helpful information to guests—from how to find a meeting room to how to find a good place to eat. "Safety goes hand in hand with being hospitable," says Gantz. "With all the unknowns and uncertainties that come with traveling, safety has to be a given."

Pioneers in Guest Comfort

Hilton Hotels has participated in research on the effects of travel on sleep, health, fitness, and stress with some of the country's expert organizations, such as the National Sleep Foundation and American Institute of Stress. As a result, the company has developed the Hilton Health-Fit Room and the Hilton Stress-Less Room,

both of which are available at the Hilton San Francisco.

The specially equipped Stress-Less Room offers tension reducers such as indoor fountains, massage-and-heat chair pads, sound-and-light-therapy alarm clocks, yoga videos, blackout drapes that completely shut out harsh light and noise, Serta mattresses, hypoallergenic bedding, aromatherapy amenities, and more. The Hilton Health-Fit Room also includes an exercise machine and

THE HILTON SAN FRANCISCO HAS 1,900 GUEST ROOMS AND SUITES IN THE THREE TOWERS, MAKING IT THE LARGEST HOTEL ON THE WEST COAST.

ATOP HILTON'S LANDMARK TOWER ON THE 46TH FLOOR, CITYSCAPE BAR & RESTAURANT OFFERS CLASSIC AMERICAN CUISINE; INCOMPARABLE, 360-DEGREE VIEWS OF SAN FRANCISCO; AND IMPECCABLE SERVICE.

A VARIETY OF CUISINE IS OFFERED IN THE HOTEL'S MARKETPLACE EATERIES, INCLUDING THE CAFÉ, A FULL-SERVICE RESTAURANT (TOP RIGHT); INTERMEZZO, A MEDITERRANEAN BISTRO (BOTTOM RIGHT); AND MASON STREET DELI, WHICH FEATURES EAT-IN OR TAKE-OUT BREAKFAST AND LUNCH (TOP LEFT).

other fitness products, special healthy menu options, and complimentary nutrition bars.

The hotel's fitness facility comprises a virtual resort in the middle of the city. A spacious atrium, open to the sky, encloses a heated swimming pool and landscaped courtyard. Guests can maintain their workout schedules at the hotel's health club, which offers fitness equipment including StairMasters, Tetrix bikes, Lifestride treadmills, and weight machines. The club also offers a dry sauna; dressing rooms with lockers, showers, complimentary toiletries; and massage by appointment.

Just as San Francisco is beloved the world over for its scenery, the city within a city is crowned with one of the finest view restaurants: Cityscape. Atop Hilton's landmark tower on the 46th floor, Cityscape Bar & Restaurant offers classic American cuisine; incomparable, 360-degree views of San Francisco; and impeccable service. A variety of cuisine is offered in the hotel's other marketplace eateries, includ-

ing The Café, a full-service restaurant; Intermezzo, a Mediterranean bistro; and Mason Street Deli, which features eat-in or take-out breakfast and lunch.

COMMUNITY INVOLVEMENT

The Hilton San Francisco is committed to finding permanent solutions to some of the toughest urban issues facing many major cities today. The hotel adopted the city's most densely populated residential downtown neighborhood as its home, and since its founding has guided the neighborhood's development with leadership, access, and visibility.

To foster understanding between employees and the community, the hotel established an all-employee volunteer force that addresses the neighborhood's needs and participates in citywide initiatives as well. Gantz

created a dedicated position to oversee the Hilton's Hotel with a Heart program. In addition to coordinating volunteer activities, the community projects manager oversees the donation of tons of materials every year to some 85 nonprofit organizations to be reused or recycled. In recognition of his efforts, Gantz has won the San Francisco Chamber of Commerce's Special Directors' Award bestowed at the annual Ebbies (Excellence in Business Awards), for his significant contribution to improving the quality of life in the community.

Today, the city, community, and hotel are in close partnership to economically revitalize the area. With the city's investment of $750,000, the neighborhood started its own street-cleaning business, facade improvement program, public safety program, graffiti abatement program, mural projects, and community newspaper. Plans are underway to develop a 70,000-square-foot facility that will provide jobs related to the visitor industry and neighborhood-serving retail businesses, while generating revenue for the community.

While its past has been spent shaping a vision and building consensus, the Hilton San Francisco's future will be at the helm of good corporate citizenship. The city within a city looks forward to helping San Francisco reinvent its long-cherished urban vitality.

SAN FRANCISCO'S MBT ARCHITECTURE HAS DISTINGUISHED ITSELF FOR building designs of exceptional functionality and architectural excellence. In doing so, it has become a firm of choice to meet the exacting standards of companies and institutions in the San Francisco area and beyond. ◆ MBT counts IBM, Chevron, Pacific Bell, Genencor, Union Bank, Stanford University, and University of California-San Francisco among its illustrious clientele. "Having clients come back to us again and again points to our success at achieving our goals," says David Lindemulder, AIA, senior vice president and partner in the firm. "And that is to establish the highest level of quality in our client relationship, our service, our design—everything we do."

A Distinguished History

Gerald McCue, FAIA Emeritus, retired dean of Harvard's Graduate School of Design, founded MBT in 1954. Today, the firm's more than 70 employees, headquartered in San Francisco and a Seattle branch, compete with substantially larger firms for major national commissions.

Through 45 years of accomplished architecture and interiors, the practice has garnered countless awards for projects ranging from private residences to research laboratories, from computer centers to corporate office interiors. These include five national honor awards from the American Institute of Architects, the profession's highest building design recognition.

Lindemulder points to the IBM Santa Teresa Programming Center in San Jose as an example of an enduring MBT project, and he adds, "If you look at contemporary West Coast architecture, it would be considered one of the top 10." Completed in 1977 at the dawn of the computer age, it was the definitive facility for software programming. "When built, it was startling to come upon this sleek, silver machine in a pastoral setting," says Lindemulder. Even now, more than two decades later, the building continues to attract visitors and queries from around the world.

A Bright Future

In the immediate future, MBT will continue to concentrate in its specialty of designing for clients in the fields of science and technology. "We design for the human aspect," says Tully Shelley III, AIA, MBT president and chairman. "Most technology companies and institutions want their scientists to interact. We look for opportunities in a building's design that will bring people together—on their way to and from individual research areas and within shared spaces—to exchange ideas and learn from each other. That is one of the things so satisfying about the design profession. Architecture can shape and improve people's activities, achievements, and lives."

As trends in work patterns evolve, the firm's interiors group has seen a growth in the redesign of office space to increase efficiencies. Kathy Kelley, ASID, director of MBT Interiors and a partner in the firm, says, "Our designers have distinguished themselves by seeking alternative office solutions that are creative and provocative—enhancing productivity and well-being, yet meeting our clients' new, often stringent business plans."

MBT is also playing a major role in the design of new auto and rail ground transportation facilities being constructed at the San Francisco International Airport. Likewise, retrofitting of existing buildings has become a specialty. A most notable recent achievement is the firm's architectural design contribution to the seismic strengthening and restoration of historic San Francisco City Hall.

In each project, the architects and interior designers at MBT Architecture focus on fulfilling the firm's mission—to create architecture for both clients and the community at large that carefully fulfills its requisite purpose, is architecturally meaningful, and satisfies the collective need for social responsibility and environmental sustainability.

MBT ARCHITECTURE DESIGNS FOR THE HUMAN ASPECT OF SCIENCE AND TECHNOLOGY BUSINESSES, SUCH AS THE "MAIN STREET" CIRCULATION ATRIUM AT THE GENENCOR INTERNATIONAL TECHNOLOGY CENTER IN PALO ALTO (LEFT).

MBT HAS DISTINGUISHED ITSELF FOR BUILDING DESIGNS OF EXCEPTIONAL FUNCTIONALITY AND ARCHITECTURAL EXCELLENCE, SUCH AS THE VINCENT E. MCKELVEY FEDERAL BUILDING AT THE U.S. GEOLOGICAL SURVEY CAMPUS IN MENLO PARK (RIGHT).

A S THE NATION'S NUMBER ONE DISTRIBUTOR OF PHARMACEUTICAL SUPPLIES and medical/surgical equipment and supplies, McKessonHBOC has come full circle back to its roots. ◆ In 1833, John McKesson and his partner, Charles Olcott, opened a small import and wholesaling shop in New York City's financial district, which supplied therapeutic

drugs and chemicals to the tall-masted clipper ships that shuttled goods to and from the young nation. Over the years, the company grew with America's westward expansion. Pills, herbs, glassware, sponges, and even wine and whiskey comprised some of the inventory headed for isolated frontier towns near recently laid railroad lines.

McKesson continued to diversify, and at one time or another was involved in such varied concerns as wine and spirits, chemicals, dairy products, office products, pasta products, bottled water, specialty foods, veterinary supplies, commercial real estate,

third-party prescriptions, and a cooking school.

New Alliances

A 1967 merger with Foremost Dairy produced a new corporate entity, Foremost McKesson, and led to the transfer of the company's headquarters from New York to San Francisco. When the dairy portion of the company was sold in 1983, it became McKesson Corporation.

The 1980s brought divestment of peripheral enterprises, and the 1990s returned the company's focus to its core businesses: supply management, pharmaceutical services, and information technol-

ogy for the health care industry. As part of that focus, McKesson merged in January 1999 with Atlanta-based HBO & Company (HBOC), which had made its name by delivering cost-effective patient information and hospital operation systems, and is the world leader in health care information systems, both clinical and financial.

With the complementary strengths of the new alliance, one of the nation's oldest continually operating companies opened a new chapter in its life as the world's largest health care services company. More than 65 percent of hospitals in America use McKessonHBOC software to access patient information. Its software and services process the medical claims of 150 million Americans. In addition, McKessonHBOC delivers one-third of all pharmaceuticals in America and 15 percent of all medical surgical supplies.

McKessonHBOC's workforce of 24,500 is spread throughout the United States at 35 pharmaceutical distribution centers and 50 medical/surgical supply distribution centers. While 95 percent of the company's revenues come from the U.S. health care market, McKessonHBOC also has customers in 10 other countries.

"We provide the technology, pharmaceuticals, medical supplies, and information our customers need to provide high-quality care and improved clinical outcomes, while managing costs," says Larry Kurtz, vice president of corporate communications.

Investing in the Community

W hile the Fortune 100 company conducts its business globally, McKessonHBOC acts locally with an active program of philanthropy through the McKesson Foundation, espe-

ESTABLISHED IN NEW YORK IN 1833, McKessonHBOC HAS BEEN HEADQUARTERED IN DOWNTOWN SAN FRANCISCO SINCE 1968.

cially in San Francisco. Of a total budget of approximately $3 million in 1998, $1.7 million supported programs in the Bay Area.

"For many years, we've provided financial support to organizations in the Bay Area focused on the health of at-risk youth," says Kurtz. Emphasis is also placed on educational enrichment, recreation, youth development activities, cultural arts, and other quality of life issues in underserved populations. Explains Kurtz, "While we don't give big operational grants every year, we like to provide seed money for new initiatives in gifts of $5,000 to $25,000."

Entirely self-sustaining, the McKesson Foundation is endowed largely from long-held company stock that in time has appreciated in value. Operationally independent of its parent, the foundation's direction and leadership are supplied by employees from all levels of the company. Extending the personal contributions of its employees, both in time and in resources, the foundation makes grants to programs to which employees have already committed their support.

According to Marcia Argyris, president of the McKesson Foundation, "Each year, the foundation contributes more than $3 million to not-for-profit community organizations, including 230 agencies

EVERY DAY, McKESSONHBOC DELIVERS PRESCRIPTION PHARMACEUTICALS TO SOME 45,000 PHARMACIES ACROSS ALL 50 STATES.

where McKessonHBOC employees volunteer. These investments have helped fund the specific needs of health care and educational initiatives, and have transformed many great ideas into productive outcomes—even projects that once were thought unachievable."

One such project, a new public elementary school in the Tenderloin District of San Francisco, was the decade-long dream of the Bay Area Women's and Children's Center. Completed in 1998, the Tenderloin Community School serves some 500 children who were once bused to 47 schools around the city. The school's foundation-supported McKesson

Health Clinic serves as a hub for the entire community, where children and their families can access dental and medical care.

Another foundation-supported program with a significant community impact is Huckleberry House. "As the country's first runaway shelter for youth, Huckleberry House reaches out to more than 2,000 homeless kids a year in San Francisco's Haight District," says Donna Draher, McKessonHBOC director of technical services, and volunteer and cochair of the shelter's Program Support Committee. The scope of Huckleberry House's services include temporary shelter, counseling, pregnancy and sexually transmitted disease prevention education, and medical resources to help youth make the transition off the streets.

Other examples of the foundation's local community investment include support for Big Brothers/Big Sisters and several high school work-study programs. And in 1998, a chair was endowed at the University of California-San Francisco School of Pharmacy.

"These are a small, but powerful representation of how not-for-profit agencies, McKessonHBOC employees, and the McKesson Foundation are partnering to solve social challenges we as a nation confront today," says Argyris. "Together, we are making a difference."

DURING THE 1800S, THE COMPANY GREW RAPIDLY FROM ITS NEW YORK CITY ROOTS TO BECOME THE NATION'S LEADING PHARMACEUTICAL WHOLESALER.

GAP INC. STRIVES TO DELIVER STYLE, SERVICE, AND VALUE TO EVERYONE— from kindergartners and grandparents to students and professionals. That simple formula is as successful today as it was in 1969 when the company was founded in San Francisco as a single store with just a handful of employees. ◆ Today, Gap Inc. is a global company, head-

quartered in the San Francisco Bay Area, with three distinct brands—Gap, Banana Republic, and Old Navy. With revenues topping $9 billion, the company currently employs more than 110,000 people worldwide.

GAP

From jeans and T-shirts to khakis and jackets, Gap offers a balance of styles in a clean, organized, easy-to-shop environment. Merchandise ranges from clothing and accessories to personal care products for adults, kids, and babies. The Gap reach extends across more than 1,800 Gap, GapKids, babyGap, and

Gap Outlet stores in the United States, Canada, France, Germany, Japan, and the United Kingdom.

And U.S. customers can shop on-line at www.gap.com.

BANANA REPUBLIC

Banana Republic has redefined what it means to live simply and comfortably, to dress effortlessly and confidently. Product categories include men's and women's clothing, shoes, accessories, personal care products, intimate apparel, jewelry, and home accessories. Customers can shop at more than 300 Banana Republic stores in the United States and Canada, through the Banana Republic Catalog, and, for U.S. customers, at www.BananaRepublic.com.

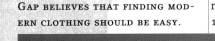

GAP BELIEVES THAT FINDING MODERN CLOTHING SHOULD BE EASY.

Old Navy

At Old Navy, fun, fashion, family, and value are part of everyone's shopping vocabulary. Through innovative marketing, merchandise promotions, community events, and its famous Item of the Week[SM.] Old Navy has become the whole family's destination for value-priced shopping. Customers can always find great clothes at great prices for adults, kids, and babies at Old Navy stores. And now in the United States, purchasing an Old Navy gift card is just a click away at www.oldnavy.com.

Gap. Banana Republic. Old Navy. Three distinct brands. One simple formula.

BANANA REPUBLIC OFFERS THE BEST OF THE TRENDS AND CLASSICS IN FABRICS OF EXCEPTIONAL QUALITY (TOP LEFT AND RIGHT).

AT OLD NAVY, FUN, FASHION, FAMILY, AND VALUE ARE PART OF EVERYONE'S SHOPPING VOCABULARY (BOTTOM).

HILL AND KNOWLTON, INC.

NE WORD BEST DESCRIBES THE SAN FRANCISCO OFFICE OF THE INTER-national public relations giant Hill and Knowlton: revitalized. In the 1997 Agency Report Card edition of the newsletter *Inside PR*, Editor Paul Holmes declared that Hill and Knowlton and leadership again belong in the same sentence. And in 1998, the publication named it one of the top international public relations agencies in the nation.

"Hill and Knowlton is once again one of the most respected brands in the public relations industry," says Richard Rice, managing partner of the San Francisco office since 1996. "And our strengthened presence in the San Francisco Bay Area is evidence that our commitment here is long-term."

REVITALIZED

Established in San Francisco in 1969 as an outpost of the full-service, New York agency established by John W. Hill in 1927, Hill and Knowlton had seemed to lose its local footing in the wake of international fallout from questionable tactics made public in the early 1990s. By the end of 1999, however, the turnaround was in high gear. With 54 offices in 32 countries, the firm's global network was a source of pride, and transnational communication for Fortune 500 companies was again a core of the firm's business. Moreover, Hill and Knowlton has become a magnet for talented professionals.

"Hill and Knowlton has been known in the past for developing its people," says Rice. "We're investing incredible amounts into Hill and Knowlton College to train our junior to midlevel employees, investing in the next generation of managers in the company."

Locally, San Francisco's oldest full-service international agency is bringing the luster back to the firm's shine. The office has picked up some high-profile clients, including Pacific Gas & Electric Company (PG&E) and E*TRADE. The San Francisco office was Hill and Knowlton's fastest-growing branch in the United States in 1997, and at the end of 1999, it had grown to about 30 employees. The most notable move for the local office, however, was the addition of an entire international high-technology practice to the firm's already well-known public affairs, health care, financial, and corporate communications practices.

A PERFECT FIT

In February 1999, Hill and Knowlton acquired the Blanc and Otus public relations agency. The acquisition of the highly regarded, San Francisco-based high-technology agency, which was founded in 1985 by Maureen Blanc and Simone Otus, was widely seen as a perfect fit.

"Hill and Knowlton sought to aggressively enhance our existing global technology practice through a specialist high-tech partner," says Howard Paster, Hill and Knowlton chairman and CEO at the time of the merger. "Blanc and Otus brings to the table an unmatched understanding of business and marketing issues related to the high-technology and telecommunications sectors."

"HILL AND KNOWLTON IS ONCE AGAIN ONE OF THE MOST RESPECTED BRANDS IN THE PUBLIC RELATIONS INDUSTRY," SAYS RICHARD RICE, MANAGING PARTNER OF THE SAN FRANCISCO OFFICE SINCE 1996. "AND OUR STRENGTHENED PRESENCE IN THE SAN FRANCISCO BAY AREA IS EVIDENCE THAT OUR COMMITMENT HERE IS LONG-TERM."

"We felt Blanc and Otus' style and their approach to clients' needs were a good match with Hill and Knowlton," adds Rice. "Look at the kinds of clients they have, and the way they take clients from birth to graduation, if graduation is an IPO. By the time their clients get to that point, they're ready for all the full range of services Hill and Knowlton has to offer. Also, we had plenty of clients that needed more specialized technology public relations. Ultimately, it was quicker to find a good, sophisticated partner than to grow it organically."

Capitalizing on its sterling reputation, Blanc and Otus, with some 90 employees, retains its brand and operates as Blanc and Otus, a Hill and Knowlton Company. Agency president and CEO Jonelle Birney and cofounders Blanc and Otus retained their agency roles and added the responsibilities, respectively, of head of Hill and Knowlton's Global Technology Practice and codirectors of its U.S. technology practice.

"As our clients continue to grow," says Blanc, "we want to provide them with the support that technology leaders demand—including corporate positioning, investor communications, and international public relations. Joining the Hill and Knowlton network provides the opportunity for us to bring a host of new services to the emerging high-tech companies we've traditionally served."

The alliance offers profound advantages for both parties and their clients. Hill and Knowlton gained a Silicon Valley insider with expert knowledge of emerging technologies and unique perspectives on the industry's convergence of enterprise, Internet, and telecommunications. On the other hand, Blanc and Otus became instantly connected to a global network with capabilities to handle high-level counseling in the areas of corporate positioning, branding, investor relations, and public policy communications.

The Key to the Future

We're stronger now than ever before, now that we have Blanc and Otus," says Rice, "especially since we've moved away from a regional structure to a team-based format. If the right team for a client is in Houston or Hong Kong, for example, we'll bring them in. This new structure worked very well for us recently when we carried out product announcements in Europe and Asia for several Blanc and Otus clients."

In the future, Blanc and Otus will play an integral part in Hill and Knowlton's growth, fueled by the continued explosion of technology business. Rice also anticipates growth in the consumer marketing business. In addition, the firm's large health care practice, corporate communications, and public policy work will continue to be a mainstay of the San Francisco office.

"Seeing the recognition that Hill and Knowlton is back, solid and stable, is a tremendous measure of success," says Rice. "Just as our clients do, we recognize that the equity of our brand is as much a measure of our success as our financial performance. And delivering services effectively to our clients is the key to our future."

WALKER INTERACTIVE SYSTEMS, INC. BRINGS ORDER TO TODAY'S INFOR-mation-driven chaos. The San Francisco-based company is a lead-ing global provider of financial, operational, and analytic software applications that help companies better manage their e-business performance. Walker identifies and delivers key information, based on the client's own performance criteria, and makes it available to those man-agers who can take immediate action.

The Walker family of e-business applications, vertical industry solutions, and integra-tion and consulting services is utilized by Fortune 1,000 compa-nies and midmarket organizations across a range of industries, includ-ing banking, financial services, paper, retail, transportation, and utilities.

THINKING FORWARD

Most companies today face a dilemma: The technology to create, distribute, and store information has ex-ceeded the capability to analyze it fast enough to impact company performance.

Walker's success in providing unique solutions to match client needs, with high ease of integra-tion into customers' preexisting systems including Web capabili-ties, has allowed it to grow from a

handful of people at the dawn of the information age to a 590-person enterprise with employees in eight locations worldwide.

Geoffrey Walker started the company in 1969 in San Fran-cisco, which remains its head-quarters today. The history of the company is tied directly to the fundamental advances of the computer age. Walker was one of the first companies to provide interfaces with the computer in real time versus paper punched cards that required overnight pro-cessing time. "It was revolution-ary," says Paul Lord, senior vice president. The company reached a significant milestone in its his-tory when IBM announced rela-tional databases in the mid-1980s; Walker was one of the first pro-viders of accounting software for the innovative technology of that era.

From its inception, Walker has always provided solutions to high-volume clients. "Our cus-tomers are the bluest of the blue-chip companies," says Lord.

E-BUSINESS SOLUTIONS

The Walker family of solu-tions today includes Smart Financials for the Enter-prise, Smart Financials for the Mid-Market, Walker Horizon Analytic Applications, Walker Immpower Smart Enterprise Asset Management, and Walker Professional Services. The com-pany's newest area of expertise,

e-business solutions, allows its customers to leverage the collaborative environment of the Internet.

Lord takes care to differentiate between e-commerce and e-business. "An e-commerce model, like Amazon.com, is very straightforward: They buy finished goods and sell finished goods. Our customers, on the other hand, produce things that require many ingredients from other suppliers. It's a very collaborative environment, which our applications support. In the world of plain old business, everything is done at an arm's-length basis and predominantly through pieces of paper—invoices, orders, and check payments. The e-business world makes things a lot more collaborative, instantaneous, and on-demand. I call this the Web lifestyle; it's a 24-hour-a-day, seven-day-a-week way of life."

Aside from being open all night, the Internet opens up entirely new opportunities for agility, enabling organizations to increase revenues, cut costs, provide better customer service, and ultimately gain a competitive edge. Walker's e-business solutions enable clients to achieve real value from the Internet by merging Internet and related technologies with core business processes and applications such as procurement and accounts receivable.

When it comes to business-critical applications such as procurement and revenue management, planning for the support of hundreds, thousands, and even hundreds of thousands of users is crucial. In a typical $2 billion company, 150 users may be accessing credit and accounts receivable information. Once this access is extended outside the credit department, a system that is not designed to scale can quickly be overwhelmed; 150 users can quickly become 1,500 internal users. If the system is opened up further, possibly to customers and suppliers, it can easily become more than 150,000 users.

"Because of our history of being able to deal with volumes and numbers of users, scalability, and reliability, we are very well placed to completely allow our customers to exploit the whole e-business paradigm shift and implementation," says Lord.

Staying Ahead of the Curve

In the rapidly changing world of technology, Walker continues to stay ahead of the curve by training its employees extensively and maintaining an attractive stock option plan for its employees. The company partners with premier hardware and software providers to enhance Walker solutions with value-added technologies. Walker specialists then work closely with customers to identify and incorporate the best practices and techniques into Walker solutions, delivering in-depth management insight.

The company's placement in San Francisco is a prime position for expansion. Top management has its eye on markets in Asia, particularly China, as well as Eastern Europe, and recently opened an office in Johannesburg.

Over decades of rapidly changing technology, Walker has withstood the test of time. The company continues to deliver a high level of customer satisfaction, serving many clients for more than 15 years. Today, as enterprises around the globe feel the vibrations from the paradigm shift of which San Francisco is the epicenter, Walker is positioned to be the chosen provider of systems that allow customers to take advantage of the opportunities presented by the Internet and e-business world.

WALKER IS A LEADING GLOBAL PROVIDER OF FINANCIAL, OPERATIONAL, AND ANALYTIC SOFTWARE APPLICATIONS.

I N THE TREATMENT OF DISEASES SUCH AS CANCER AND HEART AILMENTS, THE more doctors know—and the faster they know it—the better able they are to restore patients' health. Milpitas-based ADAC Laboratories (Nasdaq: ADAC) provides state-of-the-art diagnostic equipment and health care information systems software to aid physicians in both the

R. ANDREW ECKERT IS CHAIRMAN AND CHIEF EXECUTIVE OFFICER OF ADAC LABORATORIES (TOP).

FOUNDED IN 1970, MILPITAS-BASED ADAC LABORATORIES PROVIDES STATE-OF-THE-ART DIAGNOSTIC EQUIPMENT AND HEALTH CARE INFORMATION SYSTEMS SOFTWARE TO AID PHYSICIANS IN BOTH THE DIAGNOSTIC MEASUREMENT AND THE TRACKING OF PATIENT CARE TO SPEED PATIENTS DOWN THE ROAD OF RECOVERY (BOTTOM).

diagnostic measurement and the tracking of patient care to speed patients down the road of recovery.

ADAC was founded by four government scientists working at NASA. While at a cocktail party in 1969, the four experts in parameter estimation technology described to a nuclear medicine physician the military uses of their research to simulate flight paths of Cold War-era soviet missiles. The doctor felt the technology had medical applications in diagnostic imaging. After some investigating, the scientists resigned from NASA and started a company called Analytical Development Associates Corporation, eventually shortened to ADAC Laboratories.

"As technology leaders in each of our businesses, we're a company that continues to innovate very rapidly," says Andrew Eckert, CEO and chairman of the board. "Our purpose is to improve the quality of life and the effectiveness of

health care through the application of this advanced technology and, as we grow larger, to maintain our sense of urgency in delivering important products to the marketplace."

ADAC MEDICAL SYSTEMS

D ramatically improving the accuracy of oncology and cardiology assessment, ADAC's diagnostic imaging equipment and accompanying

customer support are the centerpiece of ADAC Medical Systems, the company's worldwide nuclear medicine business. In the $700 million worldwide market, ADAC leads the industry with nearly 50 percent of the market.

Nuclear medicine, characterized by metabolic and physiological analysis, involves a patient's ingesting a radioactive isotope with low levels of radiation. The isotope then gravitates toward certain areas of the body. "The uptake of that pharmaceutical within, say, the heart can be analyzed by our system as the data is then emitted out of the body," Eckert explains. "The beauty of the system is you're not only able to have a visual representation of the viability of the heart muscle itself, you're also able to have quantitative data behind the image so clinical personnel can compare your heart's strength with what they call a normal database and benchmark the health of your heart."

A relatively new technology that ADAC Medical Systems has introduced, positron-emission tomography (PET), utilizes the same concept as nuclear imaging, except with a sugar-based radio isotope. The sugar gravitates toward rapidly growing cells— metastatic diseases are of primary concern—enabling doctors to identify the presence of cancer. "More important perhaps," says Eckert, "is the ability to determine if the cancer has spread, which in the past had been a very difficult undertaking. PET imaging has proved to be somewhere above 90 percent in diagnostic accuracy."

HEALTH CARE INFORMATION SYSTEMS

W ith a long and illustrious history of providing information systems to radiology departments in hospitals around the country,

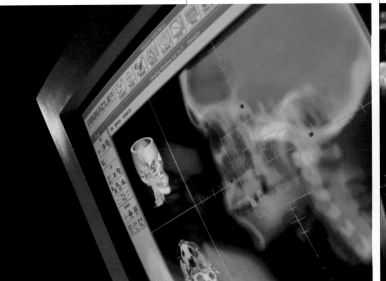

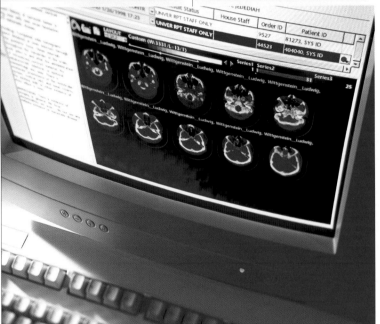

ADAC has an installed base of legacy products in some 300 hospitals nationwide.

Radiology health care providers, under pressure to increase efficiency in managed care and to provide better care at lower costs, have been turning to ADAC's Texas-based health care information systems business, HCIS, to help manage administrative work flow, track film, schedule treatments, and facilitate all other functions of a hospital's radiology department, especially since the 1997 introduction of the QuadRIS™ system.

Focused on radiology, ADAC's HCIS serves 20 percent of the health care information systems market, although Eckert projects additional growth in 2000. Looking to duplicate its radiology success in the nascent cardiology market, ADAC has introduced a product, CorCAAT™—already a technology leader—that is driven by the same need for streamlined work flow.

ADAC's latest innovation, Envoi™, allows any referring physician to call up patients' images on an Internet browser, as well as a diagnostic report of the study. "This is very powerful," says Eckert. "Traditionally, the referring physician had to wait 24 to 72 hours for film and a written report to be delivered down the hallway to the doctor's office. Now, in a period of a couple of hours—as long as it takes for the transcription to be completed—information and images can be delivered electronically."

ADAC LABORATORIES IS THE WORLD MARKET SHARE LEADER IN NUCLEAR MEDICINE AND RADIATION THERAPY PLANNING SYSTEMS, AND IS A TECHNOLOGY LEADER IN PROVIDING CLINICAL WORKFLOW SOLUTIONS, MANAGEMENT INFORMATION, AND KNOWLEDGE SYSTEMS TO HEALTH CARE ORGANIZATIONS IN NORTH AMERICA.

RADIATION THERAPY PLANNING

In the three years preceding 1998, ADAC had 10 percent of the market for radiation therapy planning. In 1998, the company's market share jumped to 55 percent, which translates into approximately $44 million in business.

Propelling ADAC into the marketplace lead was its Pinnacle3™ software, used in hospital oncology radiology departments. Developed in partnership with the University of Wisconsin, the state-of-the-art product computes radiation treatment plans for cancer patients, helping oncology physicians determine how often to treat the patient with linear acceleration-based treatment, how much radiation per treatment, location of treatment, and other parameters.

INVESTING IN FUTURE TECHNOLOGY

Even with its already long list of successful products, ADAC continues to grow. Each year, the company contributes nearly $1 million in targeted research grants to employees and nonemployees alike who submit worthy invention ideas. Several successful ideas funded in the past have been incorporated into ADAC's product offerings.

"We have a goal of a new product introduction every year," says Eckert. More ambitiously, his mission is to grow ADAC to a $1 billion company by 2003, as well as to be the company that health care professionals and patients ask for first. Yet, even with all this growth, ADAC's 1,100 employees around the world never lose sight of the company's mission: to make a difference and improve lives.

Semiconductor Equipment and Materials International (SEMI)

As employees begin their workday at the Silicon Valley headquarters of Semiconductor Equipment and Materials International (SEMI), their colleagues in the organization's Asia offices are still sleeping. Colleagues in Europe are just leaving their offices, while Moscow colleagues are going to bed, and those on the East Coast are in the midst of their workday.

"With us, the clock never stops," says Stanley Myers, president of the global, nonprofit trade association representing the semiconductor and flat panel display equipment and materials industries. In addition to its headquarters in Mountain View, SEMI's 190 employees work in cities worldwide where the semiconductor industry has a significant presence, including Tokyo; Seoul; Singapore; Beijing; Hsinchu; Brussels; Moscow; Austin, Texas; Boston; and Washington, D.C.

Pervasive Products

If you look at the worldwide semiconductor equipment and materials industry, which enables the technology and processes used in manufacturing computer chips, it's a $60 billion-to $65 billion-a-year industry," says Myers. "It permeates all aspects of life today, and will continue as one of the key technological and economic drivers into the next century."

Semiconductors, also known as integrated circuits and computer chips, form the foundation of technology today. Smart cards, computers, Internet appliances, actuators on automobile air bags, and computer monitors are just a small sampling of everyday applications.

The industry's newest products are showcased each year at SEMICON West, annually the Bay Area's largest convention of any kind. Other SEMI expositions around the world include SEMICON events in Korea, Taiwan, China (alternating in Beijing and Shanghai), Europe (Munich), two in Japan (Osaka and Tokyo), and one in Singapore, known as SEMICON Test, Assembly & Packaging. In addition, SEMI cosponsors numerous other international events with other associations, such as the Display Works exposition in San Jose for the flat panel display industry. SEMI also sponsors an annual CIS (Commonwealth of Independent States) Executive Mission and Exhibit in Moscow. Combined, these events attract almost 300,000 visitors annually.

Governed by a 24-member board of directors, SEMI's volunteer leadership is comprised of senior executives of some of the world's best-known electronics companies. In addition, SEMI counts on the expert participation of some 4,000 executive-level volunteers from around the world.

"Of our 4,000 volunteers, less than half of them are involved in such things as boards, committees, and conference program planning," says Myers. "The majority are involved in standards-setting activities."

Setting Industry Standards

Working with SEMI has been likened to working with the United Nations, where the language of commerce at board and committee meetings must be translated simultaneously into a cacophony of Romance and Asian languages. Those logistics are merely a precursor to the herculean task of achieving global standardization of specifications used in semiconductor manufacturing.

Established in 1973, SEMI's Standards Committee was formed to deal with a daunting materials problem. Approximately 2,000 different specifications for silicon wafers had been developed by the user community, making it difficult for the supplier base to meet customer requirements. This lack of uniformity caused difficulties in the manufacturing process and in maintaining appropriate inventories.

The SEMI Standards Program now provides a forum for industry professionals from Asia, Europe,

and North America to create industrywide specifications. More than 150 committees, subcommittees, and task forces meet hundreds of times to coordinate efforts, culminating in the publication of the multivolume book of SEMI standards.

PROMOTING THE INDUSTRY

Other significant activities in which SEMI engages include its Market Statistics Program, which provides participating member companies with accurate, current benchmarks for market size and growth; technical and business education through conferences and training courses; information resources—videos, newsletters, and Internet products—providing timely business, marketing, and technical information; government relations to advocate free and open market access worldwide and to address member concerns on import/export controls, trade policy, and tax issues; and the unique SEMIndex, a stock index updated every 15 minutes, comprised of 66 of SEMI's global public semiconductor member companies with individual market capitalizations of $50 million equivalent or more.

"For a group like us, taking on this investor index is revolutionary," says Myers. "Most indices are put on by big institutional investors, but ours is a specialized global technology stock index." Eleven months after the index's January 1999 introduction, it had grown by nearly 150 percent.

NEW CHALLENGES

The new millennium will be characterized by major innovations in technology made possible by the advances in semiconductor manufacturing processing. SEMI's member companies will continue to play a significant role in those advances. Technically, the industry is preparing to move to a new generation of highly complex semiconductors and to produce them on larger wafers of silicon (300 mm) than has ever been attempted. It will be an expensive transition, but the payback will be swift because of the increased manufacturing productivity. Aside from the technical challenges, there will be new management challenges as smaller companies forge partnerships that over time will make new technology more affordable through a sharing of efforts and costs. These are the challenges of the 21st century already being addressed by SEMI in its conferences, symposia, standards development meetings, expositions, and other activities designed to add value to the technology of its members.

"No industry in the history of the world has become so truly global in scope," says Myers. "At the same time, no other industry has better reflected the progress that can be made when manufacturers of final products become partners with the developers of their manufacturing processes. It is the goal of SEMI to explore every avenue through which this partnership can progress."

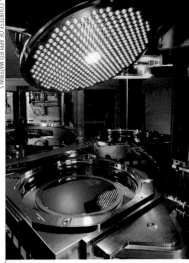

COURTESY OF APPLIED MATERIALS

THE PROCESSES USED TO CREATE SEMICONDUCTORS ARE SIMILAR TO SILK-SCREENING AND PHOTOGRAPHY. THE MICROSCOPIC TRANSISTORS AND OTHER ELECTRONIC COMPONENTS THAT MAKE UP A SEMICONDUCTOR ARE CREATED BY ALTERNATELY LAYERING AND ETCHING DIFFERENT PATTERNS OF MATERIALS AND METALS ON THE WAFERS (TOP).

GROWN AS A SINGLE CRYSTAL, THE HIGH-PURITY SILICON INGOT IS SHAPED AND CUT INTO INDIVIDUAL WAFERS, ON WHICH SEMICONDUCTOR CHIPS WILL BE BUILT. THE LATEST WAFER SIZE—300 MILLIMETERS (12 INCHES)—CAN HOLD HUNDREDS OF CHIPS (BOTTOM).

Custom Chrome, Inc.

I T ALL STARTED IN 1970, IN A MOTORCYCLE SHOP BEHIND A GARAGE ON West San Carlos Street near Bird Avenue in San Jose. Four friends noticed that a growing number of motorcycle owners wanted to customize their bikes to make a personal statement through the uniqueness of their motorcycle's appearance. ◆ To meet the needs of these

customers, the four friends opened one of America's first self-service motorcycle accessory stores, Coast Cycle, in a retail space adjacent to the motorcycle shop—the predecessor to Custom Chrome, Inc. (CCI).

A Niche in the Motorcycle Market

Finding a niche for high-quality, off-the-shelf products, Custom Chrome began to seek out manufacturers of custom parts and accessories, and collaborated with them to build unique items to Custom Chrome's specifications.

Soon, motorcycle dealers around the country discovered the growing line of custom parts and accessories available in San Jose, and Custom Chrome evolved into a wholesaler and distributor of aftermarket products for motorcycles. Before long, comprehensive catalogs followed, along with the need for larger warehousing, distribution, and product development facilities. The company outgrew numerous warehouses before settling into its current facility in Morgan Hill, 15 miles south of San Jose.

In 1982, the staff of Custom Chrome decided to focus exclusively on the Harley-Davidson

market because loyal owners of these bikes devoted more time and money to customizing their bikes than owners of Japanese or British brands. For example, early Harley-Davidson customers sought to extend their front forks, or customize their seats, or add sissy bars to the backs of passenger seats.

Today a division of Global Motorsport Group, Inc., Custom Chrome is the world's largest independent supplier of aftermarket parts and accessories for Harley-Davidson motorcycles. Custom Chrome distributes its own products, many of which are offered under the brand names of RevTech®, Premium®, Dyno

Power®, and C.C. Rider®, and also distributes other manufacturers' products under their respective brand names.

Custom Chrome has always been able to satisfy the marketplace with innovative product designs that rely heavily upon an intensive research and product development effort. In addition to its in-house designer, John Reed, and a staff of engineers and product specialists, the company also relies on the services of outside designers like Rick Doss who work exclusively for the company. One of Doss' most popular items is a teardrop-shaped headlight assembly reminiscent of a 1939 Ford automobile.

HEADQUARTERED IN MORGAN HILL, CUSTOM CHROME, INC. IS A WHOLESALER AND DISTRIBUTOR OF AFTERMARKET PRODUCTS FOR MOTORCYCLES, FOCUSING EXCLUSIVELY ON THE HARLEY-DAVIDSON MARKET.

CUSTOM CHROME'S ENGINEERING STAFF DESIGNS MANY OF THE FIRM'S PRODUCTS ON 3-D CAD STATIONS, THEN CHECKS THE PROTOTYPES AGAINST THE COMPUTER BLUEPRINTS USING CMMs (COORDINATES MEASURING MACHINE).

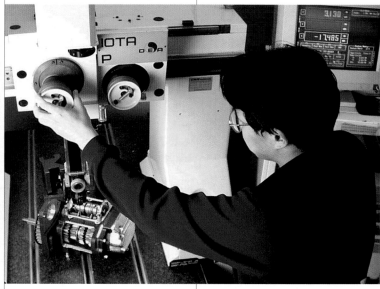

KICK-STARTING SUCCESS

Never a company to settle for initial success, Custom Chrome has always been attentive to the wants and needs of the marketplace. Over the years, some of the company's best-selling products have been suggested by people outside the company, and many of the parts sold today reflect the input received from both dealers and customers. Weekly product meetings are conducted to determine which new ideas will be developed and to establish the design specifications for new products.

For example, when Harley-Davidson eliminated the kick starter after the 1985 model, a large percentage of Harley owners longed for the accessory's nostalgic look. When it was discovered that these customers only wanted the kick starter for looks and not for its original function, the company developed a fake one that could be bolted onto the transmission and that could actually be made to swing through an arc.

Some of the latest innovations to come from the Custom Chrome Research and Development department include the new RevTech six-speed overdrive transmission assemblies and gear sets, which have revolutionized the riding experience, and Rick Doss' teardrop-shaped headlight kits that redefine the classic look of Harley-Davidson motorcycles. These are items that devotees will not find anywhere else.

Custom Chrome's product specialists also work closely with their suppliers to develop new proprietary product lines like the RevTech Pure™ line of engine oil that provides synthetic-like performance at a petroleum price, or the new Santee™ motorcycle frames designed to permit the installation of extra-wide rear wheels and tires.

Custom Chrome is the largest supplier of aftermarket replacement parts for most Harley-Davidson models as far back as 1936, and sells items from its catalog to its network of more than 4,700 motorcycle dealers and repair shops worldwide. The Custom Chrome catalog has more than 1,050 color pages, and is available in both a softbound version for use in the company's dealers' catalog racks and a hardbound version for resale to consumers. The catalog features more than 4,000 pictures and product descriptions, and is widely acknowledged as one of the finest reference books of its kind available today.

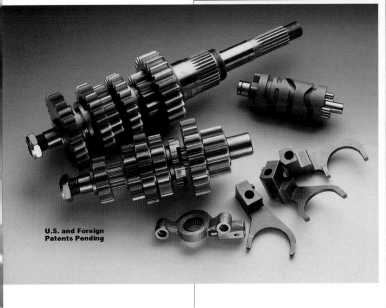

CLOCKWISE FROM TOP: CUSTOM CHROME RELIES ON THE SERVICES OF OUTSIDE DESIGNERS LIKE RICK DOSS WHO WORK EXCLUSIVELY FOR THE COMPANY. ONE OF DOSS' MOST POPULAR ITEMS IS A TEARDROP-SHAPED HEADLIGHT ASSEMBLY REMINISCENT OF A 1939 FORD AUTOMOBILE.

CUSTOM CHROME PROVIDES PARTS EXCLUSIVELY TO THE HARLEY-DAVIDSON MARKET BECAUSE LOYAL OWNERS OF THESE BIKES DEVOTE MORE TIME AND MONEY TO CUSTOMIZING THEIR BIKES THAN OWNERS OF JAPANESE OR BRITISH BRANDS. THE COMPANY PROVIDES MANY ITEMS DEVOTEES WILL NOT FIND ELSEWHERE.

CUSTOM CHROME DISTRIBUTES MANY OF ITS PRODUCTS UNDER THE REVTECH® BRAND, INCLUDING THE REVTECH 100™ ENGINE, REVTECH SIX-SPEED OVERDRIVE GEAR SET, AND REVTECH PURE™ OIL.

THE CUSTOM CHROME CATALOG HAS MORE THAN 1,050 COLOR PAGES, AND IS AVAILABLE IN BOTH A SOFTBOUND VERSION FOR USE IN THE COMPANY'S DEALERS' CATALOG RACKS AND A HARDBOUND VERSION FOR RESALE TO CONSUMERS. THE CATALOG FEATURES MORE THAN 4,000 PICTURES AND PRODUCT DESCRIPTIONS, AND IS WIDELY ACKNOWLEDGED AS ONE OF THE FINEST REFERENCE BOOKS OF ITS KIND AVAILABLE TODAY.

WEBCOR BUILDERS

IN THE CONSTRUCTION INDUSTRY, INTEGRITY IS AS CRITICAL TO THE BUILDING process as concrete and steel. As clients will attest, it is also a key ingredient of Webcor Builders, and is one reason why the company is one of the largest general contractors in Northern California and one of the leading contractors in the Bay Area. ◆ Established in San Mateo in

1971, Webcor has put its innovative stamp on some of the Bay Area's most high-profile buildings in recent years, becoming the builder of choice for some of Silicon Valley's hottest names, including Oracle Corporation, Electronic Arts, Symantec, Adobe Systems, and Electronics for Imaging (EFI), to name just a few.

In San Francisco, a city proud of its architectural heritage, Webcor has erected eye-catching structures to critical acclaim. Examples include the W Hotel and Portside Condominiums, nestled in the shadow of the Bay Bridge. The company's growing interiors sector—Webcor Interior Construction Group (ICG)—claims such exacting clients as LucasArts, Virgin Megastore, and Electronic Arts.

"We want to focus on the San Francisco Bay Area," says Andrew Ball, president of Webcor. "We've resisted the temptation to expand around the United States and around the world because we think it's a drain on the company's resources, to move our best people around. So we'll continue to focus on this area and take care of our clients."

PEOPLE ARE A PRIORITY

Since its founding, Webcor has placed a priority on people—both employees and clients—and this focus has made all the difference in the firm's growth, serving the company well in weathering the debilitating recession of the early 1990s, and helping the firm manage the explosion of new business when the economy improved.

"What the recession did for the building trade," says Ball, "was scatter our skilled workforce. Here at Webcor, we kept our skilled workers on the payroll and chose to lose money instead of laying workers off. Talented, well-trained people are our most important resource, and that policy bred a lot of loyalty. Some have been with the company 25 years."

The commitment to employees starts at the very beginning of their tenure at Webcor, when they are mentored by a company veteran of 10 or more years. The company invests in education, training, and high-tech tools for all employees.

The personal integrity of the Webcor management team permeates the entire company and extends into the community. Heavily involved in charity work throughout the Bay Area, Webcor believes in giving back to the community. Companywide projects include Habitat for Humanity; Christmas in April, to which the firm donates resources, time, and expertise for one day each year to renovate homes and community

"WE GET INVOLVED MORE IN DESIGNING AND ASSISTING WITH ENGINEERS AND ARCHITECTS," EXPLAINS JOHN KERLEY, WEBCOR BUILDERS SENIOR VICE PRESIDENT, BUSINESS DEVELOPMENT. "THAT'S WHY WE CALL OURSELVES BUILDERS. WE'RE MASTER BUILDERS WORKING WITH THE TEAM TO PROVIDE A COMPLETE PROJECT," SUCH AS THE ELECTRONICS FOR IMAGING CAMPUS (TOP).

WEBCOR BUILDERS HAS CONSTRUCTED OFFICES FOR SOME OF SILICON VALLEY'S HOTTEST NAMES, INCLUDING THE ORACLE CORPORATION WORLD HEADQUARTERS (BOTTOM).

STEVE WHITTAKER

WEBCOR HAS ERECTED EYE-CATCHING STRUCTURES TO CRITICAL ACCLAIM, INCLUDING THE W HOTEL IN SAN FRANCISCO'S BURGEONING YERBA BUENA NEIGHBORHOOD.

facilities; and Bayshore Christian Ministries, a nonprofit tutorial and leadership center for children in East Palo Alto.

"You set a standard for yourself," says Ball, who volunteers with Boy Scouts of America," then you surround yourself with people who carry on those values."

MASTER BUILDERS

Webcor has banked on its credibility in the negotiated bid approach to win project assignments. Un-

like hard bid firms, where contractors compete against each other to submit the lowest price proposal, the negotiated contractor is selected by the owners to oversee and work on the entire structure from the design phase to completion of construction.

"With their approval, we get involved more in designing and assisting with engineers and architects. That's why we call ourselves builders. We're master builders working with the team to provide a complete project," ex-

plains John Kerley, senior vice president, business development. Often, owners can realize up to 20 percent savings in the negotiated bid process.

A case in point concerns the fast-track Treat Towers project for Spieker Properties in Walnut Creek. The compact construction site presented numerous design challenges for Webcor Builders. Original plans pushed parking for 700 cars underground, an expensive proposition. "We freed up a lot of square footage from the

building and put in a freestanding garage without an increase in cost," says Kerley. The plan eventually yielded 1,175 parking spaces.

"We structure ourselves so we can deliver service for our clients' needs," says Kerley.

When this process succeeds, it leads to additional work. And Webcor has been very, very busy. The national industry bible *Engineering News-Record* reported Webcor's growth in a 1997 article: "When Webcor and A.J. Ball Construction merged in 1995, Webcor jumped on *ENR*'s Top 400 list from 318 in 1995 to 95 in 1996. But it was the high-tech market that catapulted Webcor to 66 [in 1997]."

INNOVATIVE SOLUTIONS FOR CUTTING-EDGE CLIENTS

One of the company's most successful endeavors has been the five buildings, conference center, and parking structures built in Redwood Shores for Oracle Corporation, one of the largest software companies in the world.

"Oracle is a success story, in that we were asked to build building after building," says Ball.

Other multiphase projects for major high-technology companies include the San Mateo headquarters for computer games maker Electronic Arts, and the Foster City campus for EFI, whose technology revolutionized color copiers.

"It's fun building for high-tech companies like these," says Ball. "For one thing, they require the utmost in cutting-edge techniques and facilities. They're not just on the edge, they're beyond it."

Webcor is extremely popular with trailblazing companies because of its own forward-thinking approach to some of the industry's trickiest problems. Take the aforementioned Treat Towers project, for example. The ambitious time line called for continued construction through the rainy season of 1997-1998. Taking the time and expense to weatherize the site in the fall enabled construction to continue without being mired in mud. Using its own Internet server and T-1 line, Webcor provided employees with laptop computers and Palm Pilots,

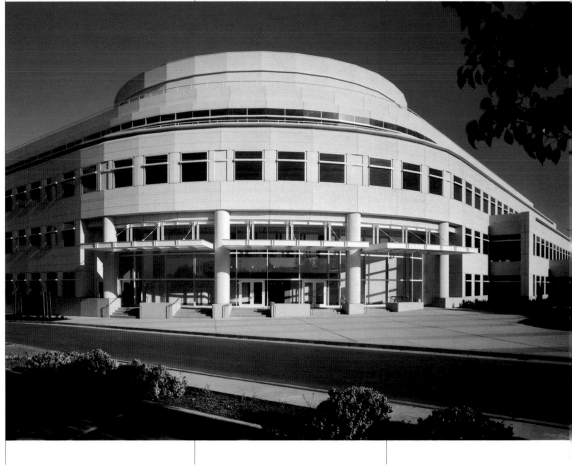

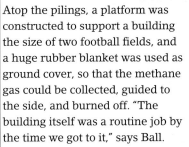

then hooked up its offices, via the Internet, to Doppler radar. The result: Concrete was poured between rainstorms, and the project proceeded through the winter, ahead of schedule.

Another innovative solution was developed on the Home Depot project in Colma, California. The building site, a former garbage dump, was unstable and gave off methane gas. Webcor drove more than 740 pilings, each 200 feet long, to bedrock. It looked like a porcupine forest, phone callers said.

Atop the pilings, a platform was constructed to support a building the size of two football fields, and a huge rubber blanket was used as ground cover, so that the methane gas could be collected, guided to the side, and burned off. "The building itself was a routine job by the time we got to it," says Ball.

For all of the company's innovations in construction methods— consistently delivering quality projects early and below budget without sacrificing desired design elements—Webcor's measure-

ment of success continues to be client satisfaction. "At the end of the day, if the client isn't satisfied, you really have nothing," says Ball.

Fortunately, Webcor Builders has yet to encounter a dissatisfied client, or one who did not appreciate the firm's employees' enthusiasm for their work. As Ball expresses it, quite simply: "We love to build." For three decades, the company has been doing just that, and in the process, Webcor has made a significant mark on the San Francisco Bay Area.

MERT CARPENTER PHOTOGRAPHY

BAYER CORPORATION

OT MORE THAN TWO MILES AWAY FROM THE WORLD-RENOWNED BERKELEY campus of the University of California, amid West Berkeley's industrial neighborhood, the modern, 30-acre site housing the laboratories and production facilities of Bayer Corporation harbors the nerve center for groundbreaking biotechnology research, develop-

CLOCKWISE FROM TOP:
IN ITS EFFORT TO CHANGE THE WORLD WITH GREAT CARE, BAYER DEVELOPED THE BIKUNIN PROJECT FOR CYSTIC FIBROSIS.

"DISEASES HAVE NOT CHANGED, TECHNOLOGY HAS," SAYS DR. WOLF-DIETER BUSSE, BAYER'S SENIOR VICE PRESIDENT OF BIOTECHNOLOGY. "OF THE 450,000 KNOWN BIOLOGICAL DISEASES, LESS THAN HALF CAN BE TREATED. WE BELIEVE THAT ALL THE PROTEINS RELEVANT TO HUMAN DISEASE ARE LIKELY TO BE DISCOVERED WITHIN THE NEXT FIVE YEARS."

NOT MORE THAN TWO MILES AWAY FROM THE WORLD-RENOWNED BERKELEY CAMPUS OF THE UNIVERSITY OF CALIFORNIA, AMID WEST BERKELEY'S INDUSTRIAL NEIGHBORHOOD, THE MODERN, 30-ACRE SITE HOUSING THE LABORATORIES AND PRODUCTION FACILITIES OF BAYER CORPORATION HARBORS THE NERVE CENTER FOR GROUNDBREAKING BIOTECHNOLOGY RESEARCH, DEVELOPMENT, AND BIOLOGICAL PRODUCTION.

ment, and biological production. Scientists in Bayer's laboratories are searching for—and finding—treatments for some formidable diseases in genetically engineered pharmaceuticals.

For example, Bayer is the sole producer of Prolastin, made from human blood plasma, which saves the lives of congenital emphysema sufferers around the world. And plasma-based Thrombate III treats thrombotic conditions by dissolving blood clots.

MEDICINE FOR THE MILLENNIUM

The facility's first and most important genetically engineered medicine was Kogenate, which allows hemophiliacs to live near-normal lives. A technological breakthrough when Bayer established the process for producing it, Kogenate is the world's largest molecule produced in the biotechnology industry, and was licensed from Genentech in 1984.

"We invested $500 million here in Berkeley to develop Kogenate and build a world-class, state-of-the-art production facility," says Dr.

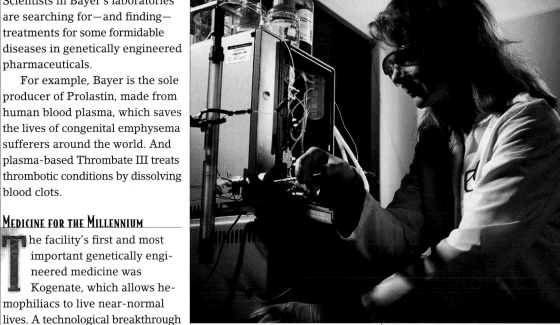

Wolf-Dieter Busse, Bayer's senior vice president of biotechnology.

Kogenate, which became widely available in 1993, replaces the missing Factor VIII in the blood of people with hemophilia. "A new, improved version of Kogenate will soon be released, and a third version is currently under development, says Michael Kamarck, senior vice president, biological operations. All the while, Bayer scientists have been exploring ways to treat the disease with gene therapy, to some day eliminate the need for drug transfusions altogether."

Other products under development either by or in partnership with the Berkeley facility are being evaluated for treatment and cure of such major illnesses as multiple sclerosis, diabetes, cancer, and several forms of asthma.

Partnerships with other firms at work in similar or complementary fields help extend the reach of Bayer's drug development program. Alliances and partnerships, critical for a research organization such as Bayer, allow the company to broaden its base of potential products by sharing research findings that may be a by-product

of another company's development process. Bayer has established an alliance with Millennium Pharmaceuticals, Inc. of Boston, in an innovative, production-oriented approach to rapidly move compounds based on genomic research toward clinical trials and to market. Bayer has existing partnerships with a number of Bay Area and world-wide companies. In addition, in 1998, Bayer acquired the Emeryville unit of Chiron Diagnostics, a division of Chiron Corporation.

The Next Step

"Gene therapy is the next step," says Busse. "Also, with future vaccines and biological paradigms that we're just beginning to see, in the far distant future, we'll be able to significantly extend people's lives."

Lest anyone start scrambling for their actuary tables, Busse cautions that the development time from research stage to the eventual widespread availability of therapeutics, both chemical and biological, is painstakingly slow, with no guarantee of success. In some cases, promising medicines that have taken a dozen years to develop can fail in phase III clinical trials, the last stage before a drug can be approved by the Food and Drug Administration.

To ensure that Bayer remains on the forefront of the drug discovery process, its biotechnology pipeline is packed with eight products in various stages of development. Also, $350 million has been committed toward a precedent-setting, 30-year development agreement to build out the facility, approved in 1991 by the City of Berkeley.

Taking Care of Environment and Community

Honored in 1997 by the California Environmental Protection Agency for the "extraordinary ways" the company has "reduced, reused, recycled, and purchased recycled

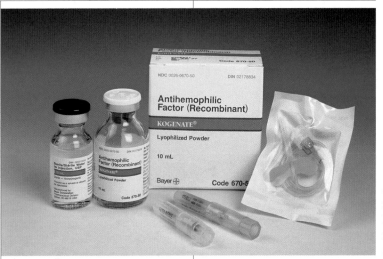

products," Bayer was also one of only two companies to receive the Governor's Environmental and Economic Leadership Award in recognition of its waste-reduction efforts, ride-sharing programs, and participation in Coastal Cleanup Day. Furthermore, the East Bay Municipal Utilities District (EBMUD) recognized the company for its water conservation programs and sensitive management of water usage.

Contributions to community-based organizations and the creation and financial support of a local foundation that offers support for West Berkeley programs are part of Bayer's commitment to the city. The company also provides funds for science education programs in grades K-8, established and supports a school-to-work biotechnology education program in high school and junior college, and contributes funds for

housing, child care, and job training to the City of Berkeley.

Changing the World with Great Care

Part of the $9 billion, global company's pharmaceutical division, Bayer's Berkeley-based Biotechnology and Biological groups focus on the discovery and development of protein therapeutics, blood-based medicines, and gene therapy products resulting from recombinant DNA technology, or genetic engineering. A separate consumer care division, based in Morristown, New Jersey, produces over-the-counter vitamins and drugs, including aspirin, which was invented by a Bayer chemist in 1897. Other major businesses for the research-based company include chemicals, life sciences, and imaging technologies.

Despite its tremendous size, Bayer has not lost sight of its core mission of changing the world with great care. From the discovery of aspirin to the development of Kogenate, Bayer scientists remain intensely focused on improving human health around the world.

"Diseases have not changed, technology has," says Busse. "Of the 450,000 known biological diseases, less than half can be treated. However, hundreds of new genes are being discovered and released each day by the Human Genome Project, a joint effort between the U.S. Department of Energy and the National Institutes of Health. We believe that all the proteins relevant to human disease are likely to be discovered within the next five years."

THE BERKELEY FACILITY'S FIRST AND MOST IMPORTANT GENETICALLY ENGINEERED MEDICINE WAS KOGENATE, WHICH ALLOWS HEMO-PHILIACS TO LIVE NEAR-NORMAL LIVES.

AS ONE PART OF ITS FUNCTIONAL GENOMICS EFFORTS, BAYER BIOTECHNOLOGY USES THE FLUOROMETRIC IMAGING PLATE READER (FLIPR) FOR CELL-BASED, HIGH-THROUGHPUT ASSAYS.

ZiLOG Inc.

WITH NEW OWNERS AND NEW MANAGEMENT, DEVELOPING NEW PRODUCTS, and evincing a new attitude, ZiLOG Inc. has every intention of living up to its vision "to be the fastest-growing, most exciting computer company in the world." ◆ One of the industry's original chip makers, ZiLOG introduced the Z80™ microprocessor,

its original product, shortly after its founding in 1974. Despite possessing one of the industry's most comprehensive proprietary design libraries, ZiLOG eventually fell back with the rest of the pack, jockeying for position as a niche player, ricocheting between private and public ownership.

Fast-forwarding to 1999, ZiLOG had emerged as a vibrant, cutting-edge partner for companies in three areas: integrated controls, communications, and home entertainment. This turnaround is in part the result of Texas Pacific Group's acquisition of the company in 1998 and its recruitment of Curtis J. Crawford, former CEO of Lucent Technologies Microelectronics Group, as president and CEO of ZiLOG.

In 1999, ZiLOG's new management team steered the company to a 20 percent increase in sales and focused its energies on a new goal—making products that provide people with "extreme connectivity." ZiLOG's new family of microprocessors and microcontrollers connect people to the Internet, to home and office networks, and to interactive communication products, such as M@ilTV. In 2000, the company launched a companion initiative to create

smart networked appliances for digital homes.

Focus on Customer Service

Crawford has set employees at all levels of the company on a path of excellence that leads to servicing ZiLOG's customers. "ZiLOG creates embedded technologies that improve the performance of everyday applications," he says. "Our engineers immerse themselves into all aspects of specific markets so we can deliver appropriate, feature-rich solutions at breakneck speeds. Passion, ideas, and service fuel our drive to always focus on one goal: helping our customers succeed."

Crawford's customer-centric strategy evolves around customers' needs. "We listen to the customer and respond in a timely fashion, and are competitive in everything we do," he says. "It also means understanding customers' requirements and providing honest feedback to help them create the best solutions."

The new focus is not just talk; ZiLOG has put this philosophy into action. For example, the company recently established a customer service center in Austin, Texas, where technical support personnel provide around-the-clock assistance.

"The ZiLOG way and excellence are synonymous," says Crawford. "If we believe that—if

CLOCKWISE FROM TOP: COFOUNDED BY FEDERICO FAGGIN (LEFT), ZiLOG INC. IS LED BY CURRENT CHAIRMAN, CEO, AND PRESIDENT CURTIS J. CRAWFORD.

ZiLOG'S TECHNOLOGY WILL ENABLE PEOPLE TO LIVE IN SMART HOMES WHERE APPLIANCES AND ELECTRONICS IN THE AVERAGE HOUSE CAN BE HOOKED UP VIA THE INTERNET AND ACCESSED REMOTELY ANYTIME, ANYWHERE. TO THIS END, THE COMPANY IS DEVELOPING M@ilTV, A PRODUCT THAT TRANSFORMS A TV SET INTO A PORTAL ON THE WORLD WIDE WEB.

PLANNING A MORE AGGRESSIVE MOVE TOWARD INTERNET-RELATED PRODUCTS, ZiLOG INTRODUCED THE EZ80 INTERNET ENGINE IN 2000.

we practice that in everything we do—it gives us a competitive advantage. We are building the right strategies and serving our customers with the highest level of support in the industry."

COMMUNICATIONS AND HOME ENTERTAINMENT

While many consumers may be unfamiliar with ZiLOG, chances are their lives are touched every day by household products embedded with a ZiLOG chip.

The best-selling eight-bit microprocessor in history, the Z80 is still sold today. The venerable Z80 and the company's new flagship products for extreme connectivity—including the eZ80™ Internet Engine, the Cartezian™ Communications Engine, and high performance digital signal processors—are housed in the company's Communications division. Targeted applications in this $32 billion market include network routers and switches, Internet appliances, automatic meter reading, voice recognition for personal digital assistants (PDAs), glass break detection/security, motor control, point-of-sale swiping terminals, postal meters, and vending machines.

The Integrated Controls division provides highly integrated microcontrollers to the consumer electronics industry. ZiLOG's Z8, Z8Plus, and Wave family of wireless spread spectrum products can be found in hundreds of consumer brand-name products, such as Sears garage door openers and treadmills, Sonicare toothbrushes, Black & Decker power tools, Ray-

O-Vac battery chargers, Microsoft and Logitech computer mice, NMB and Key Tronic keyboards, and DSC and Ademco security systems, as well as GE and AT&T cordless phones.

The Home Entertainment division provides semiconductor-based solutions for TVs and infrared (IR) controllers. With more than 125 million televisions, 100 million VCRs, and five million to 10 million set-top boxes sold worldwide, the market for home entertainment is enormous. Additionally, the IR remote control portion of the market is estimated to exceed $1 billion. With the emergence of digital TV, growing demand for violence-blocking V-chips, and other special features, and increasing breadth and functionality of remote controllers, the potential for growth in the semiconductor segment of this market is enormous.

Says Crawford, "Any product that connects people to data is where we excel."

PLANNING FOR A SMART FUTURE

As ZiLOG continues to grow, the firm plans to become more consumer oriented. For instance, to capitalize on its growing reputation for excellence, the company is developing a consumer advertising effort in partnership with customers to trumpet when a product is powered by a ZiLOG chip.

The company also plans a more aggressive move toward Internet-related products—for example, its M@ilTv product that transforms a TV set into a portal on the World Wide Web. ZiLOG's technology will enable people to live in smart homes where appliances and electronics in the average house can be hooked up via the Internet and accessed remotely anytime, anywhere.

"The technologies we provide drive commerce around the world," says Crawford, "and it's exciting for us to be a part of it."

HEADQUARTERED IN CAMPBELL, CALIFORNIA, ZiLOG INC. HAS FACILITIES ACROSS THE UNITED STATES, INCLUDING A CUSTOMER SERVICE CENTER IN AUSTIN AND A STATE-OF-THE-ART CLEAN ROOM FACILITY IN NAMPA, IDAHO (TOP).

IN ADDITION TO LAUNCHING NEW PRODUCTS FOR THE HOME, THE OFFICE, AND THE INTERNET, ZiLOG IS AGGRESSIVELY PROMOTING THE COMPANY'S NEW IDENTITY AT INDUSTRY CONFERENCES AND TRADE SHOWS (BOTTOM).

PACIFIC UNION COMMERCIAL BROKERAGE (PUCB)	1975
PACIFIC UNION REAL ESTATE GROUP	1975
FIRSTAMERICA AUTOMOTIVE	1976
GENENTECH, INC.	1976
ULTRATECH STEPPER, INC.	1979
CENTIGRAM COMMUNICATIONS	1980
HILL GLAZIER ARCHITECTS	1980
INFORMIX CORPORATION	1980
ADVENT SOFTWARE, INC.	1983
HYUNDAI ELECTRONICS AMERICA	1983
HILL PHYSICIANS MEDICAL GROUP	1984
McCOWN DE LEEUW & CO., INC.	1984
XILINX	1984
CUNNINGHAM COMMUNICATION, INC.	1985
FIRST REPUBLIC BANK	1985
PATMONT MOTOR WERKS	1985

KARL SOPKE IS IN AN ENVIABLE POSITION, AND NOT JUST BECAUSE HIS fourth-floor office in the Marina District has a spectacular Bay vista with a peekaboo view of the often fog-shrouded Golden Gate Bridge. ◆ Sopke is president of Pacific Union Real Estate Group (PUREG), the darling of the residential real estate industry. The company main-

tains a leadership position in the Bay Area, and is blazing a trail of technological innovation and exceptional approaches to customer service.

Considered a destination company to which real estate agents aspire, PUREG is known for being very selective about the managers and agents in its fold. Comprised of residential and commercial brokerages, as well as lending and retirement living services, the company specializes in the upscale markets of the Bay Area, where average home sale prices are in excess of $500,000.

COMPRISED OF RESIDENTIAL AND COMMERCIAL BROKERAGES, THE PACIFIC UNION REAL ESTATE GROUP (PUREG) SPECIALIZES IN THE UPSCALE MARKETS OF THE BAY AREA, WHERE AVERAGE HOME SALE PRICES ARE IN EXCESS OF $500,000 (TOP).

PUREG HAS GROWN INTO ONE OF THE LARGEST RESIDENTIAL REAL ESTATE COMPANIES IN NORTHERN CALIFORNIA, WITH 14 OFFICES IN THE BAY AREA, INCLUDING LOCATIONS IN SAN FRANCISCO, DIABLO VALLEY, MONTCLAIR/PIEDMONT, SONOMA AND NAPA VALLEY WINE COUNTRY, AND MARIN COUNTY (BOTTOM LEFT AND RIGHT).

Opportunities for Growth

Founded in 1975 by Bill Harlan and the late Peter Stocker as part of Pacific Union Company, PUREG started as a two-office, San Francisco-based real estate brokerage. Since that time, it has grown into one of the largest residential real estate companies in Northern California, with 14 offices in the Bay Area (San Francisco, Diablo Valley, Montclair/Piedmont, Sonoma and Napa Valley Wine Country, and Marin County).

"Pacific Union Company has best been described as not a com-

pany but a guild, in that it was a collection of 10 individuals who had unique and diverse skills and backgrounds who came together because of the common thread of real estate," Sopke says. Today, the Pacific Union group of companies is involved in development, residential and commercial real estate, financial services, property management, and hotel operations.

Speaking specifically about Pacific Union Real Estate Group, Sopke says, "You have to have a track record of success to join PUREG. We have the highest average sales volume per associate of

the top 350 brokerages nationwide. We also have the highest average sales price per transaction in the nation. That speaks volumes, in terms of depth of quality."

Amazingly, the company's period of largest growth occurred during the crippling recession of the early 1990s. It eventually rose to the top as the San Francisco Bay Area crested the nation's real estate market for housing prices in 1998.

"Down markets present tremendous opportunities for growth," says Sopke. "One of the truths in our business is that top people

always survive in any market. Consumers usually do better with companies like ours, which are very disciplined when they deliver products and services to clients."

Adding to the successful operation in San Francisco, Contra Costa became the first area of expansion, with an office in Danville in 1989 and another in Lafayette in 1991. In 1990, the Montclair/Piedmont office was opened. Offices in the Wine Country opened in quick succession in Santa Rosa, Sonoma, and St. Helena starting in 1996, and the Marin County brokerage opened its Mill Valley location in the mid-1990s, adding a fabulous new office in central Marin County in April 1999. In 1997, San Francisco opened another key office.

Unlike other real estate companies that grow through mergers and acquisitions of existing companies, PUREG began expanding throughout the Bay Area in 1989 by building and creating new offices. While more time consuming, this method allowed the company to retain a consistent, customer-focused culture of excellence and discipline.

"First, we identify the market; then, we find the right manager," says Sopke. Once that manager has been recruited to the PUREG fold, he or she becomes the nucleus of the operation, and acts as a magnet to draw other top staff.

INNOVATIONS IN HOME BUYING AND SELLING

Pacific Union Real Estate Group has emerged as an industry leader because of its no-holds-barred approach to innovations. While other real estate companies were initiating policies to send their agents home and calling that a mobile office program, PUREG was backing up its policies with technology. It designed and implemented an Intranet program to allow its real estate agents to process transactions 24 hours a day, seven days a week, from their homes and on the road. PUREG's Mobile Agent and ViaLINK Program has resulted in higher agent productivity and increased earnings. More

important, it has allowed agents to service clients more efficiently and more quickly.

This customer-driven approach to business prompted the company to launch South of Market (SoMa) Living in 1998. A unique alternative to the current home-buying process, the new venture delivers Web-driven real estate services to home buyers. The company also has a proprietary retail store located at 38 Bryant Street in San Francisco's SOMA area where customers can get community information and browse the Web site at www.somaliving.com.

"We looked at the home-buying process and asked how it could be repackaged in a way that the consumer might want to select as an alternative," Sopke explains. The result, known as the Saturn approach, presents information about every aspect of the home-buying process under one roof: costs, neighborhoods, home inspections, financing—even redesign of exist-

PACIFIC UNION BUILDING

ing features to make the home more suitable for the buyer's needs. The non-commissioned staff consultants are salaried, and serve the buyer's bests interests.

"Technology never sold a piece of real estate," says Sopke, "but it certainly has allowed us to respond faster to our customers. It has been the great enabler for us."

PUREG takes the most pride in the satisfaction of its customers. "We're incredibly customer focused," says Sopke. Consequently, much of the firm's business comes from repeat customers and referrals.

"At the end of the home-buying transaction, it has to be good for everyone involved," Sopke summarizes. "It has to be a rewarding experience for our clients, our agents, our company. When it is, then everyone wins, and we go on into the future."

"AT THE END OF THE HOME-BUYING TRANSACTION, IT HAS TO BE GOOD FOR EVERYONE INVOLVED," SAYS KARL SOPKE, PRESIDENT OF PUREG. "IT HAS TO BE A REWARDING EXPERIENCE FOR OUR CLIENTS, OUR AGENTS, OUR COMPANY. WHEN IT IS, THEN EVERYONE WINS, AND WE GO ON INTO THE FUTURE."

FOUNDED IN 1975 BY BILL HARLAN AND THE LATE PETER STOCKER AS PART OF PACIFIC UNION COMPANY, PUREG STARTED AS A TWO-OFFICE, SAN FRANCISCO-BASED REAL ESTATE BROKERAGE, AND HAS GROWN INTO ONE OF THE LEADING REAL ESTATE COMPANIES IN THE BAY AREA.

Pacific Union Commercial Brokerage (PUCB)

PACIFIC UNION COMMERCIAL BROKERAGE (PUCB) WAS ESTABLISHED IN 1982 as a part of Pacific Union Real Estate Group, a division of Pacific Union Company. The goal of Pacific Union Company's founder, Peter Stocker, was to create a regional real estate company that could provide complete, comprehensive, and seamless real estate services for clients in both the residential and commercial markets. Pacific Union Company develops and owns real estate in the Bay Area, and for nearly two decades, PUCB has participated in Stocker's vision by establishing itself as one of the leading commercial brokerage firms in the Bay Area market.

Full-service experience in all aspects of real estate is a distinct advantage. PUCB is well known in San Francisco as a premier commercial brokerage firm, providing quality leasing and sales services to many of the city's landmark companies and nonprofit organizations. In recent years, PUCB has earned a reputation as a leader in finding innovative solutions for high-tech and Internet firms relocating in San Francisco.

The Network Advantage

As a part of a regional real estate company, PUCB has the advantage of working with more than 400 Pacific Union Residential Brokerage (PURB) agents in Bay Area offices who are an ongoing source of business for the Commercial Brokerage agents. Clients who have purchased a home feel confident when they turn to PUCB for their office, warehouse, industrial, or investment property needs. The process works equally as well in the reverse; when a commercial client desires to purchase a home, they then turn to PURB.

Staying on top of the market is especially important for brokers during the extreme peaks and valleys of the market-driven business. During the economic recession of the early 1990s, office vacancies rose higher than 12 percent. By the end of the decade, however, the trend had reversed and vacancies were squeezed to below 3 percent. The experience of PUCB's brokers is a valuable asset for clients who depend upon their PUCB brokers to forecast the market and advise them through market changes.

PUCB stays at the forefront of the Bay Area commercial real estate market through its research technologies. The firm is continually expanding its computer networking and research capabilities, and brokers at PUCB are computer savvy. The real estate market is going online, and PUCB brokers are leading the way, establishing a presence on the Internet at www.sfcommercial.com.

Tapping the Invisible Market

There is an invisible real estate market in San Francisco. In this market, the broker has to know what is available, even though it may not be listed yet. PUCB brokers have a highly developed ability to read the signs of the invisible market. Clients appreciate the advantage of working with a broker who thoroughly knows the local commercial market.

Realizing integrity is the foundation for a lasting client base, PUCB brokers make customer satisfaction their primary goal. Through building on client referrals and staying ahead of the market, the opportunities for PUCB's future success are boundless. Above all, the firm takes pride in its agents and employees, the services it provides to clients, and the strong reputation it has built in its first two decades of existence.

I N THE EARLY 1980S, STEPHANIE DiMARCO WAS WORKING AS A FINANCIAL analyst and portfolio manager when she saw an opportunity to create a software product to assist her colleagues in the investment management industry. She might have hesitated if not for the startling realization—in the middle of a job interview—that she had hit the glass ceiling, and was

NABIB JOE HAKIM

just at the start of her career. DiMarco decided to take the leap to test her entrepreneurial skills.

"I was at a decision point, asking myself if I was really going to start this business, when I decided to apply for a job at a big investment firm in the city," says DiMarco. "Halfway through the interview, I realized he was talking about a secretarial job, but I thought I was interviewing for an analyst job. I figured I could do a lot better."

In 1983, DiMarco launched Advent Software, Inc., an investment management software company, and in 1995, she took it public.

INVENTIVE ENTREPRENEURSHIP

A s chairman, DiMarco heads the company that is the world's leading provider of software solutions, data integration tools, and services for investment management professionals. Not bad for a company that started with just one product.

"We're in a constant state of invention," says DiMarco. "Today, we have more than 20 products and services, and we generated $71 million in revenue in 1998. The consensus for 1999 among *Wall Street Journal* analysts was that we'll do just under $100 million."

Since its inception, Advent has been on the forefront of investment management software development, making possible the automation of a wide range of investment activities. Advent's innovative solutions—for such tasks as portfolio management, partnership accounting, client relationship management, reconciliation processing, and trade order management—allow investment professionals to focus on decision making rather than technology implementation.

THE STANDARD IN PORTFOLIO MANAGEMENT

T oday, Advent Software represents the standard in portfolio management and trading and order manage

ment," says DiMarco. "And we are rapidly becoming the leader in Internet-based investment solutions. That's why more than 5,400 financial institutions around the world have chosen Advent Software as their technology partner."

With more than 600 employees in offices in New York City, Boston, and Australia, and its headquarters in San Francisco, Advent is run like the company DiMarco wanted to work for in the early days of her previous career. "I aimed to create a very ethical company where people could feel their values were respected, whatever their politics and gender," says DiMarco. "We have a great group of people here with

a common vision of striving to do a great job. That's one of our unique strengths."

At the end of the day, employees seeking a reminder of the company's heart need look no further than the company name. "When we were trying to come up with a name for the company, we were really attracted to "advent" because it was the root of two words we really liked," says DiMarco. "One was 'adventure,' and the other was 'invent.' It's been a great adventure seeing this business grow from its inception, and also, we've invented a great many products that have helped both our customers and the industry."

STEPHANIE DiMARCO IS THE FOUNDER AND CHAIRMAN OF ADVENT SOFTWARE, INC., THE WORLD'S LEADING PROVIDER OF SOFTWARE SOLUTIONS, DATA INTEGRATION TOOLS, AND SERVICES FOR INVESTMENT MANAGEMENT PROFESSIONALS.

FirstAmerica Automotive

IN SAN FRANCISCO'S SOUTH OF MARKET AREA (SoMa), AMID AN INDUSTRIAL landscape of multimedia firms and live/work loft spaces, Sonic Automotive, Inc.—parent company of FirstAmerica Automotive—stands out as a singular automobile facility. ◆ Early in 2000, the company launched the nation's first cyber-dealership from its western headquarters.

With hundreds of new and used cars in every price range, the choices offered on- and off-line are staggering.

Brands represented in the Sonic portfolio include Acura, BMW, Cadillac, Chevrolet, DaimlerChrysler, Dodge, Ford, Honda, Isuzu, Jeep, Land Rover, Lexus, Mercedes-Benz, Mitsubishi, Nissan, Oldsmobile, Plymouth, Porsche, Toyota, Volkswagen, and Volvo. Ford, Honda/Acura, Toyota/Lexus, DaimlerChrysler, Nissan, and BMW represented approximately 77 percent of Sonic's pro forma 1999 sales.

A History of Acquisition

Sonic's Western Division traces its roots back to 1976, when Tom Price acquired his first dealership, Serramonte Oldsmobile in Colma, just south of Daly City and San Francisco. Between 1976 and 1997, he owned and operated 11 automobile franchises stretching from Marin County to San Jose.

In 1996, Price's dealership group was the number two automobile dealer in the Bay Area, selling more than 16,000 cars with nine different makes. Then, in mid-1997, the Tom Price Dealership Group joined with two other Bay Area dealerships, Don Strough's Concord Honda and Steve Hallock's Concord Nissan. The new parent company was dubbed FirstAmerica Automotive and immediately snapped up three Southern California dealerships. An aggressive acquisition strategy in Northern and Southern California followed.

In 1998, FirstAmerica landed a coveted spot on the *Forbes'* Private 500 list of the nation's largest private companies. Possessing some 21 locations representing 28 franchises and eight of the nine largest automotive manufacturers, FirstAmerica was one of California's largest auto retailers.

Price, as president and CEO of FirstAmerica, had filed papers with the Securities and Exchange Commission to initiate a public offering in 1999, aiming to raise the $60 million to $100 million needed to expand throughout the West, when an unexpected turn of events rearranged the scene.

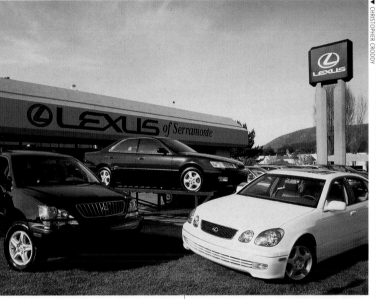

CHRISTOPHER CROODY

FORD, HONDA/ACURA, TOYOTA/ LEXUS (TOP), DAIMLER-CHRYSLER, NISSAN (BOTTOM), AND BMW REPRESENTED APPROXIMATELY 77 PERCENT OF SONIC AUTOMOTIVE'S—PARENT COMPANY OF FIRSTAMERICA AUTOMTIVE— PRO FORMA 1999 SALES.

A Mutually Beneficial Buyout

In December 1999, FirstAmerica Automotive was acquired by Sonic Automotive, Inc., a Charlotte-based owner and operator of automotive dealerships. Price is now vice chairman and a member of the board of directors of Sonic Automotive, Inc, an exciting move. "Sonic has demonstrated its ability to perform exceptionally well in the public arena, and our management team looks forward to making a significant contribution to the company's future success," he says.

Sonic President and Chief Operating Officer B. Scott Smith was particularly attracted by the company's impressive use of on-line marketing. "FirstAmerica has a highly developed Internet strategy as a result of dealing with technologically sophisticated customers in the major California markets," Smith says.

The match is a mutually beneficial one. Not only do the organizations share similar cultures and a common operational and financial reporting structure, but the franchises that made up FirstAmerica Automotive complement Sonic's brand diversity.

California accounted for more than 10 percent of new vehicle registrations in the United States in 1998. The size of the combined organizations allows the merged entity to increase synergies and economies of scale from pre-existing initiatives.

Sonic Automotive, Inc. has operations in Alabama, California, Florida, Georgia, Maryland, Nevada, North Carolina, Ohio, South Carolina, Tennessee, Texas, and Virginia, and operates 159 franchises and 31 collision repair centers.

A Passion for Cars

Customer satisfaction is the driving force behind Sonic Automotive, according to Price. Although his car-selling days are long behind him, he takes tremendous pride in matching products with the needs of his customers.

"You'll find that I talk about customer satisfaction first on almost anything," says Price. "I've found that if you take care of people, your business does very well."

Price's passion for cars got him into trouble as early as elementary school. "I got into this business for the love of cars," he says. "When I was in the first grade, I was sent to the principal's office for drawing pictures of cars. Now I race them, sell them, and collect them."

Price has worked in the automobile industry since 1963, including a stint at Ford Motor Company. A key professional decision came when he left the auto-manufacturing end and went into retail. But it wasn't a get-rich-quick move. In fact, as early as a year out of college, Price learned the hard way that get-rich-quick schemes don't work. "I bought some opals in Australia—opal stones, not cars—to bring back to the United States to resell," he says. The plan was thwarted when he discovered that the price had just doubled in Australia. "It was a great education," he says.

Treating Employees Right

A greater efficiency with inventories and a mighty purchasing power give the company an advantage over individual dealerships in more ways than one. "We get our money cheaper, we get our advertising cheaper," Price says. But, he adds,

On June 10, 1998, FirstAmerica Automotive opened a modern, centralized service center at the company's headquarters in downtown San Francisco. Servicing all makes and models of domestic and foreign cars, the facility hums with top-notch technicians attending to vehicles in 41 service stalls and 22 lifts.

SONIC AUTOMOTIVE'S PORTFOLIO INCLUDES NUMEROUS BRANDS OF VEHICLES, INCLUDING MERCEDES-BENZ (TOP) AND TOYOTA (BOTTOM).

"we're able to offer our employees investment in the company through stock options."

Expansion has the additional feature of attracting high-quality people to the sales team, management, and car repair center. Price believes in training programs that keep employees abreast of the latest information—a benefit that ranks among the top five reasons for employee retention in corporations nationwide. The company's commitment to a shared vision translates to patience and an open work environment that values the opinions and ideas of its employees.

At monthly rallies, the Wow Reports recognize outstanding employees who have favorably impressed customers during the month. A luncheon and awards ceremony held each quarter honor Sonic's most accomplished salespeople. The guidelines for winning the company's Pacesetter Award not only require salespeople to rank top in volume, but to exceed the manufacturer's national average for customer-service ratings.

Under Price's direction, the FirstAmerica sales teams won as many as four major manufacturer-bestowed awards for exceptional quality and customer satisfaction in a single year: the Elite of Lexus Award at Lexus of Serramonte, DaimlerChrysler's Five-Star Certification at Serramonte Dodge, the Toyota President's Award at Melody

Toyota, and the Honda President's Award at Concord Honda.

TECHNOLOGICAL ADVANTAGE

On June 10th, 1998, FirstAmerica Automotive opened a modern, centralized service center at the company's headquarters in downtown San Francisco. Just as the trendiest multimedia companies that share the neighborhood attract top talent, the auto retailer's yen for the latest service equipment brings in master mechanics.

The center hums with top-notch technicians attending to vehicles in 41 service stalls and 22 lifts, and services all makes and models of domestic and foreign cars. Customers can make appointments on-line, and are invited to take

advantage of free pickup and delivery of their cars to and from downtown San Francisco.

As E-commerce heats up the retail market, Sonic continues to improve its use of the new technology. Its Web site, anyauto.com, provides pricing information, dealership locations, *Kelly Blue Book* values, service information, and links to other automotive pages. The no-hassle quote feature allows customers to request a quote for a specific make of car and indicate desired options and financing needs. A representative then calls with a quote and availability. Users can also conduct a used-car search based on make, model, year, and price range. anyauto.com offers news and reviews, financing, on-line parts ordering, insurance selection, quotes, and dealership locators.

The site's search engine displays photos and listings of potential matches and provides contact information. Customers also have access to discount coupons and special offers. For an additional fee, they can access the services of *Vehicle History Report* (VHR) to research used cars. Using powerful technology, this instantly decodes and compares each VIN the customer wants checked to a database of more than 30 million previously totaled and stolen cars, including information on vehicles submitted to insurance companies and state title and registration agencies.

Strategic Partnerships

S onic's financing partner, the Car Credit Network, further enhances the megadealership's ability to serve customers. The team at the Car Credit Network is dedicated to revolutionizing the way cars are purchased by accessing each of the franchises Sonic owns to offer any special financing program available at any given time. Customers can visit just one location and the Car Credit Network team will service any of their new or used car needs.

Like Sonic's sales force, what truly sets the Car Credit Network apart is its staff. Each associate is committed to serving the needs of clients "with an unprecedented level of honesty and integrity not formerly found within our industry," says Michael Christian, director of operations. "This may be the one time you walk into a store and someone recommends that you not purchase a car at this time.

"Our goal at the Car Credit Network is not to sell a car, but to educate consumers on all aspects of credit and financing—primarily as it relates to a car purchase," Christian says. With all of the information from Sonic franchises available on-screen, associates can determine the best program for each consumer in a matter of minutes. "We can even help customers whose credit is not perfect. In addition, we work with lenders

that most dealers aren't even aware exist," he says.

An Exciting New Beginning

P rice's passion for cars is matched only by his dedication to his customers and employees. In an industry Price admits "is not particularly known for its customer service," he sees his expansion goals and customer-service orientation as complementary aspirations. "Efficient, consolidated megadealers are the future of automobile retail-

ing," he says. "Customers benefit from increased buying choices, new on-line services, expanded financing options, and more professionally run service centers."

FirstAmerica Automotive's new venture as part of Sonic Automotive is sure to keep this business in high gear. Combined with the industry talent and experience represented by Sonic's group, Price's expert management team will forge the leading auto retailing company in the country.

In addition to selling new and used vehicles, Sonic Automotive provides a broad range of parts and accessories to complement its customers' vehicles.

Sonic Automotive has nearly 3,000 employees in the San Francisco Bay Area.

G

ENENTECH, INC., THE COMPANY THAT PIONEERED THE BIOTECHNOLOGY industry, is located at what is aptly named DNA Way in the city of South San Francisco. Since its visionary inception in 1976, Genentech has utilized recombinant DNA technology to discover and develop innovative therapies that address significant unmet medical needs.

Today, Genentech has seven biotechnology drugs on the market—one of the healthiest, most diverse product pipelines in the industry.

RECOMBINANT DNA AND THE BIRTH OF BIOTECH

Genentech was born out of the fortuitous combination of chance and necessity. In the early 1970s, Herbert Boyer, a biochemist from the University of California-San Francisco, and Stanley Cohen, a Stanford University geneticist, collaboratively invented a process that involved splicing and recombining desired segments from human DNA, and then transporting this genetic material to a host bacterial cell where it could be cloned. This breakthrough was the basis upon which the biotechnology industry was founded.

But without the addition of financial savvy and creativity, this new science might not have become commercially viable. In 1976, Robert Swanson, a young venture capitalist from Silicon Valley who believed in the potential of this recombinant DNA technology, met with Boyer to discuss their mutual conviction that this technology could meet a great medical need. Later that year, Boyer and Swanson had incorporated the world's first biotech company, Genentech, Inc.—a name derived from genetic engineering technology.

Despite skepticism from both the academic and the business communities, the young company's first goal was to synthesize human insulin. This was accomplished in 1978, and the product was licensed to Eli Lilly & Company to provide funding for further efforts. One year later, Genentech successfully employed its new technology to produce human growth hormone, and by 1985, Genentech had become the first company to bring a biotech medicine—recombinant growth hormone—the full distance from research to market.

IN BUSINESS FOR LIFE

Since its early years, Genentech has been recognized as a leading biotechnology company in terms of scientific achievement and new product development, bringing to market more biotechnology products than any other company in the world. Genentech focuses primarily on two areas of medicine—cardiovascular and oncology—but looks also at emerging therapies where there may be significant opportunities to fill a therapeutic void in important areas of medicine. All of the company's marketed products are used to treat serious or life-threatening diseases, such as heart attack, stroke, breast cancer, and cystic fibrosis—and all are designed to improve or extend the lives of patients.

For more than 13 years, Genentech's Activase®, a recombinant tissue plasminogen activator, has been used in emergency departments across the country to dissolve the clots that cause heart

attacks in hundreds of thousands of patients. In 1998, Genentech introduced a new monoclonal antibody, Herceptin®, for the treatment of certain patients with metastatic breast cancer, offering enhanced survival time to the most seriously ill breast cancer patients. Another of Genentech's BioOncology division's products is Rituxan®, used to treat a type of non-Hodgkin's lymphoma.

Genentech leads the market with its well-established line of three growth hormone products: Protropin®, Nutropin®, Nutropin AQ®, all used to treat growth hormone deficiencies in children and adults, including growth failure associated with chronic renal insufficiency prior to kidney transplantation and short stature associated with Turner's syndrome.

Genentech's commitment to improving medical care goes beyond product delivery to providing clinically focused resources to health care professionals, and providing unique patient services and programs. Since the launch of its first product, Genentech has had programs in place to ensure that U.S. patients who need its medicines receive them, regardless of ability to pay.

EMPLOYEES: THE PEOPLE WHO MAKE SUCCESS HAPPEN

Genentech prides itself in attracting and retaining the best people in all areas of the company. The company's founders, Boyer and Swanson, laid the foundation for this reality by insisting that their new company break with pharmaceutical tradition: While offering the benefits of a well-funded corporation, it would also offer significant scientific freedom. This approach was effective then, and continues to add significant value today.

With approximately 3,800 employees, the company seeks people with an entrepreneurial drive, and nurtures that drive by encouraging employees to become stockholders and by rewarding individual initiative and ideas. But because of the potential for so many people to benefit significantly from their work, employees have a special desire to succeed. With a work-those-genes conviction, they have been characterized as driven, committed, and passionate about making a difference in people's lives.

Creating a work environment that is responsive to the needs of employees and their families has always been one of Genentech's top priorities. Included in its list of employee benefits are one of the largest—and first—corporate-

sponsored day care centers in the country, a paid sabbatical program, excellent health care benefits, and employee stock purchase and stock option plans. For these and numerous other reasons, Genentech has appeared on *Fortune* magazine's annual list of 100 Best Companies to Work for in America, and *Working Mother* has listed Genentech nine times as one of its 100 Best Companies for Working Mothers.

The biotechnology industry is rapidly expanding and evolving, as this science becomes even more sophisticated and as more beneficial and life-extending applications of biotechnology therapies are discovered. With its drive to innovate, its extremely motivated employees, and its com-mitment to science, Genentech will remain a leader in this exciting industry. Says Genentech Chairman and CEO Arthur D. Levinson, "Through the next century, we remain in business for hope, in business for results, in business for life."

ULTRATECH STEPPER, INC.

 WO WEEKS AFTER HIS 1990 RETIREMENT FROM THE CONNECTICUT-BASED General Signal Corporation, Arthur W. Zafiropoulo was asked by his former employers to return in order to turn around the fortunes of the company's Ultratech Stepper division so it could be sold. Zafiropoulo accepted the challenge, thinking he would return to his

retirement in Boston after reviving the photolithography equipment maker, whose products are used worldwide in the fabrication of integrated circuits, micromachined devices, thin film heads for disk drives, and photomasks for the semiconductor industry.

Sixteen months later, Zafiropoulo had succeeded in making the company profitable, yet no buyers had emerged. Instead of waiting indefinitely for a buyer, Zafiropoulo, with financial assistance from Boston-based venture capital firm T.A. Associates, orchestrated a $7.8 million management buyout and took the helm of the company in March 1993. Six months later, the company went public.

Ultratech's success continues to grow. As of December 1999, the company boasts a market capitalization of more than $400 million and has installed more than 2,800 systems in 23 countries. Employees today number approximately 500, and facilities include manufacturing operations in San Jose, Massachusetts, and New Jersey, with sales, service, and applications support throughout the United States, Europe, and Asia.

Zafiropoulo is determined to see this growth trend continue. "To ensure our continued leadership in these volatile markets, we continue to invest in the development of new products," he says.

His commitment to research and development and his ability to identify the key enduring features in the next generation of technology have guided the company to its current position of strength and maturity.

INTEGRAL PROCESS FOR CHIP MANUFACTURING

Of the five global lithography competitors, Ultratech has the longest history. Products that use the chips manufactured on Ultratech systems pervade every aspect of modern life, from pagers to automobile air bag sensors to computer hard disk drives.

"Essentially, we make an expensive camera," says Zafiropoulo. "The machines produce row upon row of small images onto silicon wafers in a step-and-repeat process, from which the term 'stepper' is derived. We offer the best cost-effective solution to customers in our served markets, since our steppers are priced significantly less than the competition due to the lower cost of manufacturing our tools."

Ultratech Stepper features a broad product line. Its 1X stepper machines utilize a proprietary reflective technology versus the competitors' refractive technology. Ultratech's low-cost steppers offer high-volume manufacturers a significant cost advantage coupled with outstanding performance. Ultratech's tools can mix and match with any other stepper in the world to maximize efficiency and cost savings for the customer.

A LEADER IN CUSTOMER SATISFACTION

Ultratech's customers have approved the efficiency of the company's products, leading to the its highest honor yet. In the results of a 1999 semiconductor industry customer survey performed by VLSI Research Inc., Ultratech Stepper received first-place ranking for small suppliers of wafer processing equipment. In addition, the company received the highest overall rating for lithography companies in both small and large supplier categories in a period that was most noted for its cyclical downturn. The award reflects the company's 20-year commitment to product quality and reiterates its stellar reputation for customer service.

Looking to the future, Ultratech continues to invest in new technologies. The Verdant Technologies division located in San Jose is developing an advanced laser thermal processing technology, which the company believes is the best solution to ultrashallow-junction annealing requirements at or below .13mm.

"For Ultratech Stepper to reach critical mass in order to become a significant worldwide player in our industry, our vision is to be $1 billion in sales," says Zafiropoulo. "We understand how to get to that point. Indeed, we have the infrastructure to reach that point and have continued to invest in technologies to achieve this goal in the foreseeable future. We are extremely excited at what we see the future to be for Ultratech Stepper."

CLOCKWISE FROM TOP: ULTRATECH ENGINEERS TEST THE ASSEMBLED STEPPERS USING STANDARD PHOTOLITHOGRAPHIC PROCESSES.

THE OPTICAL PATH OF THE ULTRATECH 1X STEPPERS INCLUDES A PRIMARY MIRROR, PRISM, AND LENSES.

A MULTISTATION ROBOT MOVES MATERIALS ONTO A STEPPER.

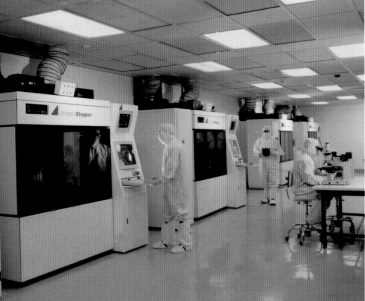

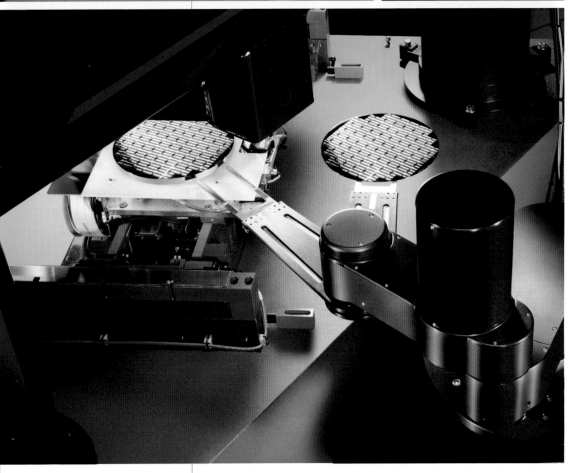

Centigram Communications

B Y THE END OF THE FIRST DECADE IN 2000, CONSUMERS WILL BE USING their cell phones to send and retrieve E-mail messages, faxes, video mail, and voicemail messages. This scenario exemplifies the concept of integrated communications—in which dominant forms of messaging can be sent and retrieved from any one of a number

of devices—at the heart of Centigram Communications' future.

Established in 1980 as a maker of text-to-speech products, San Jose-based Centigram entered the messaging communications business in 1990. The company made its initial public offering of common stock in 1991.

A leading provider of advanced wireless and wireline messaging and communications management systems, Centigram delivers solutions to service providers in the telecommunications sector by integrating voice and fax on its Series 6 communication server, and by providing access to these messages through phone, personal computer, or mobile device.

Centigram Solutions

Centigram's revenue-enhancing services are provided in 12 languages and dialects: American, Australian, British, and New Zealand English; Brazilian Portuguese; Cantonese; Danish; French Canadian; German;

Latin American and Mexican Spanish; and Mandarin.

The firm's communications solutions offer an array of choices. VoiceMemo is a feature-rich voice-messaging product that provides telephone answering, call processing, paging, and audiotext services. FaxMemo integrates with VoiceMemo to provide fax store-and-forward capabilities, while PageMemo features store-and-forward applications for pagers. CallAgent functions as a call-processing, automated attendant.

Smart Forwarding enables subscribers to receive calls to their home telephone number or to their mobile phones or work phone. Unified Inbox provides users with access to voicemail and fax mail messages from any standards-based E-mail client application, such as Microsoft Outlook, Netscape Communicator, or Qualcomm Eudora.

Short Message Service allows callers to deliver Internet and other real-time content to the

mobile user's handset. EasyAdmin is a comprehensive set of system management tools; Internet Call Manager ensures that users don't miss important calls while surfing the net; and MESA Net works as an end-to-end digital networking solution.

Key Word: Integrated

Most of our competitors will sell their service piecemeal on various servers," says Bob Puette, CEO and chairman. "But telcos want all that, if possible, on the fewest number of systems, just to be able to manage it. They'd like to have fewer vendors. So we focus on integrating those functions."

Centigram's system is scalable to meet service provider customers' needs as their business grows and succeeds. "Most of our competitors have much larger systems and can't scale down as small as we can," Puette says.

This does not mean Centigram clients are small. On the contrary, the company's 200 to 250 customers include such giants as Sprint and Bell Atlantic in the United States, and many others around the world. The company counts as its partners such industry leaders as Motorola, Lucent, Siemens, Telecom Networks, Eriline (Brazil), Alcatel, and Cable and Wireless.

With 2,500 installed systems around the world, Centigram supports slightly more wireless than wireline business at the dawn of the new millennium, which is sure to change as telecommunications technology leapfrogs onto the Internet.

Bridging Old Telephony

Exploding use of the Internet and E-mail, an ever more mobile society, and a growing consumer desire to stay connected have fueled demand for unified and simplified messaging and communication services. For

JONATHAN POSTAL

JONATHAN POSTAL

many end users, the Web will become a common interface for managing all voice, text, and video messaging services.

Centigram provides the critical technological foundation to juggle the demands of the new suite of services. Meanwhile, Puette envisions Centigram's providing the bridge between the new Internet-based communications services and traditional telephony. In late 1999, Centigram introduced Internet Call Manager to do just that.

"Say you're one of the 91 percent of the people in the United States with one telephone line at home," says Puette. "What happens when you get on the Internet? Those three minutes you spend on the phone each day turn into three hours. What do you do if you need to receive phone calls?"

With Internet Call Manager, a small, pop-up menu appears on the screen to alert the user when someone is calling. The technology gives customers several choices: They can answer the call and disconnect the Internet session, activate the voice mailbox or answering machine, or route the call to another phone.

This is all accomplished over the Internet, where one-way communications is not a problem. "In more technical terms," Puette continues, "we've interfaced the world of circuit-switched telephony with the Internet world, and made them work together in a way that allows consumers to retain one phone line and still access the whole wide world of the Web."

Puette puts the global picture in perspective. "Half of the people in the world have never made a phone call," he says.

"If you look at the teledensity in China, you see that of 1.3 billion people, the number of telephones per person is less than 10 percent. That adds up to a lot of opportunity out there."

A LEADING PROVIDER OF ADVANCED WIRELESS AND WIRELINE MESSAGING AND COMMUNICATIONS MANAGEMENT SYSTEMS, CENTIGRAM DELIVERS SOLUTIONS TO SERVICE PROVIDERS IN THE TELECOMMUNICATIONS SECTOR BY INTEGRATING VOICE AND FAX ON ITS SERIES 6 COMMUNICATION SERVER, AND BY PROVIDING ACCESS TO THESE MESSAGES THROUGH PHONE, PERSONAL COMPUTER, OR MOBILE DEVICE.

HILL GLAZIER ARCHITECTS

BASED IN PALO ALTO, HILL GLAZIER ARCHITECTS HAS GROWN WORLDWIDE in scope and reputation since its founding in 1980. Partners John Hill and Robert Glazier have taken their firm to national and international prominence by specializing in luxury hotels and resorts, golf clubhouses, and spas around the world. ◆ Chances are, subscribers to esteemed travel publications—*Travel & Leisure, Condé Nast Traveler*, or the *New York Times* travel section, for example—have read about the firm's work and seen photographs of it.

INSPIRATION ON-SITE

In the cookie-cutter world of chain hotels, Hill Glazier creations stand out as exemplary structures of quality and elegance that echo local architectural character and highlight natural site features.

"When people go to a resort, they want to feel like they're on location, not back at home," says Hill. "So what we do becomes very much a crafting of an experience for people. We try to create a sense of place. As a result, all of our projects are unique."

"All of our work is inspired by the site in which it exists," Glazier says. "For example, our project in Dubai reflects the historic architecture of the Mediterranean and Middle East." To be completed in 2001 at the edge of the Arabian Sea in the United Arab Emirates, the opulent Four Seasons Hotel Dubai is designed in the image of a Moroccan palace with a variety of distinctly Islamic details.

Another well-known project, the Loews Ventana Canyon Resort in Tucson, is located on a plateau in the Santa Catalina Mountains. The award-winning resort complements the natural surroundings of the Sonoran Desert with its vertically textured masonry blocks that recall the forms of nearby saguaro cacti and the colors of natural rock formations. The 400 rooms step up the hillside's natural contours to allow guests to experience the rugged setting, including the site's most dramatic feature—an 80-foot waterfall.

"A lot of these resorts have a story behind them," says Hill. For example, the celebrated Shutters on the Beach in Santa Monica, completed in 1994, is "designed to feel like your grandmother's beach house." Popular with both domestic and international celebrities, the property is one of the leading hotels of the world. Crisp white shutters and trim, broad eaves and brackets, and French doors leading onto terraces elegantly carry out the resort's informal beach theme.

"The client asked that we design the building to look as

HILL GLAZIER ARCHITECTS' FOUR SEASONS RESORT AT HUALALAI IN KONA, "BLENDS IN WITH SEA AND SKY SO WELL THAT IT SEEMS BARELY THERE—EXCEPT WHEN YOU WANT IT TO BE," SAYS *TRAVEL & LEISURE* MAGAZINE.

HILL GLAZIER HAS AN IMPRESSIVE PORTFOLIO THAT INCLUDES WORLD-CLASS RESORTS ALL OVER THE GLOBE, INCLUDING THE HYATT REGENCY HILL COUNTRY RESORT IN SAN ANTONIO (LEFT) AND THE RITZ CARLTON HALF MOON BAY RESORT IN HALF MOON BAY, CALIFORNIA (RIGHT).

though it had always been there," Hill explains. "Our inspiration came from the turn-of-the-century beach bungalows once found along the Santa Monica and Malibu coast. To achieve the intimate scale, the hotel was designed to appear as three small buildings rather than one large massing."

DOING THEIR HOMEWORK

No matter where in the world they have projects, Hill Glazier architects do their homework. "We spend time at the site, walking the site itself," says Glazier. "We also spend time researching the local vernacular, so we can design our resorts in keeping with historical building traditions and cultures."

The firm is so successful at incorporating local features into its projects that one of them was called "The Invisible Resort" by *Travel & Leisure* magazine: "The Four Seasons Hualalai . . . blends in with sea and sky so well that it seems barely there—except when you want it to be," says the review.

Inspired by the architecture of traditional Hawaiian villages, the resort, completed in 1996 in Kona, fulfills the concept of *kipuka*—a lushly landscaped oasis paradise surrounded by molten lava flows. The lobby, restaurants, and spa are designed as open-air pavilions to allow for unobstructed views of the Pacific Ocean. The golf clubhouse allows for views to the 18th fairway of the Jack Nicklaus Signature Golf Course. And guest rooms, organized around four informal courtyards, feature ocean views, private terraces, and traditional Hawaiian furnishings.

The resort's success has in turn led to the client's adjacent real estate success. In fact, all of Hill Glazier's resorts are extremely cost efficient, which helps to improve clients' bottom lines.

SPECIALIZING IN EXCELLENCE

A relatively small firm with only a 50-person staff, Hill Glazier nevertheless ranks fourth largest in the world in its hotel and resort design. The ranking is powered by repeat and referral clients—comprised of such five-star names as Ritz-Carlton, Four Seasons, Hyatt Regency, and Westin—with projects in such exotic locales as Tobago,

the Bahamas, Jerusalem, Canary Islands, Egypt, West Indies, Thailand, Guam, Saipan, New Caledonia, and Japan.

As successful as the firm has become, Hill Glazier has no plans to expand. "We have made a conscious decision to keep the firm the size that it is, because if it gets any bigger, Bob and I can't get involved in each project," says Hill. "We want to maintain the consistent quality of our designs, for which our firm has become known."

INFORMIX CORPORATION

BASED IN MENLO PARK, INFORMIX® CORPORATION SPECIALIZES IN ADVANCED information management technologies that help enterprises in the i.Economy solve their most complex business problems, build unique strategic advantage, and generate new revenue through both analytic and Web solutions. ◆ Organizations today are drowning in mountains of data, and the Web is only adding to the chaos. Companies are experiencing explosive growth in the number of transactions, Web clicks, and documents of all types. Informix leverages 20 years of expertise in the most advanced, scalable, online transaction processing (OLTP) engines and leading business intelligence solutions to create end-to-end Web solutions that dramatically increase companies' productivity, lower their cost of doing business, and help them deliver new products and services. Informix solutions integrate easily with companies' existing applications, and do not require armies of consultants to implement.

INFORMIX SOLUTIONS FOR THE I.ECONOMY

Informix has grown to become one of the most influential and trusted providers of information management solutions worldwide. The company's solutions are vital in many industries and are exceptionally suited for retail, telecommunications, financial services, health care, manufacturing, media, and publishing.

For 20 years, Informix has pioneered advanced database technology. The company invented the first open relational database and introduced the first commercial object-relational database, allowing businesses to process, store, and retrieve mission-critical data. Today, its advanced engines and complete solutions for transactions, business intelligence, and the Internet help many of the world's leading companies turn the chaos created by mountains of data into something very valuable: a strategic advantage.

In order to be successful in the fast, explosive, and unforgiving i.Economy, companies need to be able to get to market quickly, have Web sites that are fully scalable, and operate at the lowest possible cost. In the summer of 1999, Informix introduced Informix Internet Foundation.2000™, which became the only platform built for the Internet from the ground up. Foundation.2000™ turns companies into true Web-based enterprises with industrial-strength transactions and dynamic content management, supporting every Internet development standard.

In order to help companies build their Web sites quickly and cost effectively, while still delivering the most scalable and powerful technologies, Informix has developed end-to-end integrated solutions. Informix i.Reach™ is a Web site deployment solution that companies can use to build Web sites, as well as enable content authors to easily publish and maintain their own content—thereby reducing tenfold the cost of maintaining Web sites.

A complete, rapidly deploy-

WITH HEADQUARTERS IN MENLO PARK, INFORMIX® CORPORATION HELPS COMPANIES TURN THE SPEED OF A REAL-TIME ECONOMY INTO A STRATEGIC ADVANTAGE WITH INDUSTRIAL-STRENGTH, SCALABLE SOLUTIONS THAT LET COMPANIES GET TO MARKET SOONER THAN THE COMPETITION.

able e-commerce solution, Informix i.Sell™ is an electronic storefront solution integrating database and applications server technology with e-commerce software, tools, consulting, and services. i.Sell features dynamic product merchandising and can handle massive numbers of transactions and personalize each customer relationship based on past behavior patterns.

Information management is about more than words and numbers—most businesses depend on digital assets, including product photos, presentations, and videos. Informix has developed the only complete content management solution that addresses all of these needs. Informix Media360™ allows companies to archive, store, manage, repurpose, and distribute their rich data files easily and efficiently. Many of the world's leading media companies have come to rely on Informix technology for their content management needs.

Informix Business Intelligence Solutions

Informix delivers end-to-end, business-critical intelligence solutions based on advanced analytic engines. Its turnkey decision support solution, Decision Frontier™, is assembled from Informix Extended Parallel Server™ and Informix Red Brick® Decision Server™–the world's fastest, most flexible

and scalable analytic engines. Informix is one of the leading companies offering world-class decision-support solutions for both enterprise data warehouses and data marts. It designs these solutions specifically for transparent, integrated data warehousing in thoroughly heterogeneous environments. In addition, the company has added a complete set of powerful tools to extract, transform, and load the right data into the warehouse or data mart. Then, advanced analytic and data-mining applications take over,

uncovering business insights and helping businesses work better, faster, and smarter.

World-Class Service and Support

Informix has invested considerable resources to create a world-class customer services organization that includes around-the-clock support, direct access to engineers, more than 15 separate ISO 9000 certifications, and some of the best metrics in the industry.

Providing consistent support from geographically dispersed locations, Informix's world-class service is based on building long-term customer relationships, developing an understanding of customers' business objectives, and having a vested interest in customers' ongoing success. The firm continues to maintain a vanguard market role, a position that contributes to its growth and success and leads to high levels of customer satisfaction.

Succeeding in today's i.Economy promises greater rewards and poses greater risks than ever before. Informix helps companies turn the speed of a real-time economy into a strategic advantage with industrial-strength, scalable solutions that let companies get to market sooner than the competition.

INFORMIX HAS CREATED A WORLD-CLASS CUSTOMER SERVICES ORGANIZATION THAT INCLUDES AROUND-THE-CLOCK SUPPORT, DIRECT ACCESS TO ENGINEERS, MORE THAN 15 SEPARATE ISO 9000 CERTIFICATIONS, AND SOME OF THE BEST METRICS IN THE INDUSTRY.

INFORMIX SPECIALIZES IN ADVANCED INFORMATION MANAGEMENT TECHNOLOGIES THAT HELP ENTERPRISES IN THE i.ECONOMY SOLVE THEIR MOST COMPLEX BUSINESS PROBLEMS, BUILD UNIQUE STRATEGIC ADVANTAGE, AND GENERATE NEW REVENUE THROUGH BOTH ANALYTIC AND WEB SOLUTIONS.

Hyundai Electronics America

QUALITY AND CUSTOMER RESPONSIVENESS HAVE EARNED HYUNDAI ELECTRONICS AMERICA A LEADERSHIP POSITION AS THE WORLD'S LARGEST DYNAMIC RANDOM ACCESS MEMORY CHIP SUPPLIER (BELOW RIGHT).

HYUNDAI ELECTRONICS AMERICA IS HEADQUARTERED IN SAN JOSE WITH TWO 95,000-SQUARE-FOOT BUILDINGS THAT HOUSE SALES AND MARKETING, RESEARCH AND DEVELOPMENT, AND ADMINISTRATIVE DEPARTMENTS (BELOW LEFT).

ESTABLISHED IN 1983 TO PROVIDE A SALES AND MARKETING PRESENCE FOR Hyundai Electronics in the United States, Hyundai Electronics America (HEA) and its subsidiaries employ a workforce of 2,000 throughout the nation, including 200 at the San Jose headquarters. In 1998, revenues for HEA, including subsidiaries, exceeded $2.4 billion in markets throughout the United States and South America. From its location in the heart of Silicon Valley, HEA not only contributes high-technology leadership to the area's computer giants, but also serves as the technology pulse for its parent company in Ichon, South Korea.

Memory at Hyundai's Core

Hyundai Electronics' high-quality product line centers on memory products, including dynamic random access memory (DRAM), static random access memory (SRAM), and flash memory. The company also manufactures application-specific integrated circuit (ASIC) components. Other high-tech products are manufactured and sold by subsidiary companies.

The world's number one maker of DRAM, Hyundai supplies more than 20 percent of the market with computer memory. DRAM chips are essential components of personal computers, workstations, and servers.

Hyundai Electronics' low-power SRAM uses low voltage to retain memory. Ideal for mobile communications and battery backup applications, SRAM retains important data with a minimum amount of power. An area of tremendous growth for SRAM products is in telecommunications, networking, and mobile communications, where speed and power constraints are an issue.

Flash technology, different from DRAM and SRAM, retains memory when power is removed. Flash memory does not require batteries to retain data, and is particularly useful in such products as digital cameras and cellular telephones. Hyundai's high-performance flash memory family serves increasingly sophisticated applications that are fueling demand for higher densities and faster memory. Typical applications include disk drives, printers, modems, networking equipment, telecommunications products, PC memory cards, digital answering machines, and games.

Hyundai Electronics' System Integrated Circuits Business Unit addresses the growing need for ASICs. Using advanced process technologies, combined with superior design support and a range of packaging options, Hyundai's ASICs offer high performance and design flexibility that are cost competitive in the marketplace.

Hyundai Semiconductor America is HEA's DRAM fabrication subsidiary in the United States. Based in Eugene, the semiconductor production facility was the result of an investment of more than $2 billion. HEA's subsidiary Hyundai DynaLogic focuses on the research and development of advanced semiconductor products, such as memory, merged-memory/logic, and systems-on-a-chip devices. HEA's subsidiary MMC Technology, formed in 1998, develops and manufactures hard-drive media disks. And CyberLANE

Inc., established in 1997 as a wholly owned subsidiary of HEA, offers wireless communications solutions.

GAINING STRENGTH AND FOCUS

HEA's parent company is Hyundai Electronics Industries Co., Ltd., the world's largest DRAM memory chip maker. Hyundai Electronics not only endured the Asian financial crisis of the late 1990s, but also emerged stronger and more focused than ever before.

"The Asia crisis was business Darwinism at its best," says Ross Gaisor, senior manager of corporate communications at HEA. "It forced us to invest wisely, work efficiently, focus on core product offerings, and enhance our business practices—resulting in high-quality, cost-competitive products."

The Asia crisis also precipitated the reengineering of parent Hyundai Electronics into a global semiconductor powerhouse, focused on producing quality products, maintaining customer satisfaction, and providing cost-competitive semiconductor solutions. Toward this strategic goal, the company acquired LG Semicon Co., Ltd. in 1999 to create the Hyundai MicroElectronics Group, effectively combining Korea's leading chip makers into the world's largest DRAM supplier in terms of production capacity.

WORLD-CLASS CUSTOMERS

Hyundai's determination to become a leading supplier of high-quality memory products has paid off in increased sales to existing customers, who are leading technology companies around the world.

Primarily, HEA provides memory components to U.S. and South American computer and workstation original equipment manufacturers. IBM, Compaq, Dell, Hewlett-Packard, and Gateway are blue-chip examples. HEA has expanded its target market to other high-technology fields, such as networking, communications, and graphics. In these areas, clients include 3Com, Diamond, and Motorola.

In recognition for its high-quality products, HEA has won numerous awards from valued customers. Another source of pride for the company is its recognition for supply chain management excellence, resulting in many Supplier of the Year honors.

By maintaining inventory in close proximity to client factories, Hyundai products are deployed from a just-in-time hub on a consignment-on-site basis. The system shifts inventory risk to the supplier and allows computer manufacturer customers to receive shipment on the shop floor within two to eight hours. Using on-line technology and sophisticated warehouse management systems, HEA reduced transaction time by 75 percent within 18 months.

"Measures of our success will come through technological leadership and customer service," says Gaisor, "so that as we introduce new products in the marketplace, we become leaders throughout the semiconductor industry. That will mark how well our customers value us as a company."

McCown De Leeuw & Co., Inc.

WHEN GEORGE McCOWN AND DAVID DE LEEUW FOUNDED A PRIvate investment firm in 1984, the leverage buyout industry had just begun to take shape. Only a few dozen companies around the world had been formed with significant outside capital to acquire mature operating companies with a combination of equity and debt.

Today, industry estimates suggest more than 1,000 such firms, and a pool of capital that has grown from a few hundred million dollars to about $500 billion. McCown De Leeuw & Co. (MDC) has grown, too, from its two founders to a staff of 22 investment professionals with offices in New York City and Menlo Park. Today, the firm boasts $1.2 billion of capital under management, and remains focused on buying and building industry-leading middle market companies in partnership with management.

BUILDING COMPANIES THAT MAKE A DIFFERENCE

In an industry that quickly earned a reputation for putting return on investment ahead of most other objectives, MDC was founded on the premise of being good people to do business with. "From the beginning, ours was the antithesis of the cutthroat business model," says McCown, cofounder and managing director. "It's not that we're an altruistic firm; generating an outstanding return for our investors is critical to us. But we believe that this can best be achieved if companies are run in such a way as to make the experience for the people they touch a positive one." In the mid-1990s, this goal evolved into the current articulation of the firm's mission: Building Companies That Make a Difference.

At first unsure how the investment community would react to such a lofty mission statement, the firm's partners were astounded when its effort to raise its $400 million fourth fund garnered commitments of more than two times that amount. The firm capped the fund at $750 million, an appropriate amount given its strategy; clearly, the articulation of its mission had struck a chord.

To MDC, implementing its mission means balancing the interests of all of a company's stakeholders—employees, customers, suppliers, families, and communities, as well as its shareholders. It also means that every one of MDC's portfolio companies must be driven by a mission they passionately believe in, and one that is compatible with MDC's goals.

"We believe that what we do matters more than just making money for our investors and ourselves," says Steve Zuckerman, a managing director. "We work hard to reflect that in how we manage our own firm, and encourage all of our portfolio companies to do the same."

CAPITALIZING ON A COMPANY'S FULL POTENTIAL

MDC's office in Menlo Park on Sand Hill Road, known in Silicon Valley as Venture Capital Row, is surrounded by venture capital firms. While they share the desire to invest in and build great companies, and MDC counts as founding investors a number of prominent venture capitalists, the company does not invest in start-up ventures.

"We generally look to acquire companies valued between $50 million and $300 million, and then grow them aggressively," says Zuckerman. "And all we do is buy and build. Very few firms in the buyout business pursue this growth model as exclusively as we do."

MDC actively searches for certain characteristics in companies with which to partner. For a variety of reasons, many successful businesses are unable to take full advantage of opportunities before them. These companies may be entrepreneurial enterprises ready to enter their next phases of growth, family-run businesses whose founders would like to harvest their investments, or corporate divisions that simply no longer reflect the strategic focus of the parent company.

Among MDC's current portfolio of 14 companies, four are based in the Bay Area. MDC founded Fitness Holdings, Inc., the holding company for 24-Hour Fitness, in December, 1994, to recaptitalize the dominant fitness center chain in Northern California and to aggressively consolidate its industry. With the newly formed Fitness Holdings Worldwide, based in San Francisico, MDC combines Fitness Holdings, Inc. with Fitness Holdings Europe and Fitness Holdings Asia to create the largest owner and operator of fitness clubs in the world.

Walnut Creek-based Distribution Dynamics, Inc. (DDI) began as a distributor of industrial fasteners. MDC's involvement in 1990 led to DDI's expanded scope to become a dramatically larger, value-added distributor of C-class production line supplies to original equipment manufacturers (OEMs).

Headquartered in Fremont, E-M-Solutions is a leading provider of electronic contract manufacturing services to high-end data processing and data networking OEMs. The company represents the platform from which MDC has begun to consolidate the highly fragmented electronic contract manufacturing industry.

Headquartered in San Francisco, Aurora Foods (NYSE: AOR) is a buildup of leading grocery brands such as Mrs. Butterworth's and Log Cabin syrup and pancake mix; Duncan Hines baking goods; and frozen food products including Van de Kamp's, Mrs. Paul's, Aunt Jemima, and Celeste. With the help of MDC, Aurora continues to aggressively grow its portfolio.

GIVING BACK TO THE COMMUNITY

Consistent with its mission, MDC believes in giving back to the community. While the majority of charitable giving is done individually by the firm's principals, MDC believes corporate activity is also important. A fund is available for employees to direct firm contributions to community activities, and every young professional is expected to assume at least one leadership role within a community or charitable organization with which MDC maintains a regular donor relationship.

MDC hopes it can be a role model for the buyout industry and the business community in general, through its conviction that having a heart and noble goals can be good for the bottom line.

IN DECEMBER 1994, MDC CREATED FITNESS HOLDINGS, INC. TO RECAPITALIZE THE DOMINANT FITNESS CENTER CHAIN IN NORTHERN CALIFORNIA AND TO AGGRESSIVELY CONSOLIDATE ITS INDUSTRY. IN FEWER THAN FIVE YEARS, FITNESS HOLDINGS HAD MADE 25 ACQUISITIONS REPRESENTING 150 CLUBS, OPENED 81 NEW LOCATIONS, AND INCREASED BY EIGHT TO 10 TIMES ITS STORE COUNT, REVENUES, AND CASH FLOW (TOP).

WITH THE HELP OF MDC, SAN FRANCISCO-BASED AURORA FOODS—A BUILDUP OF LEADING GROCERY BRANDS SUCH AS MRS. BUTTERWORTH'S AND LOG CABIN SYRUP AND PANCAKE MIX; DUNCAN HINES BAKING GOODS; AND FROZEN FOOD PRODUCTS INCLUDING VAN DE KAMP'S, MRS. PAUL'S, AUNT JEMIMA, AND CELESTE—CONTINUES TO AGGRESSIVELY GROW ITS PORTFOLIO (BOTTOM).

HILL PHYSICIANS MEDICAL GROUP

S TARTED IN 1984, HILL PHYSICIANS MEDICAL GROUP IS ENTERING THE new millennium as one of the largest medical groups in Northern California, and the largest individual practice association (IPA) in the nation. Hill Physicians serves nearly 400,000 HMO enrollees throughout Northern California with 2,500 physicians and 20 affiliated

hospitals. The medical organization is committed to quality, afford-ability, and accountability.

THE BEST OF BOTH WORLDS

I n the early 1970s, business school graduate Steve McDermott designed and es-tablished regional emergency medical systems that created trauma centers, paramedics, and the 911 system throughout the San Francisco Bay Area. A few years later, he helped organize emergency departments through-out California, in the process building the largest emergency medical group in the state.

The experience in emergency medicine taught McDermott that creating large-scale medical groups and regional medical de-livery systems was feasible. Though his concept is now widely accepted, 15 years ago, this view

was a radical departure from tra-ditional medical practice.

In 1984, the newly formed Hill Physicians Medical Group, then located in Oakland, expressed interest in sharing McDermott's vision. "We believed there was an opportunity to create a regional medical delivery system of private doctors that would compete with Kaiser Permanente and deliver high-quality, cost-effective medical care to a very wide geographic area," says McDermott, Hill Physi-cians' executive director. Over the years, he has received numerous requests from doctors and hospitals to help them organize physicians.

Insisting that strength lay in unity, McDermott resisted the creation of many small groups. "That's not efficient, and you can't create sys-tems and infrastructure without size and scope," he says. "Instead, little by little, we were able to convince doctors in different com-munities to become members of Hill Physicians."

As an IPA, Hill Physicians offers doctors a middle ground between the confines of a clinic practice, exemplified by early HMOs, and the isolation of solo independent practice. "We're able to cull out the best of both worlds: highly moti-vated professionals working in

their own offices, yet connected in teams in a way that is more consumer friendly and cost effective," states Arthur Stanten, M.D., a general surgeon who has served as chairman of Hill Physicians since 1992.

Fifteen years after Hill Physicians' founding, the health care industry had undergone tumultuous upheaval, imploding with the consolidation of insurance companies and hospital corporations. Many physician groups have gone out of business, casualties that drowned in the wake of the industry's churning waters. A primary factor in Hill Physicians' success has been its focus on its customers, its disciplined management structure, and its demand for mutual accountability among all participants in the system.

RETIRING THE PAPER TRAIL

Hill Physicians is now harnessing the power of the Internet to further strengthen the connection between its partners. Working with Healtheon Corporation, the pioneering provider of advanced Internet-based solutions for the health care industry, Hill Physicians is electronically connecting its member doctors to provide information in a timely manner to all parties involved in a patient's treatment. Through Healtheon, Hill Physicians is able to accept electronic claims from physician offices, validate the claims for eligibility and authorization before

they enter Hill Physicians' claims processing system, and provide on-line claim status reports back to the physicians.

"Current medical care delivery is a paper-based, 19th-century modality in which information is generally not available at the time you need it," says Hill Physicians' Chief Medical Officer Bill DeWolf, M.D. "What we're implementing is on-line, real-time access to clinical information that removes the inefficiencies of the paper-based system and enhances the ability to make clinical decisions."

CONNECTING IS KEY

Hill Physicians' ongoing goal is to bring an integrated approach to the medical delivery process. In keeping with this aim, the company has created a senior leadership position devoted to the concept: the director

of integrative medicine, who is responsible for building programs that connect the mind, body, and spirit, and who examines ways in which Eastern and Western medicine can intersect for holistic healing.

Patient information and education constitute a large part of the integrated philosophy. Toward that end, the medical group developed a health education program in 1991 to educate and inform patients about wellness and disease management. Tom Long, M.D., chief of pediatrics for Hill Physicians, explains, "Fundamentally, this leads the patient and his or her family to feel more empowered by the interaction with our doctors. It's important to remove the vulnerability and powerlessness they typically feel."

The Bay Area is a hub in the World Wide Web, and medical information is the number one use. Hill is meeting consumer interest for on-line information through its interactive Web site, located at www.hillphysicians.com.

Hill Physicians is sensitive to the criticism of HMOs. However, it sees managed care as the catalyst for improving quality, increasing preventive efforts, and creating medical systems that are more responsive to the consumer/ patient. "The concept of managed care is a good one," McDermott says. "In fact, managed care is pro-consumer and holds us all accountable to standards of quality and affordability. Hill Physicians' job is to deliver on that promise."

"CURRENT MEDICAL CARE DELIVERY IS A PAPER-BASED, 19TH-CENTURY MODALITY IN WHICH INFORMATION IS GENERALLY NOT AVAILABLE AT THE TIME YOU NEED IT," SAYS (FROM LEFT) HILL PHYSICIANS' CHIEF MEDICAL OFFICER BILL DEWOLF, M.D., WITH CHARLES FISKE, M.D., AND DEBORAH WAFER, M.D. "WHAT WE'RE IMPLEMENTING IS ON-LINE, REAL-TIME ACCESS TO CLINICAL INFORMATION THAT REMOVES THE INEFFICIENCIES OF THE PAPER-BASED SYSTEM AND ENHANCES THE ABILITY TO MAKE CLINICAL DECISIONS."

EXAMINING BABY JORDAN RACKMIL, TOM LONG, M.D., CHIEF OF PEDIATRICS FOR HILL PHYSICIANS, EXPLAINS, "FUNDAMENTALLY, INFORMATION AND EDUCATION LEAD THE PATIENT AND HIS OR HER FAMILY TO FEEL MORE EMPOWERED BY THE INTERACTION WITH OUR DOCTORS. IT'S IMPORTANT TO REMOVE THE VULNERABILITY AND POWERLESSNESS THEY SOMETIMES FEEL."

ILINX WAS FOUNDED IN 1984 TO PIONEER WHAT WAS THEN A REVO-lutionary new kind of semiconductor, the field programmable gate array (FPGA), a blank slate of silicon on which customers, using software tools, could very quickly create the logic for their own unique integrated circuits. Today, Xilinx offers an extensive array of programmable logic solutions, and its products are regarded as enabling technologies throughout the electronics industry.

Xilinx became a publicly traded company in 1990, and over the years has established an uninterrupted record of financial growth, return on shareholder investment, profitability, market expansion, and technical achievement. Headquartered in San Jose, Xilinx employs about 1,600 people worldwide and has annual revenues approaching $1 billion. The company has facilities throughout North America, Europe, and Asia-Pacific.

Customers for Xilinx products include U.S. technology giants such as Cisco Systems, Hewlett-Packard, IBM, Lucent Technologies, and Motorola, plus international leaders such as Alcatel, Ericsson, Fujitsu, Nokia, Nortel, Siemens, and Sony.

Revolutionizing FPGAs

Xilinx invented FPGAs to give designers of electronic equipment—data processing and communications systems, for example—more flexibility in creating custom-integrated circuits. Built on memory technology, FPGAs are standard parts that can be reprogrammed an infinite number of times using software tools and a PC or workstation. This permits designers to quickly refine their circuits and test them on a functioning part.

With FPGAs, companies can reduce development cycles by weeks or months, and get their products to market sooner than they would by manufacturing mass quantities of custom chips with fixed circuits. Until recently, this flexibility came at a cost: FPGAs were three to four times more expensive, and not as fast, as fixed-circuit logic chips. All that has changed, however.

"As the industry's leading innovator, Xilinx has always enhanced the capabilities of its programmable logic products and consistently reduced costs for customers," says Xilinx President and CEO Wim Roelandts. "But in 1996, we embarked on a new strategy of being first to implement the most advanced semiconductor manufacturing processes. In a short amount of time, that move has accelerated our product advancements tremendously."

THE MAIN XILINX CAMPUS IN SAN JOSE WAS RECENTLY EXPANDED AND IS HOME TO MORE THAN 1,000 EMPLOYEES.

Now Xilinx's programmable logic devices are smaller, faster, and less expensive than ever before, while offering unprecedented new levels of logic capacity and performance. From 1997 to 1999, for example, Xilinx increased the logic capacity of its FPGAs 20-fold—from about 100,000 to more than 2 million logic gates in its newest Virtex-E family of FPGAs. This technical achievement is rapidly expanding the appeal of the company's products, which traditionally had been geared toward high-value, low-volume products such as large telecommunications switches, test and measurement instruments, and data processing systems.

Today, however, Xilinx programmable logic chips can be found in a number of products, including personal computers, network servers, portable telephones, DVD players, medical diagnostic systems, Internet routers, and satellite stations. On one hand, Xilinx products address the needs of customers who require the very highest levels of performance to build products such as the next generation of wireless communications systems. On the other, Xilinx products that are designed for high-volume, low-cost applications are allowing more and more equipment makers to

compete in the price-sensitive consumer electronics market.

Xilinx has developed its broad portfolio of offerings by investing tens of millions of dollars annually in research and development. The company leads the programmable logic industry in its spending on new product development, and typically earmarks 12 to 14 percent of revenue for research and development.

"Our vision is really quite simple," says Roelandts. "As we continue to refine our technology, we believe programmable logic will be used in virtually every kind of electronic product within the next decade."

TECHNOLOGY FOR THE 21ST CENTURY

Meanwhile, Xilinx has laid the foundation for an exciting new set of applications, one that marries the ability of Xilinx chips to be reprogrammed remotely with the ballooning number of networks around the world, including the Internet. This confluence of technologies is ushering in a revolutionary model of product design and commerce that could dramatically slow product obsolescence.

A number of Xilinx on-line, upgradable systems are now available, and others are on the drawing

board. For example, the company is working to make it possible for PC manufacturers to offer consumers the option of adding the latest advances in computer hardware simply by going to a Web site and downloading new programming files for the Xilinx FPGAs inside their PCs. Internet service providers will be able to send subscribers new hardware functions that mimic the special microprocessor necessary to run a new computer game. The service could also send the software to run the game and collect a fee for it, much like cable companies do for pay-per-view television. In addition, Xilinx is developing the technology that will allow communications satellites to be repaired or upgraded remotely from Earth. A digital file to reprogram a Xilinx FPGA would go into space instead of a shuttle crew.

As the 21st century unfolds, Xilinx will continue to deliver the kind of innovative technology that is necessary to fulfill the promise of the digital age. Likewise, the company will carry on its long tradition of acting as a responsible neighbor in the Bay Area and the other communities where it does business by supporting meaningful activities such as arts, education, health, good government, and community welfare.

XILINX INVESTS SIGNIFICANTLY IN RESEARCH AND DEVELOPMENT TO KEEP PACE WITH CUSTOMER DEMAND FOR NEW PRODUCTS (LEFT).

WITH MORE THAN 150 MILLION TRANSISTORS, THIS XILINX FPGA IS AMONG THE MOST COMPLEX CHIPS EVER MANUFACTURED (RIGHT).

First Republic Bank

WHILE MANY OTHER BANKS ARE CLOSING BRANCHES, CONSOLIDATING, and ultimately reducing their service levels, First Republic Bank is opening branches and inviting customers in for a cup of coffee with their own personal bankers. ◆ The San Francisco-based bank specializes in private banking, luxury home loans,

business banking, investment management, and trust services. First Republic's concept and delivery of relationship banking has panned out brilliantly as customers seek alternatives to reduced or impersonal service from other banks.

"We rely upon satisfied customers for growth, and it works," says Katherine August-deWilde, First Republic's chief operating officer and executive vice president. "About 75 percent of our business is through repeat business and referrals. We know—because our clients tell us—that our service is extraordinary compared to other banks."

Expertise in the Home Loan Market

Founded by James H. Herbert, president and CEO, and Roger O. Walther, chairman of the board of directors, the bank opened its doors in July 1985. For 15 years, First Republic has operated in the Los Angeles, San Diego, and Las Vegas mar-

kets, and in 1998, it established an expansion in New York City. In 1992, the bank was listed on the New York Stock Exchange under the FRC symbol.

Since its inception, the bank has garnered an image of expertise in serving California's luxury real estate market, the nation's largest. First Republic created the Prestige Home Index™ to track the values of luxury homes in Los

Angeles/Beverly Hills, San Diego, and the San Francisco Bay Area. Quarterly press releases keep customers, realtors, and the real estate press informed of the results.

To expand its customer base and range of services, First Republic affiliated with longtime New York-based Trainer Wortham & Co., which functions now as a wholly owned subsidiary of the bank. This venerable investment advisory firm, founded in 1924, assisted First Republic's strategic entry into the New York metropolitan region.

Today, the bank is among the 100 largest in the country, offering stability and a strong capital foundation. Products and services include a full range of home, construction, and commercial loan products; private banking services; competitive money market accounts and customized CDs; on-line banking at www. firstrepublic.com; trust services; and investment management services available through Trainer Wortham.

FOUNDED IN 1985 BY PRESIDENT AND CHIEF EXECUTIVE OFFICER JAMES H. HERBERT (ABOVE, ON LEFT) AND CHAIRMAN OF THE BOARD ROGER O. WALTHER, FIRST REPUBLIC BANK HAS GARNERED AN IMAGE OF EXPERTISE IN SERVING CALIFORNIA'S LUXURY REAL ESTATE MARKET, THE NATION'S LARGEST.

FIRST REPUBLIC BANK'S MENLO PARK BRANCH WON A 1998 GOOD DESIGN AWARD FROM THE CITY OF MENLO PARK AS A RESULT OF MAJOR RENOVATIONS TO A 1930S-ERA BUILDING.

"IT'S A PRIVILEGE TO SERVE YOU"

With its company slogan—"It's a privilege to serve you"—First Republic differentiates itself from other financial institutions in its core business philosophy, its commitment to one-on-one service, and the flexibility offered to its customers.

"The most unique feature of our company is our level of service," says CEO Jim Herbert. "With bank mergers and branch closings continuing to sweep the country, it's unusual to find a bank as stable, independent, and customer oriented as First Republic Bank."

While the institution continues to evolve, its commitment to customer service matches pace. First Republic's highly individualized private banking program, Preferred Banking, matches each customer with a personal banker who can marshal the bank's deposit, loan, and investment resources. Bankers make the process of doing business as easy as possible; extending trust, discretion, and flexibility helps them build long-term relationships.

High-caliber customers continue to create demand for First Republic's brand of service. Many busy professionals, as well as corporate CEOs and well-known personalities, find refuge in the bank's professional, private attention. Each year, satisfied customers appear in the pages of the bank's annual report, offering personal testimonials to the level of service and discretion that First Republic provides.

COMMITMENT TO EDUCATION

Since First Republic's inception, community involvement focusing on children and education has been a cornerstone of its mission. In addition to financing the construction or renovation of more than 10 primary and secondary schools, the bank provides scholarships through the First Republic Scholars Program and has helped establish the BASIC Fund, a highly successful scholarship fund for children of low-income families.

The bank has supported the National Foundation for Teaching Entrepreneurship (NFTE), which created an innovative program that teaches business skills to at-risk youth. Through First Republic sponsorship, San Francisco became the first public school system in the country to offer this program. The bank also supports a number of other organizations, including the Exploratorium, San Francisco's Raphael House, and Habitat for Humanity.

First Republic Bank is committed to winning customers one at a time with a level of service that simply cannot be found elsewhere. With that goal in mind, First Republic is poised for continued success for years to come.

Patmont Motor Werks

B Y HIS OWN ADMISSION, STEVE PATMONT IS LIVING OUT THE TRUE American success story. As co-owner and chief inventor at Patmont Motor Werks (PMW), he has created a company that is run just the way he likes it (with wife Hannalore as equal partner, and sons Gabe and Tim as vice presidents); is just the right size

WITH A NOISELESS, VIBRATION-FREE RIDE, PATMONT MOTOR WERKS' (PMW) REVOLUTIONARY, ELECTRIC-POWERED HOVERBOARD IS CAPABLE OF REACHING A TOP SPEED OF 13 MPH AND HAS A RANGE OF 10 MILES. LIKE ALL OF PMW'S OTHER SCOOTERS, IF THIS CYBER-SCOOTER RUNS OUT OF JUICE, IT IS EASILY USED AS A PUSH SCOOTER, AND CAN BE PLUGGED IN AND RECHARGED AT ANY WALL OUTLET (TOP).

PMW IS A FAMILY-RUN BUSINESS: FOUNDER AND PRESIDENT STEVE PATMONT (STANDING) WORKS ALONGSIDE (SEATED FROM LEFT) DR. JERRY PATMONT, A MEMBER OF THE BOARD OF DIRECTORS; HANNY PATMONT, CORPORATE VICE PRESIDENT; GABE PATMONT, EXECUTIVE VICE PRESIDENT; AND TIM PATMONT, ASSISTANT VICE PRESIDENT (BOTTOM).

(70 employees); and produces environmentally friendly and fun, yet functional products: motorized and manual scooters, called Go-Peds.

The company's mission is clearly stated on its Web site: "Enhanced global happiness through enthusiastic productivity and efficient distribution of innovative designs." With barely one-tenth of 1 percent of the planet in possession of one of his inventions, Patmont has a lot of global happiness yet to enhance. Still, he is resolute about being able to manage the company's growth in order to maintain excellence in design and manufacturing, which he feels will be compromised if the company is forced to grow too quickly.

"We've steadily grown at a rate of 25 to 35 percent a year," says Patmont. "It's a nice, stable growth that keeps our supply just a little below demand. If the market suddenly grew way beyond that, we wouldn't be able to maintain excellence, and at that point, the business would be better left to someone else."

Products for People on the Go

O riginally planned as an intermediary vehicle with which people at leisure could tool around while away from their larger vehicles, Patmont's inventions are finding uses that are much more practical. Employees at the New York Port Authority, an early large account, use their Go-Peds to get around quickly and efficiently in the warehouse environment. With the aging of the population,

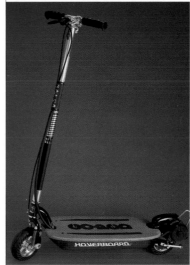

Patmont has begun to hear more frequent uses of Go-Peds as motorized canes.

Handcrafted with care in the Livermore complex, and at Go-Ped Europa in Ireland, these skateboard-bicycle hybrids combine the concept of footboards on wheels with bicycle handle controls to produce transport that is faster than walking, more environmentally friendly than motorcycles, and more portable than bicycles, especially with the collapsible steering column design.

A Go-Ped for Every Need

W ith five consumer models to choose from, and two specialized products, the uses for Go-Peds are unlimited. The most basic model, the Know-Ped, is for beginners, and is a nonmotorized push scooter of exceptional quality for a reasonable price. The oldest PMW product, the Go-Ped Sport model, continues to be the best-seller, and is the lowest-priced motorized version. With a gas-powered, two-cycle sport engine that kicks out more than one horsepower, the Sport can carry up to 400 pounds. A built-in trailer hitch allows it to hook up to a two- by three-foot Tow-Ped wagon.

The Go-Ped Liquimatic model employs a hydraulic torque converter to provide a smoother ride and, unlike the Sport model, allow it to idle when at a standstill. For off-road riding, the Big Foot model features 10-inch, pneumatic tires; a heavier and sturdier frame; and a manual clutch. Popular with rural residents, Big Foot is especially useful when owners' mailboxes are at the end of a long gravel or dirt road.

Available in very limited quantities, the X-Ped is designed for athletic participants of extreme sports. Based on the Sport model,

CLOCKWISE TOP LEFT:
GABE PATMONT DEMONSTRATES
THE X-PED, WHICH IS DESIGNED
FOR EXTREME SPORTS.

GABE AND TIM PATMONT HELP
IN THE DESIGN AND ASSEMBLY OF
NUMEROUS GO-PED LINES, INCLUD-
ING THE BIG FOOT MODEL FOR
OFF-ROAD RIDING.

STEVE AND HANNY PATMONT
ARE EQUAL PARTNERS IN PMW.

MARK FERGUSON, MANAGEMENT
INFORMATION SERVICES DIRECTOR,
TESTS A HOVERBOARD WITH A
TOW-PED ATTACHED.

the X-Ped uses Big Foot's bigger frame.

Also made in limited quantities, the Go-Quad is essentially a motorized go-cart with the same motor, wheels, and braking system as the Go-Ped, only with four wheels instead of two, and a seat.

Just in time for the new millennium, PMW announced its latest design in late 1999: the revolutionary, electric-powered Hoverboard. With a noiseless, vibration-free ride, the Hoverboard is capable of reaching a top speed of 13 mph and has a range of 10 miles. Like all of PMW's other scooters, if this cyberscooter runs out of juice, it is easily used as a push scooter, and can be plugged in and recharged at any wall outlet.

BUILDING A SUCCESSFUL BUSINESS

espite the lack of a university degree, Patmont has built a successful business out of products he designed and for which he holds several patents. Lack of a degree has also not stopped him from holding careers in such areas as computer engineering, ultralight (hang glider) design, and airline mechanics.

Although Patmont counts himself among America's success stories, he sounds a cautionary note about forces in American business that undermine the success of entrepreneurs. He cites the government's lack of adequate enforcement of its antipiracy policies, and notes that the legal and insurance industries are less interested in fostering support of emerging industries and inventions than in protecting their own interests. But Patmont does not complain about competition, feeling that it ultimately breeds better products.

Patmont also points to the company's employees as a reason for its success, and adds, "I want to create a place where employees are confident that they're being treated well, because they are our path to excellence." PMW provides benefits such as medical and dental coverage, 401k plans, and flexible hours, and additionally rewards its employees with pizza Fridays and annual flu shots—not to mention that employees can bring their dogs to work.

Patmont's employee- and customer-focused approach to the business not only earns him

a dedicated workforce and loyal customer base, but in 1994, it led to the company's Small Business Exporter of the Year award from the United States Small Business Administration.

Patmont offers advice to others seeking the success that PMW has achieved: "Set your dreams as high as you can, and don't be afraid to change your mind daily. You might surprise yourself. We sure did."

CUNNINGHAM COMMUNICATION, INC.

WITH THE PROLIFERATION OF NEW MEDIA COMPETING FOR EVER shrinking audiences, traditional methods of public relations have lost much of their effectiveness. Despite this challenge, Cunningham Communication, Inc., founded by Andrea "Andy" Cunningham, carves a leading-edge niche in the industry from its headquarters in Palo Alto's high-tech corridor on Page Mill Road.

It all started in 1984 when, Andy managed the public relations team that launched the Apple Macintosh, the computer that made desktop publishing accessible and inexpensive. In short, she was at the vanguard of a revolution in communications. With the advent of the Internet came the opening of a Pandora's box of media options.

Cunningham Communication has evolved into a communications consulting firm with 150 employees in Palo Alto; Austin, Texas; and Cambridge, Massachusetts, generating approximately $25 million in revenue in 1999. Combining traditional public relations practices with innovative communications methods and research, the company is a leader in the markets it serves. The company's selective client list includes such technology giants as Hewlett-Packard, Motorola, and Cisco, as well as start-ups and Internet companies such as Maxager and VarsityBook.com.

The agency encompasses four practices: the momentum positioning group, which develops the client's leadership profile; the public relations practice, which communicates the client's positioning to the outside world; the cultural alignment group, which helps close the gap, if any, between the client's ideal and actual position; and the syndicated research group, which takes the findings from the momentum positioning group and compiles quarterly report cards on the client's industry.

A NEW CONCEPT IN PUBLIC RELATIONS

In a radical departure from traditional public relations, Cunningham Communication now spends as much time providing strategic counsel to clients as it does communicating to the news media. "When there are so many ways to communicate, so many ways to get information, the only way you can really manage a client's image is by influencing the behavior of the company," Cunningham says. "We're very interested in a company's substance— what makes it tick—and we work with a company to identify an ideal position in the marketplace and then help them create momentum towards that ideal position."

Three years ago, Cunningham's agency invented a concept called Momentum Management™, a statistically rigorous methodology that measures a company's position—or leadership momentum— in its marketplace. Cunningham Communication's Momentum Management measures a company's performance against its competitors along seven dimensions of leadership, and against a slate of 35 specific attributes. The resulting leadership profile serves as a diagnostic tool to help a company identify areas of strength and weakness, so that it can strategically target and repair trouble spots.

"The Internet has introduced new rules of leadership and how to be different in the mind of a customer," says Cunningham. "It's simply impossible today to separate the substance from the perceptions. We think momentum best captures these new conditions of leadership and how companies can manage their success in a world running on Internet time. We consider our relationship with a client to be a partnership. And when our clients win, we win."

CLOCKWISE FROM TOP: UNDER THE LEADERSHIP OF ANDREA "ANDY" CUNNINGHAM, CHAIRMAN AND CEO; RON RICCI, PRINCIPAL; AND JOE HAMILTON, PRESIDENT AND COO, CUNNINGHAM COMMUNICATION, INC. CARVES A LEADING-EDGE NICHE IN THE INDUSTRY FROM ITS HEADQUARTERS IN PALO ALTO'S HIGH-TECH CORRIDOR ON PAGE MILL ROAD.

348

SEGA OF AMERICA

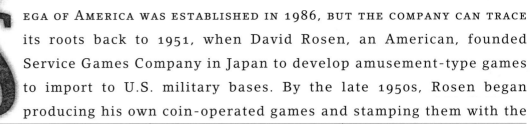

EGA OF AMERICA WAS ESTABLISHED IN 1986, BUT THE COMPANY CAN TRACE its roots back to 1951, when David Rosen, an American, founded Service Games Company in Japan to develop amusement-type games to import to U.S. military bases. By the late 1950s, Rosen began producing his own coin-operated games and stamping them with the

brand name SEGA (derived from "Service Games", which he adopted as the company's new name. In 1966, Sega produced its first worldwide hit game, Periscope.

In 1986, to capture the rapidly growing American market, Japan-based Sega Enterprises Ltd. created Sega of America, a wholly owned subsidiary, to adapt and market video games and to develop software products specifically for the American market. Today, one of the most well recognized brands among American youth, Sega maintains its domination of the industry by continually revolutionizing gaming technology.

TECHNOLOGICAL ADVANCES

tateside, technological advances include the 1990 release of the 16-bit, next-generation console, Sega

Genesis, and the December 1994 launch of the related Sega Channel, a joint venture with Time Warner and TCI that provides video games to Sega Genesis owners through a nationwide, subscription-based cable network. Furthermore, in 1995, the company introduced the Sega Saturn video game system that brought arcade-quality gaming to the home, and in 1996, introduced the companion Sega Saturn Net Link modem for on-line gaming and full Internet access.

In 1995, SegaSoft was created as a joint venture of Sega of America and its Japanese parent, CSK Corporation, to develop interactive content. The following year, Sega Entertainment, Inc. was born to create original titles and to customize Sega content in the real-time strategy, simulation, action, and sports gaming categories.

The announcement of the collaboration with MCA and the DreamWorks creative team of Steven Spielberg, David Geffen, and Jeffrey Katzenberg rocked the industry in 1996 with the unprecedented entwining of movie-making and gaming. The new company, Sega GameWorks, creates family-oriented, location-based entertainment centers.

SEGA DREAMCAST

he latest generation video game system, launched in the fall of 1999, Dreamcast completely changed the face of the gaming industry in the quality of and categories of interactive entertainment offered via television, outperforming all in-home gaming platforms and most arcade systems. Partnering with global leaders in business and technology—Microsoft, Hitachi, NEC, VideoLogic, and Yamaha—Sega created the most realistic and authentic three-dimensional gaming experience ever conceived, supported by breakthrough gaming components.

Designed to appeal to both the hard core and the casual gamer, Sega Dreamcast can display revolutionary new types of realistic three-dimensional graphics. A sophisticated sound processor surrounds players with 64 channels of music, voices, and sound effects at a quality rivaling professional audio equipment. Also, Sega Dreamcast's built-in 56k modem will unite all Sega fans with a range of intense action gaming that only a video game console can offer.

"Sega Dreamcast is Sega's bridge to worldwide market leadership for the 21st century," says Peter Moore, Sega of America Senior vice president and COO. "The Sega you see today is driven by two important goals: delivering the best new gaming content this industry has ever seen, and bringing our consumers a community."

DESIGNED TO APPEAL TO BOTH THE HARD-CORE AND THE CASUAL GAMER, SEGA DREAMCAST CAN DISPLAY REVOLUTIONARY NEW TYPES OF REALISTIC THREE-DIMENSIONAL GRAPHICS, AND ITS BUILT-IN 56K MODEM WILL UNITE SEGA FANS AROUND THE GLOBE WITH A RANGE OF INTENSE ACTION GAMING THAT ONLY A VIDEO GAME CONSOLE CAN OFFER.

B

ORN OUT OF THE REVOLUTION TAKING PLACE IN SILICON VALLEY'S BIO-
technology industry, and fueled by advances in human therapeutics
at Stanford University, the University of California-San Francisco,
and firms like Genentech, Inc., Affymax Research Institute is striving
to make the drug discovery process quicker and more efficient.

Biotechnology pioneer Dr. Alejandro Zaffaroni had already successfully launched several biotech companies by the time he founded Affymax in 1988. As chairman and CEO until 1995, he saw that the process for making human protein products, such as human growth hormones or insulin, could be harnessed as a tool to identify new medicines.

"Fundamentally, we're developing technology that can be applied to making drug discovery more efficient and cost effective," says Dr. Gordon Ringold, Zaffaroni's successor as CEO.

TECHNOLOGY THINK TANK

B efore Affymax was established, the process for developing new medicines—pioneered by chemists making aspirin at Bayer in 1902—had remained virtually unchanged for the better part of the century. Molecules had to be handcrafted one at a time, then tested one at a time.

"Alex recognized that no one had really adapted high-throughput, miniaturized, parallel processing—like you would find in semiconductor technology—to drug discovery," says Ringold. "So instead of making one molecule at a time, you could make thousands at a time, and the idea was to think of chemistry as a combinatorial assembly." Combinatorial chemistry, in which myriad combinations of building blocks are mixed and matched to create new molecules, is the basis for the revolutionary technology at Affymax.

In 1995, the world's largest pharmaceutical company, United Kingdom-based Glaxo Wellcome, recognized the significance of Affymax's research and purchased the company and its entrepreneurial approach to science. "Think of us as the technology think tank for Glaxo Wellcome," says Ringold.

In acquiring Affymax, Glaxo Wellcome not only enfolded one of the scientific leaders in the industry, it also gained a window on the technological mother lode of the Silicon Valley. Moreover, it brought into its fold a pool of talent that is both entrepreneurial and multidisciplinary. Already, several high-technology applications, which were once not deemed core to the drug discovery process, have been successfully spun off into entirely separate companies.

"We believe some of the greatest inventions come at the intersection of traditional disciplines," says Ringold, "which is why we have engineers, computer scientists, chemists, pharmacologists, and biologists all working together, side by side." The Affymax laboratory is more apt to resemble the best of a combined research and manufacturing environment, the result of approaching the process as a systems problem—a radical concept in the industry.

Glaxo Wellcome provides Affymax with the infrastructure and support to eventually bring the fruits of its technology to market. The company has also continued to foster Affymax's independence and nontraditional environment, supporting incentives for its scientists.

"Ultimately, we are motivated by a desire to improve health care through the discovery of important medicines," says Ringold. Without a doubt, the treatment of diseases in the new millennium will be made possible by application of the Affymax technologies to the medicines of tomorrow.

"AT AFFYMAX RESEARCH INSTITUTE, WE BELIEVE SOME OF THE GREATEST INVENTIONS COME AT THE INTERSECTION OF TRADITIONAL DISCIPLINES," SAYS CEO DR. GORDON RINGOLD, "WHICH IS WHY WE HAVE ENGINEERS, COMPUTER SCIENTISTS, CHEMISTS, PHARMACOLOGISTS, AND BIOLOGISTS ALL WORKING TOGETHER, SIDE BY SIDE" (TOP).

FUELED BY ADVANCES IN HUMAN THERAPEUTICS AT STANFORD UNIVERSITY, THE UNIVERSITY OF CALIFORNIA-SAN FRANCISCO, AND FIRMS LIKE GENENTECH, INC., AFFYMAX IS STRIVING TO MAKE THE DRUG DISCOVERY PROCESS QUICKER AND MORE EFFICIENT (BOTTOM).

HOTEL NIKKO
SAN FRANCISCO

Like a pearl, Hotel Nikko San Francisco derives its elegance from its smooth simplicity. As General Manager John Hutar puts it, the Nikko is "simply everything, simply" (left).

In acknowledgment of its Japanese roots, the Nikko offers Asian accents amid Western luxury and comfort (right).

JUST AFTER ONE O'CLOCK ON A RECENT TUESDAY, SEVERAL LIMOUSINES AND an airport shuttle van arrived, one after another, at the entrance to the elegant Hotel Nikko San Francisco. Moments later, the hotel's marble-clad lobby was filled with arriving guests: a well-known actress from New York, an equally famous architect from Atlanta, a group

of businessmen from Singapore, three foreign government dignitaries, and two somewhat overwhelmed women from Cheyenne, who were visiting the city for the first time. While not exactly a normal occurrence, the simultaneous arrival of so many important guests did not faze the efficient front desk staff. While one staff member summoned General Manager John Hutar to welcome the guests, others started checking them in. Within minutes, each guest had been escorted to his or her deluxe Hotel Nikko room or suite, and the staff was ready for the next arrivals.

For Hotel Nikko San Francisco, this was business as usual. Every member of the hotel's staff has been trained to make every guest —whether a head of state or a head of household—feel welcome. All are treated to the high-quality service that has become the Hotel Nikko San Francisco trademark – efficient but, most of all, unobtrusive. It's a delicate balancing act.

Another balancing act is making sure that there is a room available when a regular Hotel Nikko guest makes a last-minute decision to visit San Francisco. "Many of our guests wouldn't think of staying anyplace else," Hutar notes, "and we will do anything we can to avoid disappointing them."

That is just one way the Hotel Nikko staff anticipate the needs of its guests. There are many others. For example, the staff have threaded the needles in the sewing kits in each of the hotel's 532 rooms and suites. They have placed an umbrella in room closets to be sure that guests are not inconvenienced by unexpected inclement weather. And, so that guests can relax after a stressful day of business meetings or shopping, they have provided a selection of CDs next to each in-room stereo.

A Marriage of East and West

With guests arriving from around the world, Hotel Nikko must be welcoming to all. "We like to think of ourselves as an international luxury hotel with a Japanese heritage," says Hutar. Japanese touches include the soothing sounds of cascading water in the lobby, a manicured Japanese garden at poolside, and a Japanese-style

suite complete with rock garden, sliding Shoji screen doors, and tatami beds on request.

The hotel's fitness center combines the best of East and West. Western fitness amenities include a glass atrium-enclosed swimming pool, a Jacuzzi, a tanning cabana, and a fully equipped exercise room. Japanese health facilities within the fitness center include ofuro soaking tubs and a kamaburo dry sauna relaxation room with four polished wooden pallets placed on warm, rounded pebbles. Guests can also indulge in a shiatsu deep muscle massage.

The marriage of East and West can also be found in the hotel's famed restaurant, ANZU, located on the second level overlooking the lobby. The fine dining experience at ANZU presents the best of land and sea: the highest-quality prime beef alongside a menu of fresh sushi, plus a wide variety of other delectable offerings. A broad selection of wines and sakes complement the cuisine. Even in the morning, guests can choose from a traditional American or Japanese breakfast. ANZU has become a favorite of San Francisco's locals as well as the hotel's guests.

Each Sunday morning, ANZU plays host to local FM radio station KKSF 103.7, which broadcasts live at the hotel's Smooth Jazz Sunday Brunch. From 10:00 a.m. until 2:00 p.m., brunch guests enjoy a wide range of dishes representing the West (salads, roasts, and omelets) and the East (sushi and dim sum), and a wide variety of music from the smooth jazz playlist of KKSF.

Even the hotel's innovative Z BAR combines the best of East and West. It is becoming famous for its signature sake martinis, as well as more traditional cocktails and the finest wines from around the world. Its sushi bar is under the direction of a master sushi chef, one of only a handful in the nation.

World-Class Hotel

Like a pearl, Hotel Nikko San Francisco derives its elegance from its graceful simplicity. As Hutar puts it, "simply everything, simply."

At Hotel Nikko, guests find dedicated staff members—referred to here as hoteliers—and attentive service in an environment of understated elegance and luxury. Whether hosting meetings in its 20,500 square feet of meeting space or providing accommodations for corporate business travelers, leisure visitors, and wedding parties, Hotel Nikko San Francisco "strives to be a place to relax, recharge and regroup," emphasizes Hutar. "Eventually, it is a place where people return." The hotel boasts one of the city's highest ratios of return guests, many of whom have become Nikko loyalists.

Hotel Nikko San Francisco also believes in good citizenship. Even before the hotel opened on October 1, 1987, a staff recruitment drive took place at nearby Glide Memorial United Methodist Church, arguably San Francisco's preeminent downtown social service provider.

On opening day, poet Janice Mirikitani, the wife of Glide's Rev. Cecil Williams, presented Hotel Nikko with a poem to acknowledge its deep community roots. Now prominently displayed in the lobby, "The Hands That Built the Nikko" commends: "From this broken ground/Rise marble passages/And sand gardens that swirl in silent peace./Our hands like eternal camellias/Will blossom at your door."

What is Hotel Nikko San Francisco's greatest asset? The magnificent building? The incredible atrium pool and health club? ANZU? "None of the above," states Hutar. "It's clearly our people. As much as we would like to think it's all of our physical attributes, it's our staff that is the heart and soul of this hotel. They are the ones that bring our guests back."

"WE DEFINE OURSELVES AS AN INTERNATIONAL LUXURY HOTEL WITH TOUCHES OF JAPAN," SAYS HUTAR. THOSE TOUCHES INCLUDE THE SOOTHING SOUNDS OF CASCADING WATER FROM A FOUNTAIN IN THE LOBBY, A MANICURED JAPANESE GARDEN SURROUNDING THE POOLSIDE SUNNING AREA, AND A JAPANESE-STYLE SUITE COMPLETE WITH ROCK GARDEN, SLIDING SCREEN DOORS, AND TATAMI BEDS ON REQUEST.

MARK DARLEY

MARK DARLEY

THE RESEARCHERS AT SYSTEMIX, INC. LOOK FORWARD TO THE DAY THEY find a cure for cancer and acquired immune deficiency syndrome (AIDS). SyStemix, a biotechnology firm in Palo Alto, is a wholly owned subsidiary of Novartis and is one of the world's leading companies in gene therapy research. The company was founded in 1988 by

cellular biologists from nearby Stanford University, who concentrated on cultivating and purifying hematopoietic stem cells (HSCs)- the mother cells of the human blood system.

"Today, our efforts are broadly focused on gene therapy," says Dr. Michael S. Perry, president and CEO of SyStemix and its sister company in Maryland, Genetic Therapy Inc. (GTI). "We're developing innovative treatments for seriously debilitating diseases that currently have no reliable medical solutions. Our long-term vision is to provide genuinely curative treatments to patients and their families."

Through its expertise in cell biology and genetics, SyStemix is well positioned to maintain leadership in the discovery, development, and commercialization of cell and gene therapy products with superior medical benefits. The company's strength is further enhanced by two substantial sources of support: the long-term commitment of its parent company, pharmaceutical giant Novartis, and the molecular biology expertise of GTI, which functionally consolidated operations with SyStemix in 1998.

The Field of Gene Therapy

In the mid-1960s, medical researchers began to realize that reliance on purely metabolic approaches to treating diseases would limit treatment efficacy; therapeutic strategies must target underlying causative genetic defects. Driven by rapid advances in molecular genetics, cell biology, and virology over the last 25 years, gene therapy has become a predominant concept in targeting a curative treatment for diseases.

"This new therapeutic modality will revolutionize the practice of medicine," says Perry. "By and large, traditional medicine is tar-

geted at treating the symptoms of disease. With gene therapy, though, we have the potential to offer a cure."

The first gene therapy trial was conducted some 10 years ago. "This field is still in its infancy," explains Perry, "and the evolution observed in such a brief period of time is indeed remarkable." Historically, gene therapy was envisioned to treat classical inherited genetic diseases. Advances in technologies essential to the delivery and regulation of genes, along with an improved understanding of the functional relationship between genes and diseases, have expanded the scope of diseases that may benefit from gene therapy approaches.

Technical Approaches

To support the development of therapeutic applications, SyStemix and GTI are pursuing two types of gene therapies: cell-based or *ex vivo* (outside the body), and *in vivo* (inside the body). Cell-based gene therapies involve taking cells from a patient or donor and genetically modifying them prior to injecting them back into the patient to produce a therapeutic effect. *In vivo* gene therapies comprise the direct administration of genes into the patient.

Vector systems are used both *ex vivo* and *in vivo* to introduce therapeutic genes into the target cells of patients. Viral vectors are disabled viruses that have been stripped of the genes that cause disease and allow replication—a shell that retains the virus's biological characteristic of efficiently infecting, or penetrating, cells. The vector carries and delivers the therapeutic gene. Research is also ongoing in the use of synthetic components as delivery vehicles for genes, as well as combining synthetic and viral elements to create what are called hybrid vectors.

"To develop a successful gene therapy product," Perry explains, "understanding the functional relationship between a particular gene and a disease process is merely

"GENE THERAPY IS GOING TO REVOLUTIONIZE THE PRACTICE OF MEDICINE," SAYS DR. MICHAEL S. PERRY, PRESIDENT AND CEO OF SYSTEMIX AND ITS SISTER COMPANY, GENETIC THERAPY INC. (GTI) (TOP).

A SYSTEMIX, INC. RESEARCH SCIENTIST ANALYZES GENES BY GEL ELECTROPHORESIS TO BETTER UNDERSTAND THE RELATIONSHIP OF GENES AND DISEASES (BOTTOM).

the tip of the iceberg." It is essential that technologies are refined to ensure that the gene can be effectively and safely introduced into the patient; the gene is expressed appropriately; delivery of the gene can be targeted to the intended physiological site; and the expression of the gene can be controlled to achieve therapeutic levels. SyStemix and GTI are focusing their research and development efforts on each of these enabling components to build a broad range of effective gene therapy products.

TARGET DISEASE APPLICATIONS

The types of diseases we're going after are the truly debilitating ones—major medical needs that remain unmet by today's state-of-the-art health care technology," says Perry.

Treatment of human immunodeficiency virus (HIV) infection and related complications presents one of the greatest challenges to medicine today. Despite recent advances in AIDS treatment regimens, resistance to drug combinations and lack of immune function recovery continue to impede progress in winning the HIV battle.

The clinical program in HIV gene therapy takes advantage of SyStemix's extensive expertise in HSC research. HSCs have the potential to reproduce themselves as well as to give rise to all types of cells present in the bone marrow and peripheral blood, including red cells, platelets, lymphocytes, and monocytes. Hence, HSCs offer the ability to pass on any genetic modification to their progeny. In the HIV project, patients' HSCs are modified with antiviral genes, thus allowing their progeny cells to carry the same antiviral gene modification protecting them against HIV viral replication. The goal of the therapy is to restore the patient's immune system. "Ultimately, what we aim to provide is a long-lasting, self-renewing hematopoietic stem cell that will comprise a single treatment with the potential to yield lifelong benefit to AIDS patients," says Perry.

Aside from the HIV project, SyStemix and GTI are focusing their efforts in two key therapeutic

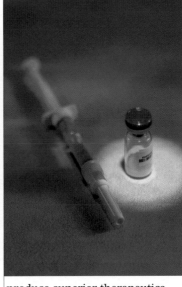

areas: cancer and vascular (both coronary and peripheral) disease. These two areas present promising opportunities for gene therapy products to provide significant advantages over traditional pharmaceuticals or as complements to current approaches.

PERSPECTIVE FOR THE FUTURE

At the end of 1999, there were no gene therapy products on the market anywhere in the world, although many major pharmaceutical companies were racing to commercialize the first of such products. While Novartis, through its biotech companies SyStemix and GTI, is very much a participant in this race, its primary focus is on the quality of the therapeutic solution.

"Our goal is to ensure that we tackle each of the technical hurdles that are required to ultimately

produce superior therapeutics, specifically where traditional pharmaceutical approaches fall short," says Perry. "Remember, this field is very young and the technology is still evolving; we want to develop gene therapy in such a way that the technology will be mature enough, robust enough, and selective enough to provide safe and effective therapeutics that will advance medicine beyond the limits of current symptomatic patient treatment. Our aim is to deliver cures as we move into the next millennium."

With a commitment to innovation well into the future, SyStemix, united with Novartis' broad expertise, has the technical assets as well as the strategic mission to build on its foundation in the biotechnology industry. Indeed, it is a company poised to lead the gene therapy medical revolution.

SYSTEMIX AND GTI ARE DEVELOPING PRODUCT CONCEPTS FOR TWO TYPES OF GENE THERAPIES: (FROM LEFT) CELL-BASED OR *EX VIVO* (OUTSIDE THE BODY), AND *IN VIVO* (INSIDE THE BODY).

SYSTEMIX'S HEADQUARTERS IS LOCATED IN PALO ALTO.

I N THE YEARS SINCE BECOMING A SEPARATE BUSINESS UNIT IN 1989, ANDERSEN Consulting has eclipsed its rivals to become an $8.3 billion global giant with 65,000 employees in 48 countries. One of the keys to the management and technology consulting organization's success is its ability to realign and reinvent itself in response to the changing global marketplace.

"The mission of Andersen Consulting is to help our clients create their future," says Ed Kennedy, Northern California office managing partner. "This means that we strive to help our clients create value in new and innovative ways to succeed in a global, network-based business environment. To achieve our mission, we must have the courage to change Andersen Consulting and to continually re-invent our firm before it is obvious in the marketplace to do so."

The firm has also worked diligently to stay ahead of the market and technology curve. "Usually where there's change or explosive growth in an industry, companies must concentrate on their core competencies; a company can wind up with a shortage of skilled executives to focus on the shifting landscape," says Kennedy. "As

evidenced by our mission, we're in the future-shaping business. What we do is look for new and innovative ways to help clients create far-reaching value."

LEADING THE WAY IN THE E-ECONOMY

The convergence of computing, communication, and content technologies has revolutionized the way business is conducted and has changed the fundamental economic assumptions on which business is based.

"As the industrial economy evolves into the electronic economy, tremendous rewards are possible—but only for those organizations willing to face this new marketplace reality head-on," says Kennedy. "The E-economy is already upon us and the time to

act is now. At Andersen Consulting, we intend to do whatever it takes to ensure that our firm and our clients and their customers take full advantage of this new age."

With 2,300 employees in Northern California, the world's high-tech epicenter, Andersen Consulting has blazed a trail linking clients' strategies to their business processes, people, and technologies—in short, helping clients navigate the brave new worlds of the wired economy.

In a recent cover story, *Forbes* magazine attributed Andersen Consulting's ascent to the top of the management consulting industry with its early recognition of the importance of information technology in business management, crediting the company with having overhauled the "digital plumbing" of 5,000 clients throughout the 1990s.

"We've gone through waves," says Kennedy of the technology revolution. "First it was hardware, then software. Each wave brings with it positive change, business opportunities, and new ventures. Now the wave is about entirely new business models—E-commerce is just getting started."

While the rest of the world may just be getting started, Andersen Consulting has been preparing and laying the groundwork for leading in the E-economy for the past several years.

Its Palo Alto location on Page Mill Road houses one of the firm's high-tech think tanks, the Center for Strategic Technology, and one of its Internet Centers of Excellence, a hub for E-commerce consulting.

GLOBAL REACH, LOCAL PRESENCE

The San Francisco office, one of Andersen Consulting's largest locations, serves as the primary base for the firm's Northern California operations, which include the

PROFESSIONALS AT ANDERSEN CONSULTING ENVISION THE BUSINESS IMPACT OF NEW AND EMERGING TECHNOLOGIES.

DAWN NEAL

TARR & FARAH PHOTOGRAPHY

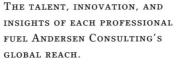

THE TALENT, INNOVATION, AND INSIGHTS OF EACH PROFESSIONAL FUEL ANDERSEN CONSULTING'S GLOBAL REACH.

Palo Alto office as well as locations in Sacramento and San Ramon. Sacramento is the seat of the firm's government practice for the western United States, while San Ramon houses the telecommunications industry practice, and includes the Communications and High Tech Solution Center.

From these locations, Andersen Consulting serves clients all over the Bay Area and the world; the firm's global reach is one of its greatest strengths. For instance, Andersen Consulting has worked on the supply chains of all of the world's 500 largest companies. Furthermore, half of the world's mail is processed with the help of Andersen Consulting, and one in five of the world's telephone numbers is billed by systems constructed by Andersen Consulting. Every four hours, an Andersen Consulting system goes live somewhere in the world.

Remarkably, given the complex issues, cross-cultural platforms, and high degree of change in their work, Andersen Consulting's professionals consistently offer quantifiable results. "We take a global approach, implement solutions locally, and build predictability into an unpredictable world," says Kennedy. "Clients hire us for our pragmatic, yet visionary approach. A client that is a large multinational corporation employing 20,000 people across 10 different countries needs to run its business in a future-focused, yet predictable fashion consistently throughout the world. These companies come to us because we can work with them to achieve their goals."

When scouring the world's best universities for potential employees, Andersen Consulting looks for a combination of vision and concrete skills. Once contenders have been winnowed and selected to join the firm, Andersen Consulting spends more than $575 million annually training new and current employees. "It's a long-term process and an investment in constantly developing our people," says Kennedy. "Each consultant working with a client ultimately represents all of us at Andersen Consulting."

In helping companies and employees create their futures, Andersen Consulting is creating its own.

DAWN NEAL

ANDERSEN CONSULTING'S DEEP EXPERIENCE IN INDUSTRY, TECHNOLOGY, AND BUSINESS DELIVERS FAR-REACHING CLIENT SOLUTIONS.

INCYTE PHARMACEUTICALS, INC.

Roy Whitfield and Dr. Randy Scott like to say that insight was such a driving force behind the revolutionary bioinformation company they cofounded in Palo Alto that they named it Incyte. Aside from the obvious homonym, the name plays on "cyte," the Latin root word for cell, the building block of all living organisms. Scott was a founding scientist at Invitron, a St. Louis-based biotechnology firm founded in 1985. Whitfield was president of Ideon, a subsidiary. At its zenith, Invitron grew to 220 employees, but by the late 1980s, it was clear the company needed to shift to meet the changing landscape of biotechnology.

Scott and Whitfield joined forces to build a new company. However, by the time they had mustered the venture capital to execute a management buyout in 1991, the new company had lost several of its scientists.

Undaunted, Whitfield and Scott launched Incyte to focus on protein research since, at the time, protein development had the most promising pharmaceutical applications. However, six months after the company's launch, Whitfield and Scott came to a crossroads: Should Incyte choose to continue on the path of protein development, or instead choose to blaze a trail and focus on genes?

"We saw that advances in technology of high throughput discovery had reached a stage where it was feasible to focus on genes rather than proteins," says Scott, Incyte's president and chief scientific officer. "And we saw that information was power. We decided we could create an information model and sell it to multiple customers on a nonexclusive basis—Roy calls it the Dolby stereo model. Instead of making stereos, Dolby patented their sound system and licensed it to stereo makers. Pretty soon, the company was making more money than the stereo manufacturers. We want to revolutionize the health care industry by applying the same techniques while becoming the premier company to supply genomics information and technology."

Genomics is defined as the sequencing and identification of the total genetic information possessed by an individual organism, and the analysis of the relationship between gene activity and cell function. Each cell in the human body contains a complete copy of the genome, which is estimated to contain 140,000 genes, according to the latest research by Incyte.

"In 1989, only about 1,000 genes were known," says Whitfield. "In September 1999, we announced

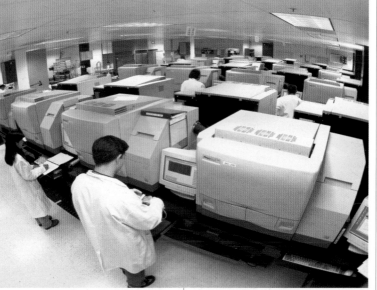

INCYTE PHARMACEUTICALS, INC.'S HIGH-THROUGHPUT SEQUENCING FACILITY OPERATES 24 HOURS A DAY, SEVEN DAYS A WEEK, USING STATE-OF-THE-ART MACHINES TO IDENTIFY THE CHEMICAL BASES THAT FORM THE BACKBONE OF DNA.

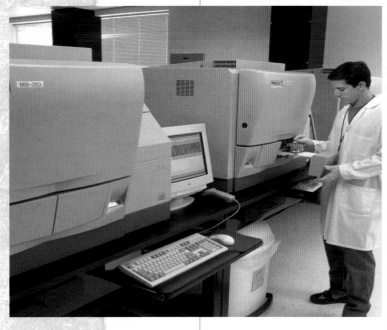

that there were more than 140,000 genes, and that scientists have only scratched the surface.

"Imagine an automobile that doesn't stop at traffic lights. Why is that? You take the car to a mechanic who would have a manual describing 10,000 parts. He or she can look at all the parts in the brake to figure out what's wrong," Whitfield explains. "We don't have a similar owners' manual for the human body. We don't know all the parts involved. But with genomics, the first step is cataloging the knowledge level of the human body. Once we do that, it will change the way medical research is conducted."

Continuing the analogy, Incyte is cataloging and marketing the instruction manual that describes all the genetic parts of the human body, and providing the diagnostic equipment to test those genetic parts for its pharmaceutical, biotechnology, and academic research partners. The company insight to switch from proteins to genes proved pivotal. "Let other biotechnology firms discover drugs," says Scott of Incyte's decision at the time. "We'll discover information."

In the information business, a premium is placed on time. "As we identify the human genome, we're developing the long-term reference set," Scott says, expressing Incyte's commercial viability. "Meanwhile, pharmaceutical companies will pay a lot of money to get their hands on an early copy of that reference set."

BIOLOGY IN SILICON VALLEY

A public company since 1993, Incyte is now at the forefront in the field of bioinformatics—the use of computers to retrieve, process, and analyze biological information. The company's 1,200-employee workforce is the leading provider of an integrated platform of genomic technologies designed to aid in the understanding of the molecular basis of disease.

Other Incyte products include genomic databases and analysis tools; bioinformatics platforms, including full data- and project-management capabilities; the world's largest warehouse of resource clones, or reagents, for wet lab studies; proteomics, or systematic analysis of protein expression of healthy and diseased tissues; and custom sequencing of clients' tissue libraries.

"Our mission is to understand the molecular basis for life. That

understanding will lead to disease discovery, comprehension, and treatment," says Scott. "In 10 to 20 years, if we can establish the molecular basis of disease, we should have drugs, compounds, and genetic therapies to treat or prevent most of the world's diseases."

While Scott sees these as exciting times, he feels that he's just at the start of the marathon. "Right now we're in the information age, but in 20 or 30 years, it's going to be the genomic age, when there will be tremendous discovery and advancements based on human genomics."

INCYTE HAS DEVELOPED AN AUTOMATED, COMPUTER-CONTROLLED ROBOT THAT BAR CODES AND PREPARES SAMPLES TO BE PROCESSED BY THE SEQUENCING FACILITY.

THE BLACK, CORKSCREW SLIDE HIDDEN FROM VIEW BEHIND THE RECEP-
tionist's desk is the first clue that Macromedia is not a typical San
Francisco company. As visitors wait in the lobby, they are apt to be
startled by employees—grown adults—swooshing down the two and a
half revolutions to the floor below. These adults, however, are the

brains behind the radical applications that allow artists to maximize the Internet's fullest creative potential.

"Most of the World Wide Web today is silent, static, no graphics—it's all text," says Rob Burgess, CEO and chairman of Macromedia. "Human beings are sensory creatures. We like to interact, yet the Web doesn't fully touch our senses. Someone needs to build the technology to make it a more sensory-rich experience. This is the notion behind Macromedia."

Chances are, Net surfers who come across dynamic Web sites that have the look and feel of television commercials or Web sites advertising movies have found

works made possible by software from Macromedia. Graphics that move, whiz-bang special effects that dance or explode, buttons or design elements that change when the cursor passes over them—these are some hallmarks of Macromedia software.

Making Customers Happy

Graphic designers and artists working in the medium of computers embrace Macromedia's Web publishing suite of software—the most up-to-date in the industry—for allowing them creative expression.

"Customers love our products," says Burgess. "One customer told me Dreamweaver changed his life,

because he went from spending 90 percent of his time trying to make things work, to 90 percent of his time creating on the Web and actually doing his craft."

While Macromedia's goal is ultimately to enrich consumers' Web experience, the tools themselves are targeted at professional designers and artists. "Other large software companies have products for consumer Web development for the bottom 80 percent of the market," says Burgess. "We concentrate mainly on the pros.

"Artists need to express themselves," says Burgess. "These products are allowing them to do that, and they're thrilled. We love making our customers happy."

MACROMEDIA ENGINEERS ARE THE BRAINS BEHIND THE RADICAL APPLICATIONS THAT ALLOW ARTISTS TO MAXIMIZE THE INTERNET'S FULLEST CREATIVE POTENTIAL.

COMPETITORS LEFT BEHIND

"The stuff we've done is pretty tricky," says Burgess. "In order to compete with us, a company would first need to make a multimedia player that could function on Apple, Windows, Internet Explorer, and Netscape. It's hard to make a player that's small yet expressive enough.

"If you were successful at that," Burgess continues, "then you would need to get distribution. Nobody wants to develop for a player that nobody has. And you have to get distribution among several companies that are fierce competitors: Real Networks, Microsoft, @Home, America Online, Apple—all the factions." An indication of its success in market penetration, Macromedia's Flash player, which gives a computer the capability to play the visually and aurally enriched Web sites built with Flash software, is used by 77 percent of all Web users, according to a 1999 survey by independent research firm Media Metrix.

"If you get past that hurdle, then you have to make authoring tools that output to that format. These are three very difficult things to do; they take years to build," says Burgess.

DYNAMIC LEADERSHIP

With offices around the world, more than half of Macromedia's 600 employees are based in the company's South of Market headquarters. The company is an anchor tenant of San Francisco's Multimedia Gulch, based there since 1992.

One of Burgess' first moves upon arrival in 1996 was to winnow the company's product line from 10 disparate software products to three that focus the development on the Web. These tools include Director, the industry standard for creating powerful multimedia, used by movie directors to create preview trailers; Authorware, the leading visual, media-rich authoring program for on-line learning, used by corporations to build Internet and intranet sites to train employees and customers; and FreeHand, the industry's most powerful design program for print and Internet graphics, used by illustrators and artists.

This streamlining effort left Macromedia's software engineers free to concentrate on developing such Internet-native products as Fireworks, for creating Web graphics; Flash, for vector graphics and animation; and Dreamweaver, for professional Web site layout, design, and production.

CONTINUOUSLY INVENTIVE

While the company has seen many of its products succeed in making the Web more dynamic and interactive, Macromedia is spurred to constantly improve its existing product line and to develop new solutions.

"I'm very interested in taking a step forward in the consumer experience," says Burgess. "I'm also very interested in revolutionizing the relationship we have with our customers, making that a mutually beneficial experience."

There's not a moment to lose in the fast-paced industry. Burgess feels the company is just beginning its work, and he is in a hurry to have it all happen.

CHANCES ARE, NET SURFERS WHO COME ACROSS DYNAMIC WEB SITES THAT HAVE THE LOOK AND FEEL OF TELEVISION COMMERCIALS OR WEB SITES ADVERTISING MOVIES HAVE FOUND WORKS MADE POSSIBLE BY SOFTWARE FROM MACROMEDIA.

ICHAEL HARRIS, A FORMER EMERGENCY ROOM PHYSICIAN, BOUGHT HIS first San Francisco apartment building in 1991. The Bush Street property on the south slope of Nob Hill had seen better days. But after a few years of hard work, Harris was on his way to a future in the furnished corporate apartment business. ◆ An old brass

plaque on his first building identified it as Pierre Crest, a name Harris took on as the working title of the restoration operation. Upon its purchase, he immediately set about restoring the 28-unit building to the elegance and character of the neighborhood, which once was the tony address for the newly minted nabobs who made their fortune building the transcontinental railroad. For the next three years, Harris painstakingly upgraded the common areas of the building. Eventually, he got his first opportunity to renovate one of the actual apartments when a long-time tenant vacated number 102.

"The first corporate suite was really a product of serendipity," says Harris, who had discovered an antique light fixture around the same time the apartment was

vacated. A heavy, cast bronze ceiling fixture with a gilt finish and sculpted frosted glass, the light fixture was 18 inches wide and 22 inches high, and had been rescued by a salvage firm from what must have been a grand old building. But Harris' own house was already filled with unique and beautiful light fixtures. "For lack of a better place to install it, we put it in the newly remodeled unit, number 102," he recalls.

To complete the upgrade of the apartment, Harris gathered furniture, linens, a telephone, and appliances, and placed an ad in the San Francisco Bay Guardian. "A summer law clerk from Yale answered our ad, loved the building," says Harris. "She was our first tenant." Pierre Suites/Nob

Hill was born, and Harris was in the corporate apartment business.

That same summer, another unit became available. Within a year, seven studios had been turned over, remodeled, and rented on a monthly basis as furnished units. Clients came from nearby Financial District firms looking for housing for workers on long-term assignments or relocating from outside the Bay Area. Visitors came from around the world, looking for a home base for a season in San Francisco. Vacancies were infrequent.

In April 1996, Harris acquired adjoining properties on Pine Street, around the block from the original Bush Street building, and increased his inventory to 60 units. Three years later, a total of

35 units had been turned into furnished suites and apartments.

No Two Suites Alike

E ach unit has a unique cast," says Harris. "No unit is the same. And no unit is kitschy." In fact, each corporate apartment is furnished lovingly with custom-made and custom-ordered items or those found one piece at a time at auctions and antique stores.

As Harris explains it, the "Pierre look" hinges on quality hardwood furnishings and superior amenities. Furniture that can be found throughout the properties may include such antiques as a claw-foot bathtub, American Federal drop-leaf table, American Eastlake armoire, or English Regency marble-top washstand. Accent pieces include antique Chinese porcelains, custom-designed hardwood mantel clocks, custom Irish cable-knit wool blankets, and one-of-a-kind bronze and stained-glass light fixtures. Kitchens feature gas ranges and are fully stocked with quality cookware.

Upon arrival, guests are provided with a hospitality package of pasta, California wine, giant almonds, chocolates, bean soup,

and certificates for complimentary free-range rotisserie chicken from the Crowne Plaza Hotel's restaurant nearby. Custom-roasted coffee accompanies the in-room coffee grinders. Even the laundry detergent and fabric softener are complimentary. For that matter, the washing machines and dryers are free.

"We want our guests to feel at home the minute they arrive," Harris emphasizes. "We sweat the details so our guests don't have to think about them. They just have to show up."

As integral to the Pierre look as quality furnishings is its superb service. Not wanting any details to go unattended, Harris and his staff of two full-time resident managers continually survey guests and visitors on how their product might be improved.

An Oasis within an Oasis

I n addition to housekeeping services, free laundry facilities, paid local phone, DSL, cable television, VCR, stereo system, and access to a video library of classic movies and CDs, guests have full access to amazing urban gardens.

Both properties harbor a lush fountain courtyard with a reading

settee. And gardens at both locations offer comfortable seating for optimum enjoyment of the greenery. Each garden features commercial-size gas grills that are fully stocked with mesquite chips. At the Bush Street property, the garden at the back of the building is dominated by a five-story avocado tree that guests are welcome to harvest, sometimes from right outside their apartment window.

Harris' pride and joy, however, are the gardens at the Pine Street property. At the back of the building, guests can literally smell the roses—not to mention the lilies, honeysuckle, mint, and persimmons. On the rooftop, a veritable orchard of dwarf trees bears cherries, apples, apricots, and plums. Grapes, blueberries, and herbs round out the edible offerings.

"I have always dreamed of this," exclaims Harris. "I get to work on my gardens for business purposes, and I get a place to live here with my Australian shepherd in the middle of San Francisco. It's my own little oasis."

For Harris, living well is its own reward. However, being able to share those values—aesthetic and philosophical—is the ultimate measure of his success.

CLOCKWISE FROM TOP LEFT:
THE "PIERRE LOOK" HINGES ON QUALITY HARDWOOD FURNISHINGS AND SUPERIOR AMENITIES.

GUESTS HAVE FULL ACCESS TO AMAZING URBAN GARDENS WITH COMFORTABLE SEATING AND COMMERCIAL-SIZE GAS GRILLS.

AT THE BACK OF THE PINE STREET BUILDING, GUESTS CAN LITERALLY SMELL THE ROSES—NOT TO MENTION THE LILIES, HONEYSUCKLE, MINT, AND PERSIMMONS.

IN 1996, DAN ODISHOO AND KEN DUDWICK WERE HAPPILY MANAGING THE Clorox business at Foote, Cone & Belding (FCB) in San Francisco, when FCB's Chicago office unexpectedly accepted the global consolidation of S.C. Johnson, a longtime Clorox business rival. ◆ In one of the most dramatic testaments to client/agency partnership in recent history,

instead of conducting an agency review, Clorox asked Odishoo and Dudwick, in tandem with DDB Worldwide, to transplant their entire team and open the San Francisco office of DDB.

Bringing with them about 30 of the key people who worked on the Clorox account at Foote, Cone & Belding and a reported $70 million in billings from their primary—and at that time, only—client, Managing Partners Odishoo

and Dudwick hung out the DDB shingle, never missing a day of business through the transition.

RELENTLESS PROBLEM SOLVERS

For DDB San Francisco, attention to detail starts at the top. Unlike senior management at most advertising agencies of DDB's size, Odishoo and Dudwick have a strong guiding hand in every aspect of their clients' campaigns.

"Ken and I are working partners," says Odishoo. "We hate the thought of not solving a client's business problem—so we do whatever it takes to find solutions. And we're the kind of competitors who hate to lose. So no matter how many times we get knocked down, we'll always get up trying harder."

With Odishoo and Dudwick in their corner, clients are assured a high level of service with generous doses of listening skills, street smarts, energy, and creative instincts. Furthermore, the two men's spirit of cooperation and personal responsibility is infectious—with the account management, planning, media, and creative teams embracing the business challenges that their clients face as their own.

At DDB San Francisco, work is judged by whether or not it is helping move the client's business ahead. If a creative approach translates to in-market sales, Dudwick and Odishoo feel they have succeeded.

FOR DDB SAN FRANCISCO, ATTENTION TO DETAIL STARTS AT THE TOP. THE COMPANY'S MANAGING PARTNERS AND FOUNDERS, KEN DUDWICK (LEFT) AND DAN ODISHOO (RIGHT) HAVE A STRONG GUIDING HAND IN EVERY ASPECT OF THEIR CLIENTS' CAMPAIGNS.

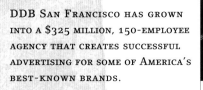

DDB SAN FRANCISCO HAS GROWN INTO A $325 MILLION, 150-EMPLOYEE AGENCY THAT CREATES SUCCESSFUL ADVERTISING FOR SOME OF AMERICA'S BEST-KNOWN BRANDS.

"We're not interested in creating ads for the sake of producing a hot reel or portfolio," says Dudwick. "Certainly our work has to be entertaining, but we also have to find a consumer point of connection with the product—what it is about the product that's meaningful for the consumer. We find that connection, then develop advertising around it."

PARTNERSHIPS THAT PAY

Judging by the agency's steady, sustained growth—essentially quadrupling in size and tripling in revenues in less than four years—DDB's business formula works not only for its clients, but for itself.

DDB San Francisco has grown into a $325 million, 150-employee agency that creates successful advertising for some of America's best-known brands. Smart Ones frozen foods, Glad bags, Bagel Bites, Formula 409, Armor All, STP, Pine-Sol, Ore-Ida potatoes, and, of course, Clorox Bleach have DDB San Francisco to credit with their business-building advertising.

Importantly, DDB's exponential growth has been organic, a testament to its philosophy of focusing on how to increase sales for its current clients. In mid-1999, the Clorox Company offered the

most rousing endorsement possible—awarding DDB the company's entire global advertising business, totaling a reported $250

million. This new business win includes Brita water filtration products, Fresh Step cat litter, and Hidden Valley salad dressings, among others, along with all media buying and planning responsibilities. Heinz echoed this endorsement by awarding DDB San Francisco two of its new frozen food assignments in late 1999.

"If you want an advertising agency that will work with you in a partnership, with people you will like and respect, and who will judge their work by your business results, then we're the agency to call," Odishoo explains.

WITH DDB SAN FRANCISCO IN THEIR CORNER, CLIENTS ARE ASSURED A HIGH LEVEL OF SERVICE WITH GENEROUS DOSES OF LISTENING SKILLS, STREET SMARTS, ENERGY, AND CREATIVE INSTINCT.

AT DDB SAN FRANCISCO, THE SPIRIT OF COOPERATION AND PERSONAL RESPONSIBILITY IS INFECTIOUS— WITH THE ACCOUNT MANAGEMENT, PLANNING, MEDIA, AND CREATIVE TEAMS EMBRACING THE BUSINESS CHALLENGES THAT THEIR CLIENTS FACE AS THEIR OWN.

KNOWN FOR ITS INNOVATION AND ACHIEVEMENT, SAN FRANCISCO IS A PLACE for leaders; entire industries have been born there. The San Francisco Partnership helps those leaders realize their full potential in the fast moving, ever changing world of business. ◆ In early 1996, a group of top business leaders envisioned an economic develop-

ment organization that would be a partnership between the city's private and public sectors, combining the Office of the Mayor, the president of the San Francisco Board of Supervisors, and top executives of some of the city's most prominent and civic-minded companies. Its members recruited Mara Brazer as president, and appointed Don Fisher, chairman of Gap, Inc., to chair the organization.

After identifying three major industry sectors—professional services, multimedia, and life

THANKS IN PART TO THE SAN FRANCISCO PARTNERSHIP, MULTIMEDIA GULCH NOW BOASTS THE CENTER OF THE ON-LINE UNIVERSE: A DYNAMIC CLUSTER OF FIRMS, A FOCUS ON CREATIVE CONTENT AND TECHNICAL INNOVATION, AND A LOCATION CLOSE TO SILICON VALLEY THAT ALLOWS FOR GREATER INTERACTION AND COLLABORATION.

sciences—the San Francisco Partnership asked Arthur Andersen Management Consulting Agency to explore San Francisco's competitiveness in these areas. At the economic summit held in April 1996, Mayor Willie L. Brown Jr. embraced these key sectors as the city's strategic direction for growth and opportunity.

FINANCIAL AND PROFESSIONAL SERVICES

San Francisco is often considered the financial center of the West. In spite of high-visibility mergers, financial services here continue to explode, making San Francisco home to 2,300 financial institutions. Pro-

fessional services have a strong base here as well. From 1995 to 1998, business service jobs grew 28.6 percent to 59,400 jobs, while engineering and management service employment grew more than 19 percent to 31,100 jobs.

MULTIMEDIA

Since the formation of the San Francisco Partnership, the most significant change in the San Francisco business landscape has come from the multimedia industry. A city known

for collaboration and creativity, San Francisco has experienced a 52 percent increase in permanent multimedia jobs, from 11,600 in 1995 to 17,600 in 1998. These numbers do not reflect independent contract work, which often can double or triple a company's workforce.

To nurture the multimedia industry, the San Francisco Partnership hosted a multimedia summit in 1998 with Mayor Brown and San Francisco Supervisor Leslie Katz. After a marathon of interactive discussions with 300 Bay Area CEOs, an action agenda was announced to support the industry. Included in this plan was the devel-

opment of the San Francisco New Media Campus. The Partnership established the campus in the South of Market (SoMa) area, also known as the genesis of Multimedia Gulch; it will feature Epicenter, a business-to-business resource center, as well as a women's technology incubator and office space ranging from below market to market rates.

Another recent triumph for the Partnership's efforts involves Sega of America. In 1999, the computer-game maker moved its U.S. headquarters to Multimedia Gulch, bringing more than 800 jobs and related businesses to San Francisco.

"Sega's move to our fine city solidifies San Francisco as the global hub of multimedia," says Brown. "Companies are drawn here not only for the talent and quality of life, but for the unique cluster of peers and partners they can find here."

LIFE SCIENCES

The San Francisco Bay Area maintains a long-standing tradition of technological advancement and achievement in the life sciences. With one-third of the nation's life sciences companies located in the Bay Area, the region has become the world headquarters for scientific and technological innovation. Here, a highly skilled workforce, unlimited access to strategic partners, and a unique concentration of research and development facilities combine to turn ideas into reality, thus ensuring the industry's growth. With the strong presence of the University of California-San Francisco (UCSF)—the birthplace of the nation's $83 billion biotechnology industry—San Francisco is uniquely positioned to become the nucleus of life sciences in the 21st century.

The Partnership is working to attract new life sciences companies to Mission Bay, home of the new

UCSF research campus, and the entire eastern waterfront. These areas offer some of the best investment and development opportunities in the city. The mixed-use waterfront urban area, with its spectacular Bay views and convenient proximity to major freeways, will feature a mix of biotechnology research and development, office, and multimedia uses.

BUILDING A BETTER BUSINESS CLIMATE

The paths between London and Tokyo, not to mention Seattle and San Diego, meet halfway in San Francisco, home to almost 800,000 people. Three of the nation's top-rated universities—the University of California-San Francisco, the University of California-Berkeley, and Stanford University—infuse the labor force with skilled and educated workers.

In order to build a better business climate and to help the city keep its competitive edge, the Partnership initiated two tax credit programs: the Target Employment Area, a valuable state income tax credit for businesses located in an enterprise zone; and the extension of the New Jobs Tax credit from two years to four.

"Since the group's inception, the Partnership has assisted 738 national and international companies representing more than 42,826 potential new jobs," says Mara Brazer. "We work free of charge to strategically apply economic benefits and incentives that companies are entitled to by being located in San Francisco."

Creating a favorable environment for potential businesses, the San Francisco Partnership provides enormous advantages in crucial areas ranging from site selection to business incentive programs. As San Francisco maintains its edge as the city of choice for knowledge-based companies, the Partnership plays a critical role as an advocate for businesses, listening to them and responding with innovative programs, as well as providing a direct line between the city and its business community.

Yerba Buena Center for the Arts presents arts and arts education programs that emphasize the diverse artists and communities of the San Francisco Bay area (top).

As the financial hub of the West, San Francisco's financial district is where deals are made. More than 2,300 financial institutions, including the Pacific Exchange and some of the nation's largest banks, call San Francisco home (bottom).

I N THE MARKETPLACE, TIMING CAN BE EVERYTHING. WALTER BURTON AND DOUG Scott appear to have perfect timing in the founding and development of their young company, Platinum Television Group. Conceived in 1997, the media services company produces national television shows, corporate training programs, demo products, and other fee-based media

services. It has expanded rapidly into Internet services, instructional videos on CD-ROM, direct mail, and publication marketing.

As Burton, who serves as vice president of the company, says, "Virtually anything a client can conceive, Platinum Television can achieve."The approach has paid off. The company's revenues have skyrocketed more than 250 percent each quarter since it was established.

NICHE MARKETING

Currently, the company's largest segment of business is its highly successful consumer educational TV programming under the umbrella of its American Lifestyle Series. *New Home Journal, This Week in Real Estate*, and *The Auto Report* are half-hour shows that have achieved almost 100 percent penetration in the top 200 markets across the country via cable, local networks, and major affiliates in all 50 states and in much of Canada. The shows are designed on a national platform that includes advice and tips from

high-profile experts in the field. On the local level, *New Home Journal* and *This Week in Real Estate* feature a wealth of information on communities, mortgage rates, property taxes, pricing, building specifications, how to negotiate

buying or selling a home, and moving companies. Publications such as *The Auto Report* instruct car buyers on issues such as dealerships, guarantees, and rebates. Notes Scott, Platinum Television Group president, "We have found

a niche to bring the local consumer up to date with the latest information in his or her city, town, and community."

Both Scott and Burton are in their early thirties, and as children of the technological age, their vision is unlimited. "The incredible possibilities of the Internet have barely been touched, especially as it becomes interactive through the consumer's television," says Burton. "We believe that we are on the leading edge of this huge new market." The future promises exciting opportunities for the rapidly growing company.

A Vast, New Market

Scott and Burton, who first met when they both worked for the same TV production company, are broadening Platinum's reach beyond television channels to the Internet. In a joint venture with Quatro Systems, Inc., an established Internet development company in Philadelphia, the duo has formed icasttv.com to bring television programming to the Internet. Launched in September 1999, icasttv.com is targeting various industries, beginning with new home construction. "Essentially, through the Internet, we are offering 24-hour programming to an audience that is absolutely exploding in numbers," says Scott. "We are marrying the cutting edge of technology in the Internet with

educational programming to link consumers to industries vital to their everyday lives."

The newest site, ihometv.com, is a virtual TV show broadcast 24 hours a day, seven days a week over the Internet. ihometv.com viewers can select a city of interest and watch real footage of the newest and most exciting homes and communities that city has to offer.

In the Air

Platinum Television Group's newest division—Inflight Entertainment Network— targets consumer- and industry-driven video news release (VNR) programming for all United Airlines domestic and international flights. Specializing in flights to and from California, companies chosen for the network are given the opportunity to relay their messages for 17,000 flights and 2.4 million passengers monthly.

"We look for good stories and solutions to issues and topics of today's consumer," says Scott. This division exemplifies how diversified this young company has become. "We started as a production company specializing in a few television programs, and have expanded to a full-service new media company with various types of programs, as well as CD-ROM development and E-commerce capabilities," Scott says.

Real estate and auto sales are

truly local. While there may be broad national trends, each market has its own personality and its own needs. Platinum Television identifies those local trends and incorporates them into each show. In addition, sponsors and advertisers include large national companies as well as local advertisers. In preparing the show for each market, the company's in-house TV crews cover each city and town thoroughly.

Platinum has developed its own full-time staff in production, editing, research, script writing, and other necessary areas. "We do our own shooting and editing," says Burton, adding that the company does work with local agencies for acting talent. "By keeping our production in-house, we have control over quality, and we think it is important to maintain our reputation in the eyes of viewers, show participants, and advertisers."

Those advertisers are vital to the company's TV success. Platinum advertises its shows extensively in national and local media, usually with four-color ads. According to Scott, the company has more than $7.5 million in advertising in the printed press, as well as through other related Web sites, primarily through trade-out arrangements. The exposure in advertising and to TV viewers continues to draw big-name experts to participate in the shows.

BANK OF AMERICA

N OCTOBER 17, 1904, A.P. GIANNINI OPENED THE BANK OF ITALY IN A remodeled saloon in San Francisco's North Beach, determined to offer banking services to the industrious "little fellows" of the working class. It was a revolutionary idea at a time when most banks catered to the wealthy and powerful. Employees went door-to-door,

explaining to people what a bank could do for them. Other bankers felt it was distasteful to solicit business, especially from immigrants, farmers, and wage earners—people who continue to make up the backbone of Bank of America's business today.

Giannini conceived of a statewide system of branch banks that could bring far-flung resources to benefit local communities. The bank became the largest in the state, and in 1930, Giannini changed its name to Bank of America, reflecting his vision of bringing helpful banking to people across the country.

Sixty-eight years later, Bank of America merged with Nations-Bank under the leadership of CEO Hugh McColl to create the nation's first truly coast-to-coast bank. The new Bank of America, with deep roots in many communities, operates in 21 states and the District of Columbia. It serves

the needs of individuals, businesses, government agencies, and financial institutions, and does business in 190 countries around the world.

Bank of America's Corporate Center is in Charlotte, North Carolina, while its Global Corporate and Investment Banking operations are headquartered in San Francisco. In 1999, Banc

of America Securities opened a new trading floor in San Francisco, the largest outside New York.

Nearly 10,000 employees work in San Francisco at the bank's 44 branches and its data center, interactive banking, and other offices. Customers access accounts at 185 ATMs in San Francisco and more than 14,000 nationwide— free of charge.

SAN DIEGO HISTORICAL SOCIETY

IN THE 1950S, BANK OF AMERICA DEVELOPED THE ELECTRONIC RECORDING METHOD OF ACCOUNTING (ERMA), THE FIRST AUTOMATED CHECK-PROCESSING SYSTEM.

GOLDEN GATE BRIDGE ARCHIVES

BANK OF AMERICA FINANCED CONSTRUCTION OF THE GOLDEN GATE BRIDGE IN THE 1930S.

A Heritage of Service to San Francisco

When the 1906 earthquake and fire struck San Francisco, Giannini set up a desk made of two barrels and a plank, and began to lend money to rebuild. Over the years, the bank's pioneering spirit brought banking services to more people than ever before—loans for business and real estate, Timeplan credit, traveler's checks, school savings, and BankAmericard, the first nationally accepted bank credit card.

Bank of America has helped communities finance schools, housing, libraries, and other needs. Locally, it has funded $10.8 billion in San Francisco notes and bonds for projects such as the Hetch Hetchy water system, the Golden Gate Bridge, and more recently, San Francisco Airport renovation and the new Giants baseball stadium.

The new Bank of America continues its tradition, pledging $350 billion for community development across the country over the next 10 years. In San Francisco, the bank recently helped launch a Microloan Program with $1 million aimed at small businesses, particularly those owned by women and minorities.

Bank of America is an innovator in affordable housing. In 1999, the bank sold one of its properties at $6 million below market value to help create one of the city's largest-ever affordable housing and mixed-use developments.

Bank of America Foundation donates more than $12 million each year to San Francisco nonprofits. In 1998, the bank announced a donation of $5 million for the development of University of California-San Francisco's Mission Bay campus.

"We should make it our business simply to care about each other," says CEO Hugh McColl, "to create an environment where all of our citizens can achieve productive, successful, proud lives; to provide excellent education and then to provide jobs; and to help those in our community who have the least."

Banc of America Securities

Banc of America Securities LLC—formerly Montgomery Securities—is the full-service investment banking and brokerage subsidiary of Bank of America Corporation. The firm employs more than 4,000 associates in offices around the country, and with affiliates, offers capabilities worldwide.

In October 1997, San Francisco-based Montgomery Securities was acquired by NationsBank. The October 1998 merger between BankAmerica Corporation and NationsBank Corporation created the new Bank of America and prompted the renaming of the investment-banking subsidiary.

"While our name has changed, our commitment to delivering high-quality, senior-level attention to our clients has not," says Lew Coleman, chairman. "We continue to operate with the same aggressive spirit that has always characterized our firm. We remain focused on growth companies, leveraged companies, middle market companies, and selected large corporate companies. At the same time, a key priority for future growth for us will be focusing on Bank of America's large base of corporate clients."

As part of Bank of America's Global Corporate and Investment Banking effort, Banc of America Securities is committed to being one of the leading investment banks in the United States. It offers everything from strategic advisory services to equity and debt capital raising, comprehensive risk management solutions, global treasury management, and trade finance tailored to its clients' needs. The firm provides investors with a valuable connection to global capital markets, with one of the largest and strongest research, sales, and trading teams in the industry.

"Our ambitious goal is to become the most creative and aggressive provider of value-added financial services to our targeted markets," says Edward J. Brown, president of Global Capital Raising and Global Markets for Bank of America.

As the financial services industry continues to evolve, Bank of America will be on the forefront, making a difference in the lives of people, businesses, and communities across America and around the world. Bank of America considers that to be its heritage and its future.

In 1999, more than 1,100 bank associates and friends participated in the San Francisco AIDS Walk.

NorthPoint Communications, Inc.

TELECOMMUNICATIONS TECHNOLOGY FOR HIGH-SPEED DATA TRANSMISSION came of age when Congress passed the Telecom Act of 1996, wresting unused space on the nation's vast network of telephone wires from incumbent local exchange carriers and unleashing a host of opportunities for telecommunications services. ◆ Taking advantage of the confluence of regulatory and technological changes, NorthPoint Communications, Inc. was born in 1997 as a competitive local exchange carrier (CLEC), offering data services wholesale to Internet service providers and other data services carriers. Its stock-in-trade, digital subscriber lines (DSL), provides blazingly rapid data transmissions equal to or faster than complex integrated services digital network (ISDN) lines, substantially cheaper than T-1 line operations, and more secure than the largely residential, shared-capacity signal of cable modems.

"We're a young, aggressive, entrepreneurial company, yet we have a depth of experience in the telecommunications industry," says Michael Malaga, chairman, founder, and CEO. All of NorthPoint's senior managers bring to the enterprise executive-level experience from established telecommunications companies and organizations.

Defining the Business

As one of the nation's first companies to focus solely on delivering data in the local exchange, NorthPoint is defining the business, network, and service qualities that characterize the CLEC as a new type of carrier.

"NorthPoint has built the largest DSL network to help meet an ever increasing demand for high-speed Internet access," says Liz Fetter, president and COO. "We are developing our business to become a leading provider of broadband services to home and business users." NorthPoint sells its service to network services providers who in turn sell NorthPoint's high-speed Internet connection to end users, who tend to be small to medium-sized companies.

With the certainty of change in these early days of the telecommunications gold rush, NorthPoint's end-user demographics are sure to evolve and the market for DSL connections to explode. In more than 60 major markets by the end of 2000, NorthPoint coverage will reach approximately 45 percent of all businesses in the United States.

Filling a Demand

In addition to the firm's continued geographic expansion, demand for high-speed Internet service in the residential market will provide NorthPoint with its next big boom. Three factors expected to open that floodgate—technological development to provide plug-and-play ease of use, regulatory changes to bring costs down even further, and distribution channels to make the service available on a retail level—are expected to fall into place in 2000.

Preparing for the opportunities ahead, NorthPoint in its relatively short life has been focusing on rapid expansion, building its network and putting the proper infrastructure in place. As an indication of its tremendous growth rate, NorthPoint's workforce has exploded tenfold, from 100 employees at the start of 1999 to about 1,000 by the end of the year.

"High-speed Internet access will change people's lives and work in fundamental ways, just as wireless technology did," Fetter predicts. "We're just at the tip of the iceberg in this business." Given the Internet-based applications being developed across the high-tech industry—from smart homes to integrated communications—NorthPoint will be an integral part of America's future.

BEGINNING AS A SMALL PUBLISHER OF LOCAL NEWSPAPERS IN THE 1930S, Towery Publishing, Inc. today produces a wide range of community-oriented materials, including books (Urban Tapestry Series), business directories, magazines, and Internet publications. Building on its long heritage of excellence, the company has become global

in scope, with cities from San Diego to Sydney represented by Towery products. In all its endeavors, this Memphis-based company strives to be synonymous with service, utility, and quality.

A DIVERSITY OF COMMUNITY-BASED PRODUCTS

Over the years, Towery has become the largest producer of published materials for North American chambers of commerce. From membership directories that enhance business-to-business communication to visitor and relocation guides tailored to reflect the unique qualities of the communities they cover, the company's chamber-oriented materials offer comprehensive information on dozens of topics, including housing, education, leisure activities, health care, and local government.

In 1998, the company acquired Cincinnati-based Target Marketing, an established provider of detailed city street maps to more than 300 chambers of commerce throughout the United States and Canada. Now a division of Towery, Target offers full-color maps that include local landmarks and points of interest, such as parks, shopping centers, golf courses, schools, industrial parks, city and county limits, subdivision names, public buildings, and even block numbers on most streets.

In 1990, Towery launched the Urban Tapestry Series, an award-winning collection of oversized, hardbound photojournals detailing the people, history, culture, environment, and commerce of various metropolitan areas. These coffee-table books highlight a community through three basic elements: an introductory essay by a noted local individual; an exquisite collection of four-color photographs; and profiles of the companies and organizations that animate the area's business life.

To date, more than 80 Urban Tapestry Series editions have been published in cities around the world, from New York to Vancouver to Sydney. Authors of the books' introductory essays include former President Gerald Ford (Grand Rapids), former Alberta Premier Peter Lougheed (Calgary), CBS anchor Dan Rather (Austin), ABC anchor Hugh Downs (Phoenix), best-selling mystery author Robert B. Parker (Boston), American Movie Classics host Nick Clooney (Cincinnati), Senator Richard Lugar (Indianapolis), and Challenger Center founder June Scobee Rodgers (Chattanooga).

To maintain hands-on quality in all of its periodicals and books, Towery has long used the latest production methods available. The company was the first production environment in the United States to combine desktop publishing with color separations and image scanning to produce finished film suitable for burning plates for four-color printing. Today, Towery relies on state-of-the-art digital prepress services to produce more than 8,000 pages each year, containing more than 30,000 high-quality color images.

AN INTERNET PIONEER

By combining its long-standing expertise in community-oriented published materials with advanced production capabilities, a global sales force, and extensive data management expertise, Towery

STEVE DAVIS

TOWERY PUBLISHING PRESIDENT AND CEO J. ROBERT TOWERY HAS EXPANDED THE BUSINESS HIS PARENTS STARTED IN THE 1930S TO INCLUDE A GROWING ARRAY OF TRADITIONAL AND ELECTRONIC PUBLISHED MATERIALS, AS WELL AS INTERNET AND MULTIMEDIA SERVICES, THAT ARE MARKETED LOCALLY, NATIONALLY, AND INTERNATIONALLY.

with chambers of commerce and other business organizations.

Despite the decades of change, Towery himself follows a long-standing family philosophy of unmatched service and unflinching quality. That approach extends throughout the entire organization to include more than 130 employees at the Memphis headquarters, another 60 located in Northern Kentucky outside Cincinnati, and more than 50 sales, marketing, and editorial staff traveling to and working in a growing list of client cities. All of its products, and more information about the company, are featured on the Internet at www.towery.com.

In summing up his company's steady growth, Towery restates the essential formula that has driven the business since its first pages were published: "The creative energies of our staff drive us toward innovation and invention. Our people make the highest possible demands on themselves, so I know that our future is secure if the ingredients for success remain a focus on service and quality."

TOWERY PUBLISHING WAS THE FIRST PRODUCTION ENVIRONMENT IN THE UNITED STATES TO COMBINE DESKTOP PUBLISHING WITH COLOR SEPARATIONS AND IMAGE SCANNING TO PRODUCE FINISHED FILM SUITABLE FOR BURNING PLATES FOR FOUR-COLOR PRINTING. TODAY, THE COMPANY'S STATE-OF-THE-ART NETWORK OF MACINTOSH AND WINDOWS WORKSTATIONS ALLOWS IT TO PRODUCE MORE THAN 8,000 PAGES EACH YEAR, CONTAINING MORE THAN 30,000 HIGH-QUALITY COLOR IMAGES (TOP).

THE TOWERY FAMILY'S PUBLISHING ROOTS CAN BE TRACED TO 1935, WHEN R.W. TOWERY (FAR LEFT) BEGAN PRODUCING A SERIES OF COMMUNITY HISTORIES IN TENNESSEE, MISSISSIPPI, AND TEXAS. THROUGHOUT THE COMPANY'S HISTORY, THE FOUNDING FAMILY HAS CONSISTENTLY EXHIBITED A COMMITMENT TO CLARITY, PRECISION, INNOVATION, AND VISION (BOTTOM).

has emerged as a significant provider of Internet-based city information. In keeping with its overall focus on community resources, the company's Internet efforts represent a natural step in the evolution of the business.

The primary product lines within the Internet division are the introCity™ sites. Towery's introCity sites introduce newcomers, visitors, and longtime residents to every facet of a particular community, while simultaneously placing the local chamber of commerce at the forefront of the city's Internet activity. The sites include newcomer information, calendars, photos, citywide business listings with everything from nightlife to shopping to family fun, and online maps pinpointing the exact location of businesses, schools, attractions, and much more.

DECADES OF PUBLISHING EXPERTISE

In 1972, current President and CEO J. Robert Towery succeeded his parents in managing the printing and publishing business they had founded nearly four decades earlier. Soon thereafter, he expanded the scope of the company's published materials to include *Memphis* magazine and other successful regional and national publications. In 1985, after selling its locally focused assets, Towery began the trajectory on which it continues today, creating community-oriented materials that are often produced in conjunction

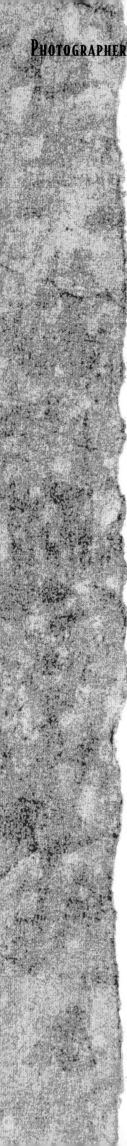

ALLSPORT was founded the moment freelance photographer Tony Duffy captured the now-famous picture of Bob Beamon breaking the world long-jump record at the Mexico City Olympics in 1968. Originally headquartered in London, Allsport has expanded to include offices in New York and Los Angeles. Its pictures have appeared in every major publication in the world, and the best of its portfolio has been displayed at elite photographic exhibitions at the Royal Photographic Society and the Olympic Museum in Lausanne.

CHLOE ATKINS has focused her work on lesbian and gay culture in the San Francisco Bay Area since 1987. Featured in numerous exhibits since the late 1970s, Atkins also gained exposure in 1992 through her award-winning billboard for the Gay & Lesbian Alliance Against Defamation. She is currently exploring her fascination with gender, identity, and costume by producing a series of Drag King photographs. When she is not working or offering courses in Continuing Education for Queer Communities at the Harvey Milk Institute, Atkins enjoys gardening and travel.

FAITH CATHCART, a resident of San Francisco, is a full-time community integration specialist for adults with developmental disabilities. Her photographs have been featured in the *San Francisco Bay Guardian*, *East Bay Express*, *Mexico City Times*, and *México Desconocido*.

PHYLLIS CHRISTOPHER received her bachelor of fine arts degree from the State University of New York (SUNY), Buffalo in 1988. She has since relocated to San Francisco, where she opened Phyllis Christopher Photography. Christopher specializes in environmental portraiture and lesbian erotica.

JIM CORWIN earned a bachelor's degree from the University of Washington and a degree in photography from Everett Community College. He spent 12 years working for photo labs in the Seattle area before opening his own business in 1990. A native of Portland, Oregon, Corwin specializes in travel, nature, people, and sports photography, and he has worked for such clients as the Boeing Company, Safeway, U S West Communications, GTE, and Microsoft. His work has been published in *National Geographic Traveler*, *Audubon*, *Mother Earth News*, and *Business Week*, in addition to Towery Publishing's *Greater Phoenix: The Desert in Bloom*; *San Diego: World-Class City*; and *Seattle: Pacific Gem*.

JASON ORPHEUS DOIY, originally from Carson City, expresses his love for San Francisco and its people through portraiture and location photography. He has worked with *Rock & Ice*, the *San Francisco Bay Guardian*, and the Associated Press.

MARK DOWNEY has covered half the countries of the world for clients such as *Time*, *Geo*, and *National Geographic*. He has photographed everything from uprisings in Los Angeles to elections in Cambodia. Downey's work has also appeared in Towery Publishing's *New York: A State of Mind*.

JOHN ELK III produces travel and location stock photography, including 250,000 images of North and Central America, Europe, Asia, and Africa. His clientele includes Hearst Publications, Houghton Mifflin Company, the McGraw-Hill Companies, the National Geographic Society, Pace Communications, Simon & Schuster, and Macmillan. Elk has lived and worked in the Bay Area for 25 years.

CHARLENE FARIS, a native of Fleming County, Kentucky, is the owner and operator of Charlene Faris Photos. Specializing in travel, historic, and inspirational photography, Faris has won numerous awards, including several from the National League of American Pen Women art shows. She was a 1994 Pulitzer Prize nominee for wedding photos of Lyle Lovett and Julia Roberts, which have now been published in more than 20 nations. Faris also completed an art project for the Hoosier Salon with a grant from the Indiana Arts Commission and the National Endowment for the Arts. Faris' images have appeared in several Towery publications, including *Orlando: The City Beautiful*; *San Antonio: A Cultural Tapestry*; and *St. Louis: For the Record*.

HOWARD GALE FORD moved from Calgary to the Bay Area in 1958 and completed a bachelor of arts degree in journalism at San Francisco State University. In his 25 years of experience, he has been nominated twice for the Pulitzer Prize in photojournalism, and was the picture editor and director of photography for the *Oakland Tribune*. Reflecting his specialization in endangered cultures, Native American land and religious rights issues, and environmental issues, Ford is currently writing a book on his 15 years of interaction with the Navajo Nation.

LEE FOSTER is a veteran travel writer and photographer who lives in Berkeley. His work has been published in a number of major travel magazines and newspapers, and he maintains a stock library that features images of more than 250 destinations worldwide. Foster's full travel-publishing efforts can be viewed on his Web site at www.fostertravel.com. His work can also be seen in Towery Publishing's *Greater Phoenix: The Desert in Bloom* and *Salt Lake City: Welcoming the World*.

LYDIA GANS, originally from Germany, lived in New York before moving to the San Francisco Bay Area in 1988. Holding a doctorate in mathematics, she worked as a university professor before beginning a career in photojournalism 10 years ago. In addition to contributing to various newspapers and magazines, Gans has published two books of photos and text: *To Live With Grace and Dignity* and *Sisters, Brothers and Disability: A Family Album*.

BRIAN GROPPE, a graphic designer whose work focuses primarily on book and poster design, has been design director for Towery Publishing, Inc. since 1986, and is principal art director for the company's Urban Tapestry Series. A 1979 graduate of California College of Arts and Crafts in Oakland, Groppe's work has been published in several of

Print magazine's Regional Design Annuals and the 1999 *Communication Arts* Illustration Annual. His professional honors include a silver award in *Photo/Design* magazine's 1992 Annual Poster Design Contest, Addy awards in 1994 and 1995 for the book covers *Chaos & CyberCulture* by Timothy Leary, and Towery Publishing's *Chicago: Second to None*, and a 1994 Addy for the Memphis in May International Festival Fine Art Poster.

RICHARD GROSS specializes in corporate, advertising, and stock photography for Fortune 500 companies. His photographs can also be seen in Towery Publishing's *New York: A State of Mind.*

STACEY HALPER received a bachelor of fine arts degree in photography from SUNY, Purchase College. Her work has been exhibited in galleries in New York, Connecticut, and Arizona, and she recently participated in a group show at the Kodak Gallery in Seoul. Halper is in the process of finishing her first short film, *Bread and Bones.* Her photographs are also featured in Towery Publishing's *New York: A State of Mind.*

GABRIELA HASBUN received her bachelor's degree in business administration from Loyola University in New Orleans in 1998, moving to San Francisco shortly thereafter. Originally from El Salvador, she is currently a student at the Academy of Art College in San Francisco, specializing in documentary work and portraiture.

LISA HOFFMAN earned a bachelor of arts degree from San Jose State University. Her studio, Studio 9 Design, specializes in a variety of productions from photography to print and Web design.

CAROL HUNT, a Santa Fe resident, is employed by St. Francis Hospital. She centers her photography on the people and culture of northern New Mexico, sports, high-rise buildings, and churches.

THE IMAGE FINDERS, founded by Jim Baron in 1986, is a stock photography company located in Cleveland, Ohio. Its files cover a broad range of subjects, including agriculture, animals, butterflies, families, food, sports, transportation, travel, trees, and the western United States.

KERRICK JAMES, specializing in destination and adventure travel photography, has been published in *Arizona Highways, America West*

© TOM MYERS

Airlines Magazine, Travel Holiday, and *Alaska Airlines Magazine,* as well as in Towery Publishing's *Greater Phoenix: The Desert in Bloom.* In his spare time, James enjoys kayaking, river rafting, and literature.

MARY LOU JANSON, a resident of Berkeley, is employed by Foster Travel Publishing, and focuses in travel writing and photography with

partner Lee Foster. This collaborative team has a client list that includes *American Way,* the *New York Times, Spa Magazine,* and *Travel & Leisure.* Educated at the University of Florida, Janson had a 10-year career as a reporter with the *Tampa Tribune* before joining Foster Travel. Her public relations achievements include the 1995 Adrian and Golden Bell Award from Hospitality Sales and Marketing Association International.

DAN KRAUSS is a photojournalist employed by the Associated Press. His regular freelance clients include the *New York Times* and the *Los Angeles Times.*

JAMES LEMASS studied art in his native Ireland before moving to Cambridge, Massachusetts, in 1987. His areas of specialty include people and travel photography, and his

work can be seen in publications by Aer Lingus, British Airways, and USAir, as well as the Nynex Yellow Pages. Lemass has also worked for the Massachusetts Office of Travel and Tourism, and his photographs have appeared in several other Towery publications, including *Greater Phoenix: The Desert in Bloom; New York: Metropolis of the American Dream; New York: A State of Mind; Orlando: The City Beautiful; San Diego: World-Class City; Treasures on Tampa Bay: Tampa, St. Petersburg, Clearwater;* and *Washington: City on a Hill.*

RON LEVINE, owner of Montreal-based Ron Levine Photography, is a 20-year veteran of commercial and editorial photography. His images have appeared in numerous international publications, including *Time, Business Week, Travel & Leisure, Forbes, Fortune, ESPN: The Magazine, Saturday Night,* and Air Canada's *En Route.* Levine's photographs of the southern United States, the Canadian Maritime Provinces, and Poland have been exhibited in museums and galleries internationally, including Colombia's Museo de la Universidad de Antioquia, Germany's Linhof Gallery, Mexico's Centro Cultural el Nigromante, and Poland's Stara Galeria. Levine served as the photography editor for Towery Publishing's *Montréal: la joie de vivre,* and his photographs also appeared in Towery's *Greater Des Moines: Iowa's Commercial Center* and *New York: A State of Mind.*

ROSEMARIE LION moved to San Francisco from Australia in 1986. With a business degree behind her, she earned a bachelor of arts degree in journalism-photojournalism from San Francisco State University and opened her own studio. Lion has been honored by Greenpeace and the *San Francisco Bay Guardian* for her work on environmental issues and women. She promotes the honor and respect of nature in order to integrate people into the environment.

CHARLIE MANZ is originally from Manila. Based in San Diego, he is currently employed at Scripps Mercy Medical Center as admission financial adviser and at Artistic Visuals, a San Diego-based stock photo company, as a freelance photographer. Manz' photographs have been published in *The San Diegan: The Original San Diego Book,* and Towery Publishing's *San Diego: World-Class City,* and *The Official Driving Guide: San Diego/Baja California.*

RORY MCNAMARA, a London-born Irish immigrant to California, works as a self-employed photojournalist. Specializing in all aspects of photojournalism and portraiture, he lists *Newsweek,* Sutter Medical Group, the *San Francisco Bay Guardian,* and Coldwell Banker among his clients.

MARY E. MESSENGER resides in the Sacramento area and specializes in stock photography with a photojournalistic slant. Her subjects include people portrayed in their daily lives and activities, as well as sports and travel. Messenger's work can be seen in Towery Publishing's *Salt Lake City: Welcoming the World.*

TOM AND SALLY MYERS have been full-time freelance photographers for 30 years, and have been published in many national magazines, including *National Geographic, National Wildlife, Newsweek,* and *Animals* (London), as well as in Towery Publishing's *New York: A State of Mind* and *Sacramento Tapestry.* Their photos appear in books and educational CD-ROM materials throughout the world, advertisements, album covers, and Hallmark cards and calendars. With their son, JEFF MYERS, the family has more than 400,000 color images in their files, covering a variety of geographic areas, including Europe and the Pacific Coast from Mexico to Alaska and inland to Colorado.

EMILY NATHAN received a degree in English literature from the University of Michigan before moving to San Francisco from Detroit in 1993.

BARBARA J. NELSON, a lifelong San Jose resident, has traveled extensively, researching wildlife, scenic portraiture, and close-ups of nature as her photographic topics. In addition to publications in *Outdoor America, Popular Photography Magazine,* and the American Museum of Natural History's *Natural History* magazine, she has published the text *Getting Started in Stock Photography.* Nelson is affiliated with Hillstrom Stock Photo Inc. located in Chicago.

JOSON NICHOLAS-LEE, a Bay Area resident since 1995, earned a master of fine arts degree from the Academy of Art College. His specialties include travel, landscape, and still life photography. Nicholas-Lee's clients include *Photolife Magazine,* Century 21, and CNN. He works domestically and internationally, collecting stock images from cities such as London, Rome, and Amsterdam.

CORBIN PAGTER completed a bachelor's degree in color technology from Brooks Institute of Photography, specializing in coastal and metropolitan scenic photography and portraiture. Having lived in the Bay Area his whole life, Pagter has developed a love for surfing that is evident in his work.

JUDI PARKS is an award-winning photojournalist living and working in the San Francisco Bay Area. Her educational background ranges from anthropology and photography to international conflict resolution and clinical psychology. Parks' work has been part of numerous museums and public collections in the United States and Europe. Her documentary series *Home Sweet Home: Caring for America's Elderly* was recently honored with the *Communication Arts-Design Annual* 1999 Award of Excellence for an unpublished series. Parks is also a professional writer, with articles appearing in more than 40 newspapers and magazines.

JOHN PERRY has deep roots in the Bay Area: His great grandfather was a conductor on the streetcar line in the 1890s. He studied literature at

the University of California, Santa Cruz before opening his own studio, John Perry Photography, which specializes in location portraits and theater promotions. Some of his recent clients include Whole Foods Market, San Francisco Conservatory of Music, and the Renaissance Entertainment Corporation.

PHOTOPHILE, established in San Diego in 1967, is owned and operated by Nancy Likins-Masten. An internationally known stock photography agency, the company houses more than a million color images, and represents more than 90 contributing local and international photographers. Subjects include extensive coverage of the West Coast, business/industry, people/lifestyles, health/medicine, travel, scenics, wildlife, and adventure sports, plus 200 additional categories.

ANTHONY PIDGEON is a self-taught, freelance photographer specializing in editorials, portraiture, and travel photography. He has contributed to *Diablo, Electronic Musician,* and the *San Francisco Weekly,* and is the house photographer for the Fillmore Auditorium.

JAMES P. ROWAN owns and operates Chicago-based James P. Rowan Photography. He has amassed a clientele that includes textbooks, children's books, and magazines, and his pictures have also appeared in Towery Publishing's *Tucson: High Desert Harmony.* Rowan annually adds thousands of images to his stock file, which currently totals approximately 300,000.

SCOTT SARACENO received his bachelor's degree in broadcasting and film from Boston University in 1990. Moving to the Bay Area in 1993, he currently works as a freelance video producer for the University of San Francisco, video coordinator for Franklin Bowles Galleries, and senior editor and cameraman for JBC Video in San Francisco. Saraceno's photo credits include working as a special assignment photographer for the *San*

Francisco Bay Guardian and as photo editor for the *Boston Network*. He specializes in architectural, still life, statuary, and portrait photography.

SHARON SELDEN, originally from Oakland has studied at Tisch School of the Arts and SUNY, Purchase. As owner of Sharon Selden Photography, she focuses primarily on offbeat and wacky subjects, as well as automobile-related sports. Selden's clients include Man's Ruin Records, Raygun Publishing, and *GearHead Magazine*, and her photographs can also be seen in Towery Publishing's *New York: A State of Mind*. She is currently writing a book about figure eight auto racing.

BRETT SHOAF, a resident of San Diego since 1958, studied photography, telecommunications, and film production at San Diego City College and Grossmont College, where he earned an associate of arts degree. Shoaf is self-employed at Artistic Visuals, and his work includes stock, commercial, and instructional/tutorial photography, as well as ad design. His clients include IVID Communications, Vortex Interactive, Shelter Island Inc., Bartell Hotels, and the San Diego Visitor Information Center. His stock photography has been published in the *San Diegan* and *San Diego Official Visitors Planning Guide*, as well as in Towery Publishing's *San Diego: World-Class City* and *Greater Phoenix: The Desert in Bloom*. With a special interest in nature photography, Shoaf has photographed the natural beauty of such places as Kauai, Switzerland, and Utah.

ROSE SKYTTA, originally from Minnesota, earned her bachelor of arts degree in English from the University of Minnesota in 1969. In the mid-1970s and early 1980s, she freelanced for community organizations, political campaigns, and San Francisco-based publications, including the *San Francisco Bay Guardian*, *San Francisco Progress*, and *Advocate*. The subjects of Skytta's photography range from neighborhood issues and gay community news to coverage of the Financial District and punk rock parties. Working now as an occa-

sional contributor to a stock photo agency and as full-time wait staff, Skytta has turned her photographic interests toward the postindustrial landscape.

ERIC SLOMANSON moved to San Francisco from New York City in 1988. His studio, Slomo Photos, produces work in photojournalism, environmental activism photography, and portraiture.

CURTIS B. STAHR has photographed the migration of the American eagle from Alaska to Florida; close to 20 national parks and monuments; and all 99 Iowa courthouses. He has walked with his camera across Canada from ocean to ocean and photographed life in each of the contiguous United States. Stahr has exhibited in 32 juried/invitational art shows and 16 one-man shows; received 11 purchase awards; and is listed in *America Artists of Renown*,

Who's Who in Photography, and *Who's Who in the World*. His work has also appeared in Towery Publishing's *Greater Des Moines: Iowa's Commercial Center*.

JIM STEINBERG is a nature and natural history photographer for Photo Researchers, Inc. A resident of Steamboat Springs, Colorado, he owns and operates the Portfolio Collection, Ltd., a stock photography studio and gallery, and is the CEO of Portfolio Publications, Inc., which produces nature calendars and fine art prints. Steinberg's clients include *Scientific American*, *Earth Magazine*, *Discover*, Microsoft, the Nature Conservancy, Gulf Oil, the Children's Television Workshop, and the American Museum of Natural History. Working as a par-

ticipating artist in the Friends of Art in Embassies for the U.S. State Department is one of Steinberg's most outstanding contributions to community service in the arts.

THOR SWIFT received a bachelor of arts degree in journalism from California State University, Fresno. He specializes in editorial portraits and journalism, contributing to the *New York Times*, *Industry Standard*, *San Francisco Chronicle*, and *Woman's World*. Swift's spare time is devoted to his young twins.

FRED VERHOEVEN, originally from Stamford, moved to San Francisco in 1991.

NIK WHEELER, a native of Hitchin, England, began his photographic career in Bangkok, where he copublished a travel supplement and guidebook on Thailand. In 1967, he worked in Vietnam as a combat photographer. Since that time, Wheeler has covered the 1968 Tet Offensive, the Jordan Civil War, the fall of Saigon, the Montreal Olympics, and the coronation of the king of Nepal. His clients include *Time*, *National Geographic*, *Newsweek*, *Geo*, *Travel & Leisure*, and *International Wildlife*, and his photographs have also appeared in Towery Publishing's *Greater Phoenix: The Desert in Bloom*. Wheeler has published four books; has copublished and photographed for the *Insider's Guide* series, including Japan, Hawaii, California, and Spain; and has appeared on *The Merv Griffin Show* and Regis Philbin's *Morning Show*.

MARGARET YAMASAKI received a bachelor of fine arts degree from the San Francisco Art Institute. She works in documentary photography and photojournalism, and her favorite subjects are everyday people doing everyday things that reach others in a very emotional way.

LIBRARY OF CONGRESS
CATALOGING-IN-PUBLICATION DATA

Young, Steve, 1961-

San Francisco : a city for all seasons / by Steve Young ; art direction by Brian Groppe.

p.   cm. — (Urban tapestry series)

Includes index.

ISBN 1-881096-78-5 (alk. paper)

1. San Francisco (Calif.)—Civilization.   2. San Francisco (Calif.)—Pictorial works.   3. San Francisco (Calif.)—Economic conditions.   4. Business enterprises—California—San Francisco.   I. Groppe, Brian   II. Title.   III. Series.

F869.S35 Y68 2000

979.4′61—dc21   00-024255

[Printed in China]

URBAN TAPESTRY SERIES

TOWERY PUBLISHING, INC.

TOWERY PUBLISHING, INC.
THE TOWERY BUILDING
1835 UNION AVENUE
MEMPHIS, TN 38104
WWW.TOWERY.COM

PUBLISHER: J. Robert Towery
EXECUTIVE PUBLISHER: Jenny McDowell
NATIONAL SALES MANAGER: Stephen Hung
MARKETING DIRECTOR: Carol Culpepper
PROJECT DIRECTORS: Ron Calabrese, Andrea Glazier, Mary Whelan, Paul Withington

EXECUTIVE EDITOR: David B. Dawson
MANAGING EDITOR: Lynn Conlee
SENIOR EDITOR: Carlisle Hacker
EDITOR/PROFILE MANAGER: Stephen Deusner
EDITORS: Brian Johnston, Ginny Reeves, Sunni Thompson
ASSISTANT EDITOR: Rebecca Green
EDITORIAL ASSISTANT: Emily Haire
PROFILE WRITER: Helen K. Chang
EDITORIAL CONTRIBUTOR: Julie B. Soller

PHOTOGRAPHY EDITOR: Jonathan Postal
PHOTOGRAPHIC CONSULTANT: Elyse Hochstadt
PRODUCTION MANAGER: Brenda Pattat
PHOTOGRAPHY COORDINATOR: Robin Lankford
PROFILE DESIGNERS: Laurie Beck, Melissa Ellis, Ann Ward
PRODUCTION ASSISTANTS: Robert Barnett, Loretta Lane
DIGITAL COLOR SUPERVISOR: Darin Ipema
DIGITAL COLOR TECHNICIANS: Eric Friedl, Deidre Kesler, Brent Salazar, Mark Svetz
PRODUCTION RESOURCES MANAGER: Dave Dunlap Jr.
PRINT COORDINATOR: Beverly Timmons